THE ECONOMIC IMPORTANCE OF INTANGIBLE ASSETS

The Economic Importance of Intangible Assets

Edited by
PATRIZIO BIANCHI and SANDRINE LABORY
University of Ferrara, Italy

Routledge
Taylor & Francis Group

LONDON AND NEW YORK

First published 2004 by Ashgate Publishing

Reissued 2018 by Routledge
2 Park Square, Milton Park, Abingdon, Oxon OX14 4RN
711 Third Avenue, New York, NY 10017, USA

Routledge is an imprint of the Taylor & Francis Group, an informa business

First issued in paperback 2018

ISBN 13: 978-0-815-39768-7 (hbk)
ISBN 13: 978-1-138-62093-3 (pbk)
ISBN 13: 978-1-351-14700-2 (ebk)

Contents

List of Contributors

Patrizio Bianchi is Professor of Applied Industrial Economics and Dean of the Faculty of Economics of the University of Ferrara, Italy.

Alberto Cottica is a partner and a researcher at Eco&Eco, Bologna, Italy.

Marco R. Di Tommaso is Associate Professor of Applied Industrial Economics at the Faculty of Economics of the University of Ferrara, Italy.

Clark Eustace is Chairman of the PRISM network and a Senior Visiting Fellow at Cass Business School, London. He was formerly a Senior Partner with the Price Waterhouse European Firm.

Francesco Galassi is Professor of Economic History at the University of Warwick, UK, and Visiting Professor at the Faculty of Economics of the University of Ferrara, Italy.

Mike Hall is a consultant member of the PRISM network and responsible for the UK activities of Fermat S.A., a leader in risk monitoring and control tools.

Roberto Iorio is a Ph.D. student at the Faculty of Economics of the University of Ferrara, Italy.

Sandrine Labory is Lecturer of Applied Industrial Economics at the Faculty of Economics of the University of Ferrara, Italy.

Susanna Mancinelli is Associate Professor of Microeconomics at the Faculty of Economics of the University of Ferrara, Italy.

Daniele Paci is a Ph.D. student at the Faculty of Economics of the University of Ferrara, Italy.

Giovanni Ponti is Associate Professor of Game Theory at the Faculty of Economics of the University of Ferrara, Italy.

Stuart O. Schweitzer is Professor of Health Services at the School of Public Health, University of California, Los Angeles, USA and Visiting Professor of Economics at the University of Ferrara, Italy.

Richard Youngman is a consultant member of the PRISM network, with a specialisation in the measurement and evaluation of intangible assets.

Stefano Zambon is Professor of Business Economics and Strategic Management at the Faculty of Economics of the University of Ferrara, Italy.

Preface

Patrizio Bianchi and Sandrine Labory

This book discusses the economic importance of intangible assets, defined as claims to future benefits that do not have a physical or financial (stock or bond) embodiment. Examples of intangibles include patents, brands, unique organisational structure, and exceptional market reputation. At the level of the economy, the main intangible assets are knowledge, innovation, organisation, human capital and social capital.

The book is the result of a two-year, interdisciplinary research programme financed by DG Information Society Technologies of the European Commission named PRISM (Policy making, Reporting and measuring, Intangibles, Skills development and Management) and aimed at both understanding better how these assets are created and developed and what are the policy implications of their growing importance in economies. The research presented in the book was performed by one of the study teams of the PRISM group, headed by Patrizio Bianchi and co-ordinated by Sandrine Labory, on the policy implications of the rise in intangible assets.

The approach of the team was twofold. First, explain the growing importance of intangible assets in contemporary economies within the framework of economics. Second, derive the policy implications. We have derived a theoretical framework for addressing the first point. Regarding the second point, the main conclusion of the research is as follows. In the past, industrial policy was oriented to substitute public actors for market forces. Nowadays, industrial development policy, or enterprise policy are devoted to create the conditions for an endogenous development of market forces to take place. Creating the conditions means two things. First, provide the rules, with regulation, competition law, property rights, and so on. Second, favour the relationships and collaboration between economic actors, be they private or public, i.e. favour the creation of networks. Many measures have been taken both at national and European level to encourage the setting up of networks, but a higher effectiveness of the policy requires that a further step be taken, paying attention to the social capital that is the necessary condition for networks to function. The social capital is a key individual and collective intangible asset that has tended to be neglected or imperfectly considered in economics. It is high time to fill this gap. The research team has therefore analysed both concepts of networks and social capital in more depth, in the various chapters that make up the book.

The Economic Importance of Intangible Assets

In the first chapter, Clark Eustace, Chairman of PRISM, presents the results of the huge PRISM research effort that has been supported by the European Commission. Patrizio Bianchi and Sandrine Labory introduce in chapter 2 the Political Economy of Intangible Assets, emphasising what intangibles mean for the value creation process and outlining the emerging problems associated with current policy issues. Chapter 3, by Sandrine Labory, analyses EU innovation and knowledge diffusion policy by considering that although the focus of innovation policy is now on networks, there is still a lack of understanding about how they work, and about how agents are motivated to take part in productive networks and social organisations. Marco Di Tommaso, Daniele Paci and Stuart Schweitzer propose in chapter 4 a view on the clustering of intangibles. There is clear evidence that intangible assets are concentrated in certain physical locations. This is due to the importance of collective intangible assets such as research infrastructures and common knowledge bases rooted in specific areas, including the 'social capital'. Chapter 5, by Francesco Galassi and Susanna Mancinelli, explains why social capital is a 'capital' public good. Co-operative efforts and the accumulation of knowledge related to a specific productive purpose makes social capital a key collective intangible asset. The spread of knowledge is not just the possible result of a spontaneous cumulative process, but also the necessary target of policy action oriented to increase investment in research and innovation. In chapter 6, Roberto Iorio outlines the rationale and workings of public intervention to favour networks in research and innovation, focusing on both the relationships between universities and business and the role of public agencies in creating and developing linkages between innovative agents. Chapter 7, by Alberto Cottica and Giovanni Pionti, focuses on how to develop mathematical models of networks. The authors highlight the limits of existing models in capturing the intangible assets generated by network relationships before offering their own improved solution.

Given the interdisciplinary stance of the PRISM group and the willingness of linking the micro and macro level, the last chapters of the book present the results of the research of other PRISM teams focusing on measurement problems at firm level. Indeed another issue emerging in this book is the need to define instruments to measure intangibles in corporate life, in order to understand how to evaluate knowledge creation, reputation, and organisational design in the value creation chain. Given that intangible assets are mainly absent from economic analyses and policy design, what is being done at firm level to make intangible assets more explicit? Stefano Zambon answers this question in chapter 8, analysing recent trends in firm reporting on intangible assets. He also points to the importance of social capital among a firm's intangible assets. Mike Hall and Richard Youngman in chapter 9 highlight the findings from research into how providers of finance can better understand their clients' intangibles. They identify areas where European policy makers should act to encourage the development of scaleable methods to more effectively provide innovation capital to European SMEs, achievable through a more widespread understanding of intangibles.

It is, finally, a pleasure to acknowledge those people who provided personal assistance and financial support to us over the two years of this project. Several colleagues and friends have invested an incredible amount of effort in moving this project from the early stages of research to the final stages of publication. Although we are unable to mention all of them here, we are delighted to make a few exceptions.

First, we thank Clark Eustace, who attentively managed the operative network of the research. We are much indebted to him, for having skilfully guided the huge PRISM Programme, of which this work has been but a small element. Clark has pioneered the research on intangible assets in Europe. He previously led a High Level Expert Group promoted by the European Commission and then created the research network, RESCUE, which later evolved into PRISM. It is now a unique research community, combining academics from strategic studies, accounting, statisticians, industrial economists and business people coming from international advisory companies, banking and industry.

PRISM's results, from the first meeting in October 2001 to the July 2003 London Conference have accumulated and widely disseminated a massive knowledge base on intangibles, making it a truly interdisciplinary, international, and open intangible college. We are indebted to all the participants in this big adventure.

We are sincerely grateful to the Directorate General Information Society of the European Commission in Brussels, which provided financial support to the entire project, to several meetings and conferences, and therefore to this book.

We also thank Mike Hall, who greatly improved the style of these contributions in transforming the authors' original translated manuscripts into their final English language version.

We are indebted also to Edward Truch, who supported this publication and for shepherding it through the publishing company.

We hope that these contributions can offer a fresh, rich, and stimulating source of material and analysis for all academics and practitioners, working day-by-day to increase our heavy baggage of weightless wealth, and above all our knowledge about value creation in modern society.

Chapter 1

The Intangible Economy: Overview of PRISM Research Findings

Clark Eustace

The PRISM initiative started in January 2000 with the establishment of a High Level Expert Group (HLEG) on the intangible economy. In so doing, the European Commission's express intention was to go beyond the borders of conventional academic research and conduct a market-centric programme of enquiry to identify the key issues for the business community and frame them.

Our first report, published in October 2000, presented new evidence on the influence of business intangibles on corporate performance and productivity, together with an assessment of the implications for companies, financial markets, public institutions and regulators.

Following on from this, a wide-reaching research programme was launched with the aim of expanding the initiative and bringing together the diverse interest groups in the business, academic and policy communities working in the area. The research agenda was also designed as a response to some of the economic and measurement issues thrown into sharp relief by the ambitious Lisbon and Barcelona accords.

By mixing macro and micro studies, academics and practitioners, the PRISM group has created a unique learning machine that helped integrate some of the previously fragmented interest groups and expand the collective academic and business mindsets engaged on the subject. Its leitmotif is to stretch and extend the boundaries of our understanding of the intangibles phenomenon, and the instruments for dealing with the issues, rather than simply to reduce the issues to what we can comprehend and measure now.

This book represents the culmination of a two-year programme of research, case study and often spirited debate aimed at gaining a deeper understanding of the socio-economic issues resulting from the influence of intangibles in the modern economy. Its focus was guided by an Advisory Council, whose views were actively courted and ascertained via a series of interdisciplinary, business-led forums and Delphi sessions. We are indebted to the senior executives and officials of the organisations listed at Appendix I, who contributed so freely and openly to the research and dissemination process.

In order to provide a context for the economic and policy chapters that follow, the opening chapter sets out a synthesis of some of the key research findings. It begins with a market-centric view of some of the transformations that are taking place in the economy today and the implications for measurement theory and practice at the macro, meso and micro levels. It is structured in line with two of PRISM's main research themes: The emerging new theory of the firm and measurement implications.

The research presented in chapters 2 to 7 is based on a collation of studies commissioned by the Economics Faculty at the University of Ferrara under the auspices of PRISM. The Ferrara work lays out a very useful analysis of the policy implications of the intangible economy and a strategy for dealing with them. In an attempt to provide a more comprehensive policy perspective, chapter 8 presents the results of Ferrara's research on the implications for corporate accounting, while the special issues for the credit analysis in the provision of debt and venture capital finance are tackled in the final chapter.

The overriding policy message pointed out by the editors of the book is that intangible assets have taken increasing importance in today's economies, and this makes the shift in policy from direct and specific intervention to 'providing the conditions for' even more essential. Providing the conditions essentially means creating the linkages between economic actors, hence favouring networks (especially concerning policy towards innovation and knowledge diffusion). What the Ferrara research suggests is that in order for the policy favouring networks to be more effective, a better understanding of how networks function is needed, and we suggest that one step forward might be made by considering the social capital[1] that allows a network to function.

1. The Emerging New Theory of the Firm

How Does the Modern Knowledge Economy Differ from What We Had Before ?

Despite a huge research effort on both sides of the Atlantic, there is no *a priori* theory or all-embracing model that even begins to explain the workings of today's services-dominated intangible economy. However, what is becoming clear to many of us is that:

- talk of a 'new economy' was more intuitive than rational, fuelled in no small part by a paucity of hard empirical data, to the uncertainties created by the

---

[1] As yet there is no consensual definition of social capital among economists. We suggest that social capital be defined as the set of collective (in the sense of shared) intangible assets available in a territory (a city, a region, a country, a set of countries). Collective intangible assets allow communication and exchange to take place without rigid, formal contracts because they provide behavioural rules (formal or informal) that avoid free-rider problems or other abuses of loose contractual relationships.

unparalleled growth in the use and versatility of ICT and the speed at which this has taken place;

- rather, a gradual shift has been taking place for many years within our economy, within the drivers of growth and productivity;

- what may have seemed like a sudden and dramatic intervention by computers and micro-chips was, probably, more like the result of a long, cumulative and path-dependent development of knowledge and technology, spanning many years. Such developments took place outside the scope and capabilities of the System of National Accounts (SNA) and therefore we missed it;

- while there are many incremental changes, with influence that is more-or-less pervasive, the central, unexplained paradox lies in the issue of sustained economic growth without inflation. A possible explanation, at any rate in the US, is that this may be the outcome of long-term, sustained investment in ICT and other business intangibles;

- a number of transformations are at work in the modern economy. While there are many incremental changes, with influence that is more or less pervasive, the central, unexplained paradox lies in the issue of sustained economic growth without inflation. A possible explanation, at any rate in the US, is that this may be the outcome of long-term, sustained investment in ICT and other business intangibles;

- on balance, the evidence points to the conclusion that the advanced economies have witnessed a significant, but largely undetected, shift in the mode of wealth creation. The principal source of economic value is no longer the production of material goods alone, but lies in the creation, acquisition and exploitation of business intangibles (typically identified with R&D and proprietary know-how, intellectual property, workforce skills, digitally-enabled supply networks, software and brands);

- the rise of intangibles challenges the existing policy/regulatory conventions and has exposed the weakness of governing today's knowledge-based economy with tools of the industrial era;

- measuring intangibles is not a specialist niche: it is central to a holistic understanding of wealth creation;

- the policy community has relied on the new economy paradigm to light the way for new policy orientation and levers. This has collapsed. As a result, the policy community is confused: there is a vacuum of ideas.

As pointed out by Bianchi and Labory in chapter 2, the implications of the phenomenal rise in importance of intangible assets in the economy have to be analysed within the context of the deep changes arising in the economy in recent decades. Not only has there been a growth in the volume of international trade and finance, but firms have been changing products more frequently and have changed their organisations, location and cultures. The penetration of information and communications technologies (ICT) has also accelerated, inducing many commentators to view these technologies as the origin of all the observed changes.[2]

The overwhelming weight of evidence would suggest that the productive economy has undergone a significant, but largely undetected, shift in the mode of wealth creation. Economic growth today is influenced less by investments in physical capital (land, machinery, stocks of goods) than by knowledge, which is now a critical factor in the productive application and exploitation of physical capital. Consequently, competitive success today requires a critical capacity to develop, manage, measure and control the flow of knowledge and intangibles.

The overwhelming weight of evidence would suggest that the productive economy has undergone a significant, but largely undetected, shift in the mode of wealth creation. Economic growth today is influenced less by investments in physical capital (land, machinery, stocks of goods) than by knowledge, which is now a critical factor in the productive application and exploitation of physical capital. Consequently, competitive success today requires a critical capacity to develop, manage, measure and control the flow of knowledge and intangibles.

With the benefit of hindsight it is increasingly clear that while the global economies are undoubtedly experiencing as rapid an era of change as at any time in history, the economic fundamentals remain in place. In particular, the classic dichotomy between market incumbents and innovative upstarts (and the changing tension between them) is still the main driver of market power in open competitive markets.

Macro Level: Transformations at Work in the Modern Economy

While the fundamentals of business economic theory appear to have withstood the hubris of the 'new' economy challenge, as outlined here and developed in the later chapters of this book we are still left with a number of unexplained factors, some apparently new. Whereas there are many incremental changes, and their influence is more-or-less pervasive, the central, unexplained paradox lies in the issue of sustained economic growth without inflation. A possible explanation, at any rate in the US, is that this may be the outcome of long-term, sustained investment in ICT and other business intangibles. However, it is also clear that a number of transformations are at work in the economy:

Firstly, we are in economies of surplus, in the sense that consumers' basic needs are essentially satisfied. Faced with increasing global competition and struggling to get to grips with the exhaustion of the old mass production model, Europe's

---

[2] Over the past decade a substantial econometric research effort has gone into exploring the complex linkages involved and, until recently, failed to demonstrate a direct causal relationship between innovative ICT investment and raised economic performance thresholds. However, recent research, notably by Erik Brynjolfsson at the MIT, has shown a correlation by taking into account the adjustment costs incurred during installation (the unmeasured investments which are complementary to computer technology). The chapter is by no means closed, and a US research centre was recently established at the MIT to address this issue.

industrial and service companies are being forced to respond to demands for mass-customisation[3] by consumers whose basic needs are now commoditised. As a result:

- the modern economy is characterised by mature markets for goods and services;
- as markets have become increasingly mature ('commoditised'), so firms are having to compete harder for monopoly profits or comparative advantage;
- this forces firms to intensify their search for new strategic assets to eliminate effective competition as well as unique factors of differentiation and market leverage. This is apparent not only in the so-called 'new economy' sectors, but in mature industries struggling to keep their business models evolving at least at the pace of the market;
- therefore, they are trying to create, maintain or invade monopolies, whether or not founded on intangibles;
- corporate strategy, as a result, is increasingly focused on 'non-price' factors of competition. Hence the critical importance of quality reputation and branding, and 'lock-on' strategies aimed at creating or stretching the market window (monopoly rent). Typical responses include raising switching costs through the deployment of proprietary 'platform' technologies and the creative use of intellectual property rights.

Secondly, the digital revolution in information and communications technology (ICT) has induced profound changes in the economics of production. Today it is possible to combine both economies of scale and the multinational delivery of discrete, highly personalised products and services. However, the much-vaunted, loose generalisation that this can be ascribed to 'globalisation', or in some way to the ubiquitous spread of services and digital technologies across the economy, is too simplistic and is masking deeper transformations. Globalisation has led not to a convergence of tastes, or even homogeneous products and services per se, but to a vast increase in the number of choices available to consumers. As a consequence, global consumer companies like Coca Cola and McDonalds as well as business services firms such as IBM and PricewaterhouseCoopers, own not one brand but 150, mostly local.

A new generation of business models has arrived, where sustainable value-creation is geared less to economies of scale than to nimbleness and speed of execution in exploiting innovation, arbitrage and scope effects. Notwithstanding the substantial pioneering research effort on both sides of the Atlantic their value-generating mechanisms, although becoming clearer, are as yet still poorly understood.

---

[3] When we use the term 'mass customisation' we are exploring a phenomenon that was considered a paradox until very recently. Mass production required a stock of homogeneous goods to exploit economies of scale, whereas customisation implies the capacity to satisfy each individual's needs uniquely. Coupling the two was considered impossible with the previous models of industrial production.

Subtly, and incrementally over several decades, this has resulted in a relative shift in the corporate value system, away from physical and financial assets (now largely 'commoditised') towards the creative exploitation of a nexus of intangible assets, quasi-assets and competencies (mainly in the form of distinctive capabilities deriving from knowledge) that have become essential ingredients of the economic production process. Concurrently, the relentless pressure on the competitive advantage window for new products and services means that value chains, which always had a limited life in competitive markets, are now eroding at a much faster rate than in the past. Hence the critical importance of:

- an effective 'innovation machine', to keep one step ahead;
- networks, as key strategic assets in leveraging comparative advantage;
- understanding the new dynamics of power, which are very different from those in a traditional, hierarchical and vertically-integrated industrial firm.

Taken together, these factors serve to move the axis of the policy debate from economic theory to the measurement domain. Most of the issues at the frontier are measurement problems, or stem from the underlying difficulty of visualising, ring-fencing and defining what it is we need to measure. They also reopen a range of theoretical issues, from the economics of the knowledge production function to the return (productivity) of investment in intangibles (and the associated dilemma of increasing returns to scale through network effects) and the tension between public goods and monopoly rent and, thus, the role and perception of IPR.

The search for a new measurement paradigm is frustrated by fundamental theoretical and practical difficulties. The science of measurement is immature and, as yet, has not achieved recognition as a legitimate academic discipline. Consequently, it has neither a cogent theoretical base nor an academic infrastructure to facilitate debate and consensus among the fragmented interest groups. As with many branches of the natural sciences, the application of measurement science to the socio-economic domain is advanced in the first place by an empirical learning process, a journey without end.[4] There is no absolute answer, no end game. This contrasts with the deterministic mindset that prevails in many quarters of the statistical and accounting communities.

Perforce, this means that we must fall back on the scientific process of empirical observation and experimentation in order to develop a practical taxonomy and language, along with the necessary metrics and tracing systems. The issue is less a question of striving for the holy grail (perfecting a 'killer' Cartesian architecture) than to reach a pragmatic accommodation on a framework around which the various interest groups can unify and move forward.

---

[4] A highly readable and relevant account of the shifting tensions between measurement theory and practice in the evolution of the natural sciences is contained in "The God Particle" by Nobel prizewinner, Leon Lederman.

Micro Level: The Emerging Corporate Asset Base

In the course of the PRISM and HLEG Delphi sessions we set out to develop a family of models, initially as an aid to common understanding of the different perspectives on the knowledge economy, but also to provide a common language for describing the phenomenon of intangibles. In the section following we offer a provisional schema of the emerging corporate asset base[5] that attempts to integrate the perspectives of the different interest groups.

Twenty years ago, Michael Porter laid out a conceptual model of the firm[6] based on the physical supply chain and the value-building process from the context of a logistical materials flow. His value system traces products from the original producer to the ultimate consumer. Our model offers a different, yet complementary perspective by focusing on the competencies, capabilities and knowledge flows of the modern business organisation, with inspiration from C.K. Prahalad and Gary Hamel (Prahalad and Hamel, 1990). In so doing, we present a new taxonomy of the corporate asset base.

Our starting point is that successful players in today's open, hyper-competitive markets must have access to a nexus of unique, or at least difficult-to-replicate, capabilities, competencies and quasi-assets in order to stay ahead of the game. These value-drivers can be conceptualised in terms of four resource groupings. The schema presents the various tangible assets, legal rights, competencies and capabilities that constitute the extended asset base of a modern enterprise. Some lie within its physical and legal boundaries while others are to be found outside within its network of influence. They also lie along a continuum. At one end we find the 'soft' intangibles that are difficult to isolate and value, often termed *embodied* intangibles, whose economic influence, and hence value, depends on complementarities with other assets. Embodied knowledge is tacit, and embodied in people who effectively lease intellectual services as an input into the firm's production process. Disembodied knowledge is codified, and can be stocked, bought, sold and otherwise traded just like material assets. In certain circumstances it can also be used as debt security.[7] At the other lie the 'hard' intangibles that are *disembodied* (OECD, 1998) and generally take the form of legal instruments created by force of law, or by contractual relationships agreed between institutional or economic units.

The right-hand segments of the schema focus on competencies and capabilities. The first (latent capabilities) represents a reservoir of potential talent and innovation that provides a source of future competitive advantage. Collectively, these attributes provide a leading indicator of the organisation's ability to respond

---

[5] Conceptually, the schema originated in the author's research into how the capital markets are responding to the question of intangibles. An earlier version (Eustace 2000) was presented as evidence to the Brookings task force on R&D and innovation, and formed the substantive basis for the US Financial Accounting Standards Board's SFAS 141 and 142 proposals.

[6] Porter (1985).

[7] Enterprises with a substantial asset base of intangible goods increasingly tap the capital markets by 'monetising' the expected future income from patents, copyrights and other licences, usually in the form of debt securities such as Eurobonds.

to market threats and opportunities that are as yet unknown, and often unknowable. Latent capabilities are what investors, in particular venture capitalists, are interested in. Flushing out, exploiting and renewing these is what distinguishes good corporate leadership.

The second group (intangible competencies) are codified and essentially proprietary capabilities now widely deployed as key factors of 'non-price' competition. They often rely heavily on the ICT infrastructure that created them and, as such, their substance and form can migrate rapidly around the world via digital networks. Following Vollmann (1996), we find it useful to divide these into distinctive, core and routine competencies:

- Distinctive capabilities: Key factors of differentiation that are difficult or costly to replicate.
- Core competencies: Competitive necessities – what you must have to compete.
- Routine competencies: Routine activities you must do, or outsource, to stay in the game.

However important these intangibles (capabilities and competencies) are in underpinning the business value chain, they pose a fundamental challenge to the existing accounting model – and one that may well prove intractable given the conceptual and practical constraints of our accounting-oriented tools. Whatever form of new math turns out to be the answer,[8] we urgently need much more interdisciplinary research – basic (mindset) and applied – on new tools and metrics. This is an acute issue for the political community. Despite a huge research effort in Europe and the USA over the past several decades, the measurement problems are not yielding readily to analysis and, if past evidence is anything to go by, victories will continue to be slow to come through.

Moving to the left-hand segments, these are characterised by assets over which ownership rights can, at least in principle, be appropriated and values assigned by reference to open-market transactions or future cash-flows. They constitute the main components of the current reporting model, and the essential basis for allocating capital and credit and a range of debt security instruments. For the purpose of the schema, the first of these tangible assets consists of physical assets (land and buildings, plant, machinery and equipment) and financial assets (cash, receivables and securities).

---

[8] The transaction focus of the accounting model has a parallel with measurement dilemma in the natural sciences at the end of the 17th Century. The old 'atomic' notions culminating in Newton were challenged by Boyle's experiments into the properties of gases, which paved the way for the new science of thermodynamics and the statistical treatment of 'corpuscular' motion.

Table 1.1 The resource base of the 21st century enterprise

Tangible assets where ownership is clear and enforceable	Rights that can be bought, sold, stocked and readily traded in disembodied form and (generally) protected	Non-price factors of competitive advantage	Potentially unique competition factors within the firm's capability to bring about
"Hard" Commodities (disembodied)			'Soft' - difficult to isolate and value (embodied)

⟵──────────────────────────────⟶

TANGIBLE ASSETS	INTANGIBLE GOODS	INTANGIBLE COMPETENCE	LATENT CAPABILITIES
PHYSICAL ASSETS PP&E Inventory Other **FINANCIAL ASSETS** Cash & equivalents Securities Investments	**MATERIAL SUPPLY CONTRACTS** Licenses, quotas & franchises **REGISTRABLE IPR** Copyright or patent protected originals - film, music, artistic, scientific, etc. including market software Trademarks Designs **OTHER IPR** Brands, know-how & trade secrets	**COMPETENCY MAP** Distinctive competencies Core competencies Routine competencies	**CAPABILITIES** Leadership Workforce calibre Organizational (including networks) Market/ reputational Innovation/ R&D in-process Corporate renewal

The last category, intangible goods, is made up of two main sub-classes: intangible commodities and intellectual property:

- Intangible commodities are essentially contractual rights, including publishing and reproduction rights, commercial databases and other marketable software.
- Intellectual property includes those assets whose characteristics are derived from the legal system, e.g. patents, copyrights, registered designs, trade secrets and proprietary technology. In this case, the cost and time of legal searches can be significant and rises dramatically where multiple legal jurisdictions are involved.

Comparative advantage and value creation are an outcome of orchestrating these resources, which today is *the* defining characteristic of business leadership and management.[9]

A key conclusion of the PRISM research is that the primary thrust of development of intangibles measurement (i.e. disclosure and reporting standards) should be devoted to the intangible goods segment of Table 1.1, whereas future academic research should focus on the right-hand segments where the value drivers are generally bundled together and interdependent to such an extent that they are difficult (but not impossible) to isolate and value. For industrial economists and econometrics, the research agenda should focus in the first place on making more explicit the 'process' intangibles that differentiate firm-level performance. A key question for IPR is where the line should be drawn on monopoly rights over competencies and capabilities, and the extent to which these can be protected in practice.

New Organisational Forms and the Importance of Networks

Organisational forms are changing in response to the new business environment, and intangible clustering is one important factor in the formation of social capital. Evidence suggests that hi-tech and bio-tech industries cluster in the same way we have seen in other industries throughout history, stretching from automobiles in Detroit to banking in London. The creation of new intangibles such as new competencies and technological breakthroughs requires interactivity. Un-codified knowledge does not travel well: only with the growth of social capital (in the shape of trust) does such knowledge start circulating within networks.

However, intangible clustering has many driving forces. Bianchi and Labory in chapter 2 stress the advantage of putting together complementary knowledge. This line of thought is developed in chapter 4, where Di Tommaso et al stress the

---

[9] In the 20th century we focused on margin, investment and asset productivity to achieve comparative advantage. This game has run its course. The winners of the 21st century game will increasingly focus on architecting capabilities – the capability to innovate and the capability to act – and managing risks such as reputational loss. We need to be less narrowly oriented in both our language and in our managerial tools around the physical and the financial.

advantage of proximity and the essential role of venture capital in financing intangible capital. In chapter 5 Galassi and Mancinelli argue that social capital is a key collective intangible asset, while Iorio, in chapter 6, analyses the role of public agencies in innovation and knowledge diffusion via a case study of space agencies.

In this context, networks have become more important but, as stressed by Labory in chapter 3, our understanding of their value mechanisms is limited:

- networks are vital strategic assets, in part because organisational strategy needs to change faster than traditional organisational forms and closed competency groupings possibly can, but also because the complexity of the projects undertaken is often beyond one firm's capabilities or resources. This theme is developed in chapter 7 by Cottica and Ponti, who examine the role of networks in transforming the processes of innovation and competition;
- the loose ties of networks, the available resources and the dynamics of power are very different from a traditional, hierarchical industrial firm.

In the final chapter, Hall and Youngman go on to argue that the complexity of under-developed or rapidly-changing industries often means that the traditional sources of capital do not work well. Capital markets tend to be more generalist and so partially rely on the expertise venture capitalists have built up. The venture capitalist's function is to acquire specialist knowledge (a key form of intangible capital) by focusing on a particular industry segment and learning more and more about less and less. Such knowledge does not necessarily travel well. Hence, a virtuous growth circle builds up whereby the capital is attracted to the ideas, often found in and around universities, which leads to the offspring of companies. As these companies grow and more venture capital and associated knowledge clusters, new players on the scene are likewise attracted to the region by the pre-existence of financial and intangible capital in the form of knowledge, ideas and skills. Silicon Valley is often cited, but this is but one of a number of examples.

2. Measurement Implications

The 'Hidden' Productive Economy Demands New Measurement Tools

Our second theme leads naturally from the first. If there are fundamentally new economic drivers, this will impact directly on the established norms of measurement practice. Our existing business routines and metrics were devised when firms operated within fixed boundaries and the management focus was geared to resources that were physical, and owned. An important feature of the 'extended' enterprise is the separation of its physical and legal boundaries, and the fragmentation of the old firm, where the physical and the legal were largely one entity, into a labyrinth of licences, contracts and other trading agreements, often involving multiple jurisdictions.[10]

One of PRISM's most notable achievements was to make a path-breaking connection between macro and micro measurement issues. It is unusual to run macro and micro studies simultaneously as in PRISM. There are large literatures in the separate fields, but little history of serious interdisciplinary work or of research papers bringing them together.

Unresolved and unexplained growth at a national level has a close parallel with unresolved and unexplained value at the company level. The root causes of the measurement gap are likely to lie in similar things – intellectual capital, investment in innovation, monopoly and property rights. The parallel also exists for perspectives on the returns to innovation. What is needed at firm level (value of firm) is also needed nationally (measurement of economic growth).

The Measurement Gap

Despite many years of serious debate our economic and statistical models have not kept pace with the demands of the market. Partly this is because the processes and causal links are complex and slow to yield to analysis, but also because the business and academic research pioneers have been frustrated by cognitive and data comparability problems. Our established macro and micro information systems are unable to produce routine, systematic information on the stocks and flows of the modern economy. Instead, we rely on ad hoc studies for tantalising glimpses of what is happening. These are akin to having some but not all of the pieces in the jigsaw, but the connection between the pieces and the whole picture remains unclear:

- Investment in knowledge-based intangibles is now a substantial budgetary outlay for national economies, firms and individuals. Studies by Hill and Youngman (2002), Croes (2000) and others have confirmed that intangible investment in the order of 10 per cent of the GDP of the developed economies goes unrecorded as such, and observe that the mis-classification of sums of this magnitude distorts our picture and understanding of economic realities.
- Nakamura (2001) estimates that in 2000, US corporate investment in intangibles was US$ 1 trillion; comparable to investment by the US business sector in property, plant and equipment. Half of this relates to R&D and software, the balance going into brands, human resources and organisational processes.
- Intangible investment in the major OECD economies is running at between 50-100 per cent of their outlays on acquiring and building physical assets. It also shows significant country variations across the EU (Hill and Youngman, 2002). Not only has this transformed the economic landscape, but it acts as a social catalyst to promote changes in work and leisure patterns.

---

[10] An important (and little researched) aspect of globalisation that will continue to play out for some time yet is the international extension of value chains.

- Creative occupations in the US rose from 1.9 per cent of the total in 1950 to 5.8 per cent in 2000 (Nakamura, 2001).
- Knowledge workers are the fastest growing segment of the OECD's labour force, with an average annual growth rate of 3 per cent during the 1990s (OECD, 2001a).
- the proportion of the Australian labour force engaged in the production of intangible capital rose from 16 per cent in 1971 to 31 per cent in 1996 (Webster, 2000, pp. 1-25).
- a recent OECD study (OECD, 2001b) on the linkages between R&D and productivity growth found that, on average, an increase of 1 per cent in business R&D generates 0.13 per cent in productivity growth. The effect is larger in countries where the share of universities (as opposed to government laboratories) is higher, in countries where the share of defence is lower, and in countries which are intensive in business R&D.

The Macro-Economic Context

It is clear there are different perspectives on today's economy, and different ways of describing it. With the benefit of hindsight, the assertion in some quarters that we are in the midst of a new post-industrial economic revolution now appears to have been more an intuitive than a rational response, fuelled in no small part by a paucity of hard empirical data, to the uncertainties created by the unparalleled growth in the use and versatility of ICT and the speed at which this has taken place.

However, some form of soft revolution does seem to have taken place. The assets which we have inadequately and inaccurately described as soft, immaterial or intangible have become key economic goods. A fundamental difference between the 20th and 21st century economies might simply be that we can no longer rely on tangible assets and the representation of production as purely a physical process to provide us with a reliable guide to the rate and direction of economic change.

The data collated by the PRISM project gives credence to the view that a gradual shift has been taking place for many years within our economy, within the drivers of growth and productivity. No longer is it sufficient to trace the investment into physical capital and the hours worked by labourers to track change. Factors which have up to now been hidden from us, mis-classified, or lumped together as 'residuals', have gradually emerged as some of the most important factors in our economy. Growth is not the result of one single policy or input factor.

For example, many associated the development of a so-called new economy with ICT. ICT is clearly having a profound impact on today's economy and will continue to do so well into the 21st century. We will for certain have to learn how to track and measure its impact. However, it is another step to suggest that this large rise in ICT investment somehow, in of itself, represents a new economy. Although the importance of the ICT sector grew during the 1990s, the sector represents only 8.5 per cent of the EU business sectors' value added (OECD, 2002).

A key perspective that may be lacking in our current thinking is the complementarity and inter-linkages which exist with ICT investment. That is to say, it may not be sufficient to track the acquisition of ICT capital items alone, since, as the OECD Growth Project observed, it is the application of ICT that matters, the effectiveness of which is heavily influenced by the requisite investment in the skills-base and in the organisation of the workplace.

In the US, a recent study by Brynjolfsson and Yang (2001) argues that conventional growth accounting does not take into account intangible investments such as the adjustment costs incurred during installation and the unmeasured investments which are complementary to computer technology. This matters if one wishes to understand productivity growth. When the ICT investment rate is slow or when the size of these intangibles is relatively small, conventional accounting does a reasonable job at estimating the rate of output and productivity growth. In the case of computer investments, however, the growth rate has been 30 per cent in real terms for the last three decades, thereby, in their view, undermining conventional growth accounting methods. They confirm that:

- the US may have created over \$1trillion of computer-related intangible assets over the past decade. However, data systems cannot tell us for sure;
- 1998 investments in computer-related assets (tangible and intangible) may have constituted as much as 10 per cent of GDP;
- a revised estimate that takes into account these intangible investments suggests that the TFP/ MFP of the US economy actually may have grown up to 1 per cent faster during the past decade than previously estimated.

However, ICT is but one important factor in explaining growth and its cross-country disparities. Other conditions need to be satisfied in such areas as innovation, business creation and human capital. The evidence that the OECD has accumulated in its Growth Project suggests that if ICT is to cause a lasting improvement in productivity and growth, it must lie in its application, not merely in its production. That is to say that countries that do not produce ICT can benefit from it just as much as those, like the US, that have a substantial ICT production industry, so long as the right complementary skills and training are in place and work is appropriately re-organised.

As Shapiro (1999) puts it, what we are witnessing is 'a shift in emphasis, as networks, interconnection, compatibility, interfaces, and intellectual property rights have become increasingly important sources of competitive advantage'. What is new is the emphasis and attention knowledge is (rightly) receiving, not that knowledge has developed some kind of fundamental new economic role. This shift to what might be called a 'new-look' economy can be clearly seen in the growth of so-called residuals which are, in the words of Moses Abramovitz, 'a measure of ignorance'. What actually may be new about today's economy perversely might simply be our degree of ignorance.

Zvi Griliches (1994) observed that the share of the economy which is measured by official statistics with a reasonable degree of accuracy is declining. Between

1947 and 1990, the fraction of the US economy for which productivity data can be deemed reasonably accurate, he argued, fell gradually from close to 50 per cent to about 30 per cent. It is presumably lower again today. As a result, he commented:

> Our ability to interpret changes in aggregate total factor productivity has declined, and major portions of actual technical change have eluded our measurement framework entirely.

Factors which were deemed to be either inexplicable or statistically insignificant (and therefore treated as residuals), seem to have gradually emerged out of the negligible category and are now too important to ignore. They have been important factors in the production model for some time but we have not paid sufficient attention. We needed the dramas of the internet and dotcom bubbles (and the subsequent fall-out) to highlight things which have been clear to others for some time. What may have seemed like a sudden and dramatic intervention by computers and micro-chips was, probably, more like the result of a long, cumulative and path-dependent development of knowledge and technology, spanning many years. Such developments took place outside the scope and capabilities of the System of National Accounts (SNA). The scale of the problem is both significant and urgent when one considers the size of the sums involved and the impact of the policy decisions that are taken on the basis of national accounts data.

At a technical level, the SNA is poorly aligned to measure today's economic realities.[11] The SNA presents a distorted picture of the working of the economy, either because it misclassifies certain activities and their outputs or because it fails even to recognise and record certain activities and their outputs. The activities in question produce intangible outputs in the form of intellectual capital (knowledge and skills) and scientific and technological originals. The outputs are also assets. In consequence, the rate of investment or capital formation in the economy is grossly understated. Stocks of these assets are ignored.

These failings are particularly serious when trying to analyse and explain the growth of the economy over time, including the growth of productivity, which is one of the principal uses of national accounts data. The role of technological progress, probably the main long-term driver of economic growth, cannot be measured when the activities that lead to advances in technology are not recorded as doing so. Human capital, also a critical factor in promoting economic growth, is simply ignored in the national accounts, and such survey data as does exist is fragmented and lacks a cogent conceptual framework. The SNA recognises a few intangible assets, such as computer software, but then misclassifies them as fixed

---

[11] A detailed treatment of the deficiencies in the SNA is contained in the PRISM WP5 papers (available at www.euintangibles.net). A summary of the proposals for SNA reform is set out in Hill (2003). Youngman (2003b) offers a wide-ranging treatment of the statistical lacunae highlighted by the intangible economy, with references to other research in this area.

assets by failing to make the critical distinction between production technology and the inputs or factors of production that are actually used within a given technology.

A fundamental reorientation of the conceptual framework and data specifications is needed. In particular:

- Measurement needs to be reoriented around the value-drivers of economic production.
- In so doing, it is conceptually important to recognise that there are investment activities which evidently lead to the formation of 'assets' (in the sense of a store of value) that are then used in production, but do not conform to the generally accepted definition of a fixed asset. When you invest in a fixed asset, you expect a flow of services. When you invest in technology or human capital, the goal is to get a step ahead, by securing some form of competitive advantage or the possibility of securing monopoly-type rents, often through property rights.
- In developing this line of thought, it is essential to separate scientific and artistic originals from the tradable rights that may be derived from those originals. The originals are in effect a public asset whereas the rights are assigned to private entities for the purpose of monopoly rent. Originals are public goods that have been accumulated over thousands of years, and are non-rival in use.
- Originals are very different from our conception of a fixed asset and cannot be monetised in the 'balance sheet' of the originator or user. What should appear in the balance sheet is the monetary representation of any patent or copyright, or de facto equivalent that guarantees property, or monopoly rights, over the original. Such an asset is created by legal, contractual or institutional instruments and is similar to a financial asset. Such an asset should not be confused with a fixed asset. Both financial assets and property rights arise directly from legal agreements and their ongoing value is impacted by changing market conditions which give rise to potentially realisable holding gains (or indeed losses).
- Recognition of innovation expenditures, such as R&D and other forms of intellectual capital formation, as value-creating activities would better align the national accounts with economic realities. R&D expenditures are treated by national accounting as current expenses. This is illogical given software development and artistic (as opposed to scientific) originals are now treated by the SNA as capital assets. Research and development adds to the stock of knowledge and should be viewed as a capital stock which is used repeatedly over a number of years in the production process, as are fixed assets. Although long-standing problems of definition mean that official R&D data is notoriously unreliable, in many countries reported expenditures by the business sector are now approaching 3 per cent of GDP[12] and the cumulative

---

[12] A recent survey of the European Roundtable of leading industrialists found that their average R&D investment was 9 per cent of turnover. This highlights one of the problems

effect of this investment amounts to a significant hidden capital stock in firms (and countries) with high R&D spend.

- Educational expenditures, including training and skills development, should not be viewed as final services consumed at the point of delivery, but as intermediate services which the student consumes for the purposes of building human capital. This capital is owned by the household sector of the economy and is in effect then leased or rented by companies as an input into the production process.

- Our first estimates, performed on the UK economy, suggest that the effect of taking this perspective on human capital formation would increase GDP by about 7 per cent and would increase the official economically-active workforce by about 10 per cent (Hill, 2003).

Corporate Accounting and Reporting

Similar cognitive and measurement problems exist with the corporate accounting framework.

Parallel with the system of national accounts, Pacioli's 500-year old mercantile model has been adapted over many generations to the needs of an industrial manufacturing economy and arguably now does a satisfactory job of tracing the transaction flows in and out of the enterprise. It records, with ever increasing accuracy, the mix of raw materials, labour and financial capital, and their cyclic flow through the process of production, sale and distribution of physical commodities. It also does a reasonably good job of tracing the value-building implications along the value chain. But there are problems:

- The reporting model is deeply rooted in the notion that sustainable growth and performance lie in the accumulation of fixed assets such as property, plant and equipment (Blair and Wallman, 2001).

- Accounting techniques have failed to keep pace with the value-delivery mechanisms of the knowledge-intensive economy. In conventional accounting practice, tangible acquisitions such as computers, land and equipment are treated as company assets. Investment expenditure on knowledge-building activities such as training and R&D are still largely treated as costs. This is despite such activities being a primary source of organisational wealth in the modern economy.

- Conventional accounting performs particularly poorly in tracing the accumulation of internally-generated intangibles, such as R&D, ICT, brands and human capital, which are now viewed as major determinants of

---

of our R&D measurement system, which is insufficiently discriminatory to be of real use for policy analysis. The need for reform of the measurement protocols for R&D and productivity of service industries is now an acute issue that requires urgent attention from the policy community and statisticians. R&D has changed as a process; collecting data on investment expenditures and related processes will need to adapt.

comparative advantage. Thus far, the accounting community has adopted the line that, in general, any internally-generated intangibles should not be treated as an asset in published company accounts.

- According to Lev (2001), if intangibles are not reflected in the financial statements, and intangible investments are fully expensed as they are undertaken, both the book value of equity and corporate earnings are understated by the conventional accounting model. This makes it practically impossible for management and investors to:

1. assess the rate of return (productivity) of investment in intangibles, and longitudinal changes in the efficiency of firm investment activity
2. evaluate shifts in the portfolio of a firm's intangible investments from long-term research to short-term development, or from product development to 'process (cost-reducing) R&D'
3. determine the value of a firm's intangible capital, and the expected lives (benefit duration) of such assets (Blair and Wallman, 2001).

Despite the evidence that this is a priority issue for corporate managers and investors, accounting regulators around the world have encountered substantial difficulties in their attempts to improve matters. In part this is due to the strong relationship at the firm level between reporting and management tools. Generally speaking, management only want to report externally on things they are confident they can predict and control, and where disclosure makes sense in the context of the business strategy and operating plan.

Broadly speaking however, there are two areas where the existing model could be expanded to provide a clearer picture of internally-generated intangibles. First, by means of historically-based data points whose position and momentum may provide at least some basis for predicting the future. Such data might include a more comprehensive breakout of investment spend on R&D, ICT or workforce development and training.[13] Alternatively, it might be liquidity ratios, load factors, innovation revenue, repeat-order profiles or customer or employee turnover rates. Past events are, however, not necessarily good predictors of future performance. Second, via asset-like indicators, which form a broad spectrum from 'hard' indicators such as annuity contracts, patents and other income-generating licences, to 'soft' indicators such as the profile of workforce qualifications. The problem with these measurements is that they only have context and meaning in relation to one's competitors. The root problem is that, in absolute terms, management cannot decide saturation levels; for example, is an investment of 5 per cent of turnover in research and product development enough, about right or too much? What are the expected returns on these investments? What are the pre-requisites for future success?

It is essential that, in contemplating the expansion of disclosure on non-financial elements of corporations through indicators such as these, the 'so what' test is applied. Repeatedly we hear the complaint from companies that they are

---

[13] As elaborated in Blair and Wallman (2001), pp 61-65.

asked to disclose on more and more areas and issues (CSR, Intellectual Capital, etc.) but without any real sense of what the actual purpose of disclosing such data might be. Who is going to use it? What are they going to do with it? What does it really mean that 10 per cent of employees of XYZ company have a PhD, versus 7.5 per cent for a competitor? Once over a threshold of around three percent, is an R&D spend of 10 per cent of turnover better than five per cent?

One place to start in this regard might be to explicitly recognise that disclosure of elements around, say, intellectual capital is not necessarily an attempt to value the company's intellectual capital (or knowledge) per se in the way financial theory would wish to reduce it to one number. Rather, the aim of disclosure and measurement in this context is to develop a language for thinking, talking and doing something about the drivers of the company's prospects for creating economic value in the future. It is about the creation of a dialogue around how value is created that is key, whether that dialogue be internal or external. Any indicators or data-points that do not lead to a useful dialogue, say between management and stakeholders, might be regarded as surplus to requirements. There is, in such a situation, no reasonable answer to the 'so what' question; there are no interest groups doing anything with data.

Recent Developments in Measurement and Reporting

Given that intangible assets are missing in economic analyses and in policy design, what is being done at the firm level to make intangible assets more explicit? Zambon in chapter 8 argues that the first signs of a co-ordinated response to the issue of measuring intangibles can be traced to the development of intellectual capital (IC) statements in the early 1990s. This movement was especially prevalent in northern European countries. Fundamentally, such statements have a function of auto-analysis for the firm, forcing it to be aware of both its implicit assets and the different links between the various types of capital. The firm therefore could more easily and consciously define a proper knowledge and competency strategy. It is also better able to evaluate its internal and external growth opportunities. The IC movement developed from the work of Sveiby's Konrad Group and Kaplan and Norton's balanced scorecard, which was the genesis of the external reporting systems promoted by pioneers such as Edvinsson at Skandia and Saint Onge at CIBC.[14] Many of the early adopters are continuing with the elaboration of IC statements and some encouraging headway, notably as a result of the Danish Commerce Agency initiative, has been made towards a framework for systematic analysis.[15]

---

[14] But the roots of IC are much older. Conceptually, IC is based on the resource view of the firm that was developed by Edith Penrose in the 1950s. The notion of the resource based view originally traces back to the economists Joan Robinson and Edward Chamberlain. They published in the UK and the US respectively within months of each other in 1933.

[15] The guidelines to analysing IC statements published by the Danish Commerce Agency were a major step forward, not only in encouraging convergence in respect of IC indicators but in providing a consistent and systematic basis for analysis and comparison

Notwithstanding these achievements, the IC movement still faces major obstacles and the prospect of any real convergence between the existing frameworks and guidelines is still some way off. Technically, some of these may well prove intractable, for example:

- The frameworks generally have very different structural architectures and do not address the same logical 'objects', which makes it difficult to aggregate or compare them, and lay down standards.
- Sophisticated users will tend to demand composite indicators with many dimensions, rather than discrete data points. Their boundaries are often ambiguous and need to change over time, which puts serious constraints on the coherence of longitudinal time series.[16]
- The indicators are based on primary data points that are generally not additive. This makes them very difficult to 'audit', or otherwise prevent double-counting and unwarranted manipulation. It also makes it difficult if not impossible to align or integrate the IC system with the company's chart of accounts.

While the potential of IC reports for both internal management purposes and external communication appears significant at face value, its adoption as a mainstream reporting tool has been limited and it is not yet clear whether it can deliver on what it promises.

In corporate financial reporting, a landmark event took place in July 2001, when two new US accounting standards (SFAS 141 and 142) proposed a different treatment of goodwill and intangibles with an indefinite life arising from business combinations. In essence, this new treatment consists of subjecting such assets not to systematic amortisation, but to an annual impairment test of their value.[17] In 2005 this accounting treatment will be extended to European listed companies via the introduction of International Financial Reporting Standards (IFRS). For the 7,000 list companies in the EU that currently report under national rules, this is the biggest change in financial reporting in 25 years. With regard to business intangibles, the regulatory change will stimulate a wider interest in the management of intangibles and their representation in company statements and will, for the first time, enable information on almost 30 different asset classes to be analysed at a fine level of detail.

It is to be expected that the proposed increase in the disclosure on intangibles on the face of the balance sheet and in the notes to (and management discussions and analyses of) financial statements will stimulate further experimentation. A

---

between firms. An English language version can be downloaded at the homepage of the Danish Ministry of Science, Technology and Innovation:
www.vtu.dk/icaccountsgibles.net.

[16] A possible solution in national statistics is the use of thematic satellite accounts as an incubator mechanism for fine-tuning new indicator clusters.

[17] A preliminary assessment of the impact of SFAS 141 and 142 on a sample of European firms is contained in the PRISM papers (Crosara and Zambon, 2003). The differences show wide variations in earnings reporting between EU countries.

further stimulus to both the management and disclosure protocols will come from the new search and consolidation facilities offered by extensible Business Reporting Language (XBRL).

The research of this book offers a useful contribution to the new economy debate. It stresses two things in particular. In the first place, that networks are the organisational form that is favoured by the modern economy, i.e. by the rising importance of intangible assets and, secondly, that social capital is an essential but often ignored intangible asset because it is as yet little understood and difficult to grasp.

References

Blair, M.H, and Wallman, S. (2001), 'Unseen Wealth', *The Brookings Institution*, Washington, D.C. (www.brookings.edu).

Brynjolfsson, E. and Yang, S. (2001), 'Intangible Assets and Growth Accounting: Evidence from Computer Investments', *Paper presented at the 4th Annual Conference on Intangibles,* NYU, May 2001.

Croes, M.M. (2000), 'Data for Intangibles in Selected OECD Countries', *Statistics Netherlands.*

Crosara, V. and Zambon, S. (2003), 'The impact of the new US accounting standards on the valuation and disclosure of the intangible assets of European companies: an explorative study', PRISM papers WP4.5.

Eustace, Clark G. (2000), 'Intellectual Property and the Capital Markets', *Cass Business School Working Paper*, 31 July 2000.

Eustace, Clark G., and Youngman, R. (2002), 'The Shifting Corporate Asset Base', *PRISM Working Paper* (available at www.euintangibles.net).

Griliches, Z. (1994), 'Productivity, R&D and the Data Constraint', Presidential address, American Economic Association, Boston, January 4, 1994, in *American Economic Review*, 84(1), 115-119.

High Level Expert Group (2000), 'The Intangible Economy - Impact and Policy Issues: Report of the European High Level Expert Group on the Intangible Economy', European Commission, Brussels:
www.beprac.com/IntangibleEconomyHLEGFinalReport.pdf.

Hill, Peter (2003), 'Intangibles and the SNA: the changes needed', PRISM papers WP5.3

Hill, T.P. and Youngman, R.D. (2002), '*The measurement of intangibles in macroeconomic statistics: WP5 proof of concept report*', PRISM papers WP5.4.

Lev, Baruch (2001), 'Intangibles: Management, Measurement, and Reporting', Brookings Institution Press, Washington, D.C.

Milgrom, P. and Roberts, J. (1992), *Economics, Organisation, and Management*, Prentice Hall, New Jersey.

Nakamura, L. (2001), 'What is the US gross Investment in Intangibles', *Proceedings of the 4th Conference on Intangibles,* Stern Business School, New York University.

OECD (1998), 'Human Capital Investment', Paris.

OECD (2001a), 'Investment in Knowledge', STI Review No. 27, *Special Issue on New Science and Technology Indicators.*

OECD (2001b), 'R&D and productivity growth: panel data analysis of 16 OECD countries', by Guellec, D. and van Pottelsberghe de la Potterie, B. (2001), *STI Working Papers 2001/3.*

OECD (2002), 'Measuring the Information Economy', Paris.

Porter, M.E. (1985), *Competitive Advantage*, Free Press, New York.

Prahalad, C. K. and Hamel, G.(1990), 'The Core Competence of the Corporation', *Harvard Business Review*, May-June, 70-91.

Shapiro, C. (1999), 'Competition Policy in the Information Economy', in *Foundations of Competition Policy Analysis*, Routledge, London.

Vollmann, T. E. (1996), *The Transformation Imperative*, HBS, Boston.

Webster, E. (2000), 'The growth of enterprise intangible investment in Australia', *Information Economics and Policy 12*.

Youngman, R.D. (2003a), 'Understanding today's economy and its residuals', PRISM papers WP5.11.

Youngman, R.D. (2003b), 'The measurement of intangibles in macroeconomic statistics: WP5 final report', PRISM papers WP5.10.

Appendix I: Advisory council members

The following organisations have contributed to the PRISM research programme, as members of the Advisory Council or through participation in the research and dissemination activities.

AIAF (Italian Association of Financial Analysts)	Italy
ARCS (Austrian Research Centers Seibersdorf)	Austria
Barclays plc	UK
BP plc	UK
Cap Gemini Ernst & Young	USA
CONSOB	Italy
Deloitte & Touche	UK
Enlightenment Economics	UK
Ernst & Young	Italy & Spain
ESPRiT GmBH	Austria
Financial Ombudsman Service	UK
Fortis Bank	UK
Georgetown University Law Center	USA
GRI (Global Reporting Initiative)	NL
Grundfos	Denmark
Haberman Associates	UK
Hermes Focus Investment Management	UK
IASB (International Accounting Standards Board)	UK
IFRI	France
IMD (International Management Development Institute)	Switzerland
Independent Audit Limited	UK
Intellectual Capital AB	Sweden
Intellectual Capital Services (ICS)	UK
ISTAT (Istituto Nazionale di Statistica)	Italy
KPMG	NL
McDermott, Will & Emery	UK
McKinsey & Co.	UK
National Science Foundation	USA
Nordic Industrial Fund	Norway
NYU Stern School	USA
OECD	France

PreVenture A/S	Denmark
PricewaterhouseCoopers	UK
Skandia Insurance Co.	Sweden
Summit srl	Italy
Telecom Italia	Italy
The Economist	UK
The Financial Times	UK
Thomson Financial Corporation	USA
UAM (Universidad Autonoma de Madrid)	Spain
UNIC	Sweden
Union Fenosa	Spain

Chapter 2

The Political Economy of Intangible Assets

Patrizio Bianchi and Sandrine Labory

In this chapter, we provide a theoretical framework for explaining the growing importance of intangible assets in the economy and for deriving policy implications. One policy implication of the phenomenon that has long been pointed out is the measurement problem: intangibles are difficult to measure both at firm and country level. We show that the growing importance of intangible assets has meant the necessity for firms to build networks with other economic actors, be they suppliers, rival firms, universities or other institutions. This makes two measurement problems more acute: the organisational capital and the social capital take more importance in such a context and should be accounted for in assessments of countries' performance. In light of these thoughts, two key issues emerge in terms of policy: do we know enough of networks and do we know enough of the social capital? The remaining chapters of the book focus on these two issues and are presented in the last section of this chapter.

1. Classical Approaches to the Intangible Economy

Intangible assets, defined as claims to future benefits which do not have a financial or physical embodiment, such as human capital, innovation, organisational and social capital, do not represent a new phenomenon in economic science. What is new is the rising importance they have taken in recent years to explain competitiveness among firms and nations, and the increased questioning in the policy debate about the way they are measured and the reliability of their indicators. In the EU and the OECD in particular, intangible assets such as human capital and innovation have been at the centre of policy makers' interests because they appear to be the key determinants of knowledge creation and entrepreneurship, hence of competitiveness and growth (European Commission, 2000a, b; 2001a, b; OECD, 2001a, b; 2003a, b; also see chapter 1).

If intangible assets are not new to economic analysis, it is because they have simply been overlooked. Adam Smith, in 'An Inquiry into the Nature and the Causes of the Wealth of Nations' stated already in 1776 that intangibles are the engine of the capitalistic economy.

The greatest improvement in the productive powers of labour, and the greater part of the skill, dexterity and judgement with which it is any where directed, or applied, seem to have been the effects of the division of labour (1960, p.4, volume I).

Smith lived during an extraordinary phase of European life. The birth of manufacturing capitalism took place during an intense phase of scientific research on the dynamism of the universe, whilst philosophical studies were simultaneously underway concerning the organisation of society and with it, the role of the state. The fervent Scottish environment in which Smith carried out his first studies pushed him to search for the general rules that kept society together. Smith dedicated his first studies at Oxford to an analysis of Newtonian sky mechanics, the exploration of a system of forces and counter forces which, whilst attracting and repelling each other, determined the heavens' motion. After that Smith turned to researching, through various experiments, the fundamental rules of a social system, and discovered its modes of aggregation and competition, identifying the dynamic factors permitting its movement across time.

This research programme, in which Smith condensed much of the philosophical and scientific knowledge of his time, concluded with the 'The Wealth of Nations', in which he identified new factors that could constitute the effective 'wealth of nations' in the context of new capitalism. Wealth could not be increased via the king's gold, or through feudal oversight, but by increasing the productive capacity of labour, through better organising 'skill, dexterity and judgement' to increase the value of production with fewer resources. This corresponds to the organisation of production according to a model of labour division that requires production objectives, development strategies, organisational design and consequently new competencies, those of the entrepreneur.

Smith describes the advantages of the modern organisation of production very precisely through his famous example of the pin factory, which related to the capacity to learn and therefore to accumulate knowledge with respect to a specific activity. One example is the knowledge accumulated from repetition, which permits task optimisation and enhanced knowledge of materials and tools in the defining and designing of new instruments and machines. The capacity also exists to develop knowledge through experience and dedicated studies aimed at improving the organisation of production, dividing up work and articulating its cycle in phases and sequential tasks, and thereby reducing lead times. The required knowledge is therefore somewhat technical, related to a single task and the function of productive transformation. There is also a specific learning effect related to the capacity to design and manage a complete productive organisation. How can this organisation be defined?

In the third chapter of his book Smith answers why and how one should organise production according to a productive model organised on the basis of the division of labour. He writes:

As it is the power of exchanging that gives occasion to the division of labour, so the extent of this division must always be limited by the extent of that power, or, in other words, by the extent of the market (p.31).

There is no unique and perfect model for organising production, although it must always be related to the exchange system to which it belongs or, even better, to the level and type of competition. Market knowledge complements technical and organisational knowledge. We must understand its configuration, the role of competitors and the nature of the traded goods. The union of technical, organisational and market knowledge determine the productivity improvements that are the basis of economic development.

Without trying to accolade Smith completely with the discovery of intangible assets, it is important to mention how the father of economics understood their role. He saw this in connection to a market and the capacity to create value through organising production specifically designed for the characteristics of that market.

In such a model, the capacity to create value is clearly related to the capacity to focus human competencies on the production of goods within an organisational model that accumulates and transfers technical, organisational and market knowledge into the productive cycle.

The explanations provided by Smith are related to productive capacity. Through different examples he reminds us that as the scope of the market increases, it is possible to define a deeper division of labour, to further develop the capacity to incorporate knowledge and therefore to increase the value of goods offered on the market.

These advantages are therefore linked to market size and have both a static and dynamic nature. 'Static scale economies' imply that the volumes produced in a given period of time are so large that labour can be divided into functional specialisation which, combined together, allow optimal use of technical, organisational and market knowledge. 'Dynamic scale economies' imply that knowledge can develop across time, given the firm's capacity to remain on the market. In both cases the source of productive efficiency is the organisation of labour, ensuring specialisation by different productive functions and their complementarity within the same economic cycle.

Specialisation and complementarity within a dynamic context are key to efficiency, and therefore to competitiveness. The capacity to design new methods of organisation, to introduce new machines, to identify new needs and to open new markets, constitutes the essential component through which this efficiency becomes a competitive advantage. Smith called these innovations 'secrets', and claimed that although advantages derived from such secrets permitted continuously high profits, they would attract new competitors. Whilst trade secrets are difficult to maintain, 'secrets in manufacturing are capable of being longer kept than secrets in trade. A dyer who has found the means of producing a particular colour with materials which cost only half of the price of those commonly made use of, may, with good management, enjoy the advantage of his discovery as long as he lives, and even leave it as a legacy to his posterity' (VII, 21, 22, p.77).

Knowledge, learning, and innovation are therefore sources of competitive advantage which combine together to represent the engine of social development. An economy becomes more dynamic as its knowledge base spreads, and as its organisation of production is increasingly based on learning. This is paradoxical though, since whilst knowledge and learning are themselves the most important productive factors for innovative competition, competitive pressures dictate however that 'secrets' need to be constantly maintained and regenerated due to entrants attempts to duplicate innovation.

Another early insight into intangibles can be seen through Smith's 'black cloth' example which aimed to define how prices fluctuate. "A public mourning raises the price of black cloth (with which the market is almost always under-stocked upon such occasions) and augments the profits of the merchants who possess any considerable quantity of it. It has no effect upon the wages of the weavers. The market is under-stocked with commodities, not with labour; with work done, not with work to be done" (VII, 19, p.76)

Let us start by explaining the phrases, 'work done' and 'work to be done', since they will be relevant hereon.

In the case of an unexpected event, it is not sufficient to be able to produce large volumes at low cost, but necessary to know how to alter production to respond to different levels of demand from that initially envisaged. In a changing world it is not sufficient to think in terms of manufactured goods, i.e. of work done, but to be able to manage resources and competencies to face what cannot yet be forecasted, i.e. it is necessary to think in terms of work to be done.

The essence of the new economy can be summarised with this metaphor. We have moved from an economy based on the work done, to an economy based on the work to be done. The industrial economy at the origins of capitalism was in fact largely based on the work to be done. Manufacturers' potential lay in their ability to organise production to meet new levels and types of demand, to accumulate knowledge, and to shield production secrets from rivals intending to compete by investing in work to be done. This conceptual clarity also appears in the work of subsequent authors such as Ricardo and Mill, as well as when political economy evolves into the economic sciences, modelled along the lines of the natural sciences. Why did these intangible factors progressively lose importance in economic analysis and in the real economy?

Firstly, the real economy changed. Competition between innovators, financiers of the early years of the industrial revolution, progressively formalised. Monopolistic practices were favoured over market liberalism whilst new investment in production prioritised legal and institutional defences to protect existing competitive advantages. In parallel, political economics became an abstract science increasingly unable to respond to the practical need of better understanding society. In addition, mass manufacturing techniques segmented production, knowledge of which was increasingly fragmented within more rigid organisations. The only measures for efficiency were the static economies of scale which represented barriers to the entry of new dynamic producers.

The current interest in the economics of intangibles is not surprising. Reasons include economic globalisation, customised production, the development of new technologies related to the rapid diffusion of knowledge, and the uncertainty affecting economies and societies increasingly exposed to world conflicts. These factors make it difficult to operate solely with knowledge based on work done, i.e.

based solely on the price of many homogenous goods. They encourage competition to respond to demands for continuously innovative and personalised goods. Entry barriers shift from the work done to the work to be done, from actual manufacturing to owning the know-how and competencies to produce goods and services, the content of which depends on an ability to incorporate technical, organisational and market knowledge into production. The capital of a firm is less and less identifiable with its machines, buildings, and physical structures. It is increasingly related to the firm's capacity to combine skill, dexterity and judgement in an organisation capable of operating in terms of work to be done. This latter form of capital has an intangible nature and depends therefore on the valuation attached to it by the market. A second paradox of intangible assets is that although a firm is more dynamic the more intangible assets it incorporates, the more it does so, the more volatile is its valuation.

There is still one crucial final element of our Smithian metaphor to explain. The division of labour exists not only within a firm but also within a community, or social organisation. It also exists within an economy, be it a city or a country, whose efficiency depends on the existence of an organisational model that allow individuals to specialise, i.e. to focus their own knowledge in a specific function, allowing complementarities to evolve between individuals within a social context. In a firm, such complementarity requires the sharing of objectives, values, norms of communication and knowledge exchange. The same is true at the level of the economy. The more norms and values are common, i.e. the higher the social capital, the greater will be the complementarities. Hence social capital represents the real glue of the social organisation and therefore of its dynamism and efficiency. It represents a collective investment, or sunk cost, which allows individual actors to put into action the common knowledge within the network.

This theory has been revitalised recently by studies of clusters, districts and networks, value adding organisations in which the productive cycle occurs outside a single firm, and involves various specialised firms, co-ordinated either by a single dedicated firm or by the internal functions of a quasi market. The following chapters dedicate much attention to industrial organisation focused on networks and to how systems of productive relations function when not commanded centrally. Social capital is more important in open productive systems generated by networks of relationships where knowledge is increasingly important. In these cases it is crucial to understand the glue that keeps various specialisations together, inducing the search for stable complementarities.

Indeed, when a system is based on totally flexible relationships, in which each contractor is always free to leave, innovation is not possible since no actor is ready to risk the appropriation by another of a jointly developed innovation. Paradoxically, this mobility constraint encourages the search for complementarity that leads in the longer term to higher efficiency and innovation. These search costs represent a common investment which subsequently becomes itself a mobility constraint. Therefore in non hierarchical systems, which increasingly characterise activity in the service and research-intensive sectors, the creation of knowledge networks require a certain degree of lock-in whereby actors are 'reciprocal hostages'.

Social capital is implied by what Marshall called Industrial Atmosphere, or the technical knowledge diffused in an area and the reciprocal trust generated by the common experience of sharing productive practices. To these aspects has to be added the sense of belonging to a community, the civic norms studied by Putnam (1993). However, it is also necessary to take into account informal knowledge within a network, and formal knowledge such as the level of education, access to R&D, formalised structures for the diffusion of scientific discoveries, and institutions guaranteeing property rights. A firm which operates in a context of high social capital benefits from a positive externality which dramatically reduces its costs of access to innovation. The importance of such externalities is so significant that a new geography of innovation exists today whereby high tech firms are concentrated in close proximity to the major university research centres.

Here emerges a third paradox. Although the advantages for a firm from networking result from its capacity to acquire knowledge, these advantages are fully exploited only when the firm appropriates the knowledge, e.g. getting property rights on it. However, appropriation implies that knowledge is no longer diffused in the network, hence the capacity to acquire knowledge no longer exists.

The three paradoxes are in fact typical of an economy based on innovation, knowledge, and learning, or in other words on intangible assets that are difficult to value. The measurement problem of such intangible assets is therefore crucial, both to allow the formulation of growth strategies for the individual firm, and to value the advantage of operating in a co-operative context such as a cluster or an area in which research structures are concentrated.

2. A New Value Creation Process

At the firm level, the last decade or so has witnessed the questioning of traditional accounting methods and the development of new indicators of firms' resources and performance (see chapter 8 in this book). The claim is that intangible assets such as human capital, innovative capacity and organisational capital are not well captured by traditional accounting methods. This is problematic both for the market perception of a firm's value and for the firm's own definition of strategy. The development of new measurement methods must be centred on the notion of intellectual capital, and therefore on the ability to accumulate and capture knowledge, which is often wrapped up within investments in social capital, which is itself also mis-measured.

At the country and policy-making level, such a proliferation of new methods for measuring firms' assets raises issues as to the measurement of a country's assets. If traditional accounting methods for firm reporting are limited, it might be that traditional national accounting methods are also limited. If intangible assets are underestimated at firm level, it might be that they are underestimated at country level too. This means that a country's stock of human capital, innovative activities, organisational capacity and knowledge are undervalued, as is GDP, growth and competitiveness.

Regarding the firm level, a first point to note is that intangible assets are difficult to define. Lev (2000) for instance defines them as claims to future benefits that do not have a physical or financial (stock or bond) embodiment such as a patent, brand, or unique organisational structure. For Lev, intangible assets are knowledge assets. This definition recalls Smith's metaphor of 'work to be done' explored in the first section.

From an empirical point of view, such a definition is clear. The problem however is that it leads to a very wide categorisation in that everything which is not physically or financially embodied is intangible. Consequently, innovation, organisational practices or human resources can be considered as intangible assets. However, these assets are also generators of intangible assets. Human capital creates ideas and therefore generates innovation, whilst a flexible organisation may allow more scope to its members to collect information, interact more with each other, generate more ideas, and hence higher innovation.

In fact, intangible assets appear to result from a combination of drivers. For example, a patent, i.e. an innovation, results from R&D activity, human resources (engineers' creativity and competence) and organisational assets (team structure, motivation, and communication possibilities influence research performance as shown by Henderson and Cockburn, 1996).

Although the management literature[1] outlines that intangible assets have not just suddenly appeared, what is new is the importance they have taken in recent years. Bianchi and Labory (2002) for example outline the deep changes arising in the economy in the last decades. Not only have volumes of international trade and finance increased, firms have been more frequently altering their products, organisation, location, and so on. Over the last twenty years the penetration of information and communication technologies (ICT) has also accelerated, inducing many commentators to view these technologies as the origin of all the observed differences. These changes have not occurred abruptly or with common cause, but rather progressively and due to different reasons which, together, have induced important alterations in the organisation of production, the nature of the firm and market structure. Changes include:

- improvements in financial markets that have made it easier to finance large investments, so that capital intensity is no longer a defence against competition;
- the continuous increase in cross-border trade that has expanded markets, so that firms that enjoyed oligopoly power at home now face global competition;
- the large fall in communications and production costs, thanks to the spread of ICT;[2]
- the diffusion of a new flexible production process invented by Japanese

---

[1] See Abernethy and Wyatt (2003) for a review.

[2] The OECD stresses that the diffusion of ICT has allowed improvements in productivity but has not created a 'new economy': 'While some of the more fanciful tales that ICT had created a 'new economy' have proved unfounded, there is growing evidence that it has been increasing productivity' (OECD, 2003a, p.12).

producers, especially in the automotive industry (particularly Toyota), which has replaced the mass production system in many industries.

The result has been increased competition at all levels, and the need to define new strategies in order to adapt to such changes. In many industries (especially high tech), increased competition has induced firms to adapt strategies to protect their market power, for example through increased product differentiation, renewal rates or by personalising the product.

Products have therefore become more complex, in the sense of having higher knowledge content. They are more often updated, and consequently contain greater innovation and incorporate services. As shown in Table 1.1, this means that the knowledge-intensive phases of production, namely the research phase and the marketing and distribution phase, have become more important. Very often both strategies are used to increase product differentiation and, via it, the specificity of the firm.

Going back to the analysis by Smith, we can claim that the main difference of the last decades, within the long-term evolution of mass production, is the shift in the strategic core of production from pure manufacturing to the phases preceding and following production. In the formerly predominant mass production system of homogenous goods, the knowledge content of goods was low. Manufacturing was the most important phase of the production process since firms relied on economies of scale for market performance. The tangible element of the factors of production was therefore to the fore whilst productivity was explained in the context of physical capital and labour employed. Firms elaborated strategy in terms of 'work done' because demand was stable and predictable which meant that production volumes constituted effective barriers to market entry. In fact it was considered impossible for new entrants to access the market of a homogenous good with the same technology as the incumbents if the latter were able to expand production up to the point where entry would be too costly (Bain, 1956; Eaton and Lipsey, 1978; Dixit, 1980; Bonanno, 1988; Bagwell and Ramey, 1990).

Since the knowledge content of goods is nowadays higher and pre-manufacturing the key to value creation, activities carried out at this phase, namely research and organisation, are very important. At the firm level, such changes have meant new forms of governance and organisation, changes in fact in the nature of the firm. Vertical integration is no longer the most optimal way of governing the production process because dynamic firms think in terms of 'work to be done'. These firms require a productive capacity with mobile frontiers to respond to requirements that are still being defined. In order to produce goods with high knowledge content, knowledge management within the firm becomes the key for increasing market power. In such a context, the aims of knowledge management are twofold.[3] The first is to collect and process as much knowledge as possible about markets, technologies, etc., and then integrate it into the product through improvements in the production process, or using Smith's words, through "the

---

[3] Kreiner and Mouritsen (2002) discuss knowledge management issues in more details.

improvement of the productive power of labour". Concentrating knowledge processing in a small team of top managers is no longer efficient since the volume of requisite knowledge is huge and such managers become overwhelmed. Rather, a decentralisation of knowledge capture and processing facilitates the effective acquisition of greater volumes of knowledge. Large firms therefore decentralise in two ways. They either delegate more responsibility to lower hierarchical levels which can specialise in the relevant knowledge of their functions, or they outsource certain activities such as their supply chain.[4]

Table 1.1 Production process and value creation

Phases of the production process (after raw materials and intermediate production):	Pre-manufacturing services (research, organisation)	Manufacturing	Post-manufacturing services (market control)
Assets related to the production phase:			
Tangible assets	Labs, facilities to perform tests or surveys, labour (quantity), machines	Physical capital Quantity of labour	Distribution channels, shops, etc.
Intangible assets	Labour (quality: ability of researchers, ability of marketers), knowledge base, capability to communicate	Communication, problem analysis and problem solving, adaptability to changes	Relations, marketing ideas

In this way for example, suppliers are responsible for their performance, can develop an autonomous capacity, and can process more knowledge about component production than could a remote senior manager in a large corporation. In short, specialisation, complementarity and the division of labour relates to knowledge and not just tasks. True, labour flexibility does not imply rigid production cycles which either add or eliminate work positions, or substitute human resources with machines. It concerns using competencies and capabilities to continuously transform the organisation of production to respond to new needs, to

---

[4] Thus nowadays about 70 to 80 per cent of a car's manufacturing costs are outsourced.

acquire and accumulate knowledge, to refocus accumulated learning, and to continuously redefine the complementarities between the various component parts of the productive process. The second aim of knowledge management is to generate knowledge, though innovation, in order to improve a product or process and to constantly renew the corporate organisation. For this purpose, interactions within the organisation and between the organisation itself and its environment are essential. Knowledge is created by exchanging ideas, thinking individually and collectively, and by generating new divisions of labour within a learning community. The best response to a changing economic environment is to organise as a dynamic network of competencies, both within the firm and between the firm and other organisations.

3. Changes in Large Firms' Internal Organisation

The changes in organisation within major multinational companies in different sectors in the late-80s and early-90s have been documented by a number of writers. Fransman (1999) for instance explains the shift from M-forms (multidivisional forms) to S-forms (segmented forms) by AT&T, IBM and NEC in the computer and communications sectors. According to the author, NEC was the first among the three to adopt the S-form as early as 1965 when it divided its activities into fourteen divisions and four product groups. The S-form is characterised by a higher segmentation and autonomy of divisions than in the multidivisional form, hence the term 'segmented'. In the S-form some strategic decisions are decentralised to divisions, contrary to the M-form where divisions are responsible for operating decisions only. According to Fransman, the aim of such decentralisation is to enable the company to more quickly adapt new product or process innovations. AT&T adopted a similar form in 1988, after its divestiture, whilst IBM adopted the new form in 1991.

Labory's (1997) examination of the automotive industry provides a similar analysis to that of Fransman (1999) and reaches the same conclusion regarding emerging organisational forms. She calls the new form however the 'N-form', N standing for network. Labory shows that the new form, of which Honda is typical, is characterised by two major aspects. Firstly, a higher autonomy is given to divisions. The strategic decisions delegated to divisions are shown to be decisions regarding local markets, since divisions are typically defined according to regions. Such delegation allows the company to better perceive and respond to changes in local consumers' tastes. Secondly, horizontal and vertical communication takes place not only between the divisions and the head office, but also at other levels of the companies. For instance, concurrent engineering, whereby a team consists of people of different functional backgrounds, is an example of horizontal communication in the product development process, since personnel with different backgrounds communicate and co-operate. At the corporate level, such horizontal co-ordination is typically achieved in the car industry by nominated functional directors responsible for different functions at world level (R&D, marketing, manufacturing, and so on).

Greater decentralisation offers the divisions more autonomy, while the communication flows are multidirectional (horizontal and vertical), two-way, and more intense than in the M-form, making the firm look like a network, with numerous communication nodes. The N-form is characterised at various levels as follows:

- Corporate level: more autonomy to divisions, and increased communication between divisions in order to exploit complementarities;
- Work level: more autonomy to workers (they can make suggestions) and horizontal communication (with teams colleagues, with other teams in workshop meetings, teams in other factories and via job rotation);
- Product development level: cross-functional project teams that increase co-ordination between the conception, manufacturing and commercialisation phases.

In addition, the network is also external to the firm, concerning relationships with suppliers (see the vast literature on suppliers' networks in the car industry, such as Asanuma, 1989 and Boyer et al., 1998) but also relationships with competitors to jointly perform R&D activities or even develop products. Concerning supply networks, a single firm alone no longer carries out every activity of the production process, but rather externalises some of its activities to external firms at various stages. Production is realised by a network of firms. The take up of outsourcing and the establishment of supplier networks has been discussed in much detail by economists (see Innocenti and Labory, 2002, for a review).

The reasons for the spread of subcontracting have been widely studied. The bureaucratic costs of the large, integrated company have been outlined (Chandler, 1990), as well as incentive (in terms of low employee motivation) and information processing costs (especially Aoki, 1988). When products become increasingly differentiated and up to date, it appears that the best strategy is to focus on core competencies (research, development and design of the product, assembly or marketing) and let other firms deal with component production, machine maintenance, and sometimes even distribution. Dis-integrated firms have thus been shown to be more efficient (lower cost or higher productivity), by Asanuma (1989) in Japan, and De Banville and Chanaron (1991) in France. Outsourcing yields other advantages though, in particular in terms of product and process innovation. For instance, Clark and Fujimoto (1991) and Michie and Sheehan (1999) show that R&D and product innovation are higher in firms which outsource.

In fact, an outsourcing strategy appears complementary to internal decentralisation activities and the creation of knowledge for product differentiation. Each firm in the network specialises in a part of the production process and develops a high competence and mastery of the knowledge relevant to that particular activity, while the membership of the network ensures the co-ordination of the various activities.

Networks can take various forms which vary according to the presence or absence of a leader, the degree of formalisation of links (contracts or informal arrangements) and the autonomy of its members and the degree of exclusivity of the network. An exclusive network is a network where firms do not develop relationships with others outside the network. For instance, within a network of a large firm that was previously vertically integrated, the suppliers exclusively sell to this firm and do not have other customers.

In economics, different types of network have been analysed from different points of view, ranging from incentives and compatibility problems,[5] to trust in partnership relationships (conditions for trust to develop and maintain) and learning issues (networks allow collective learning to take place).[6] Networks analysed empirically have been primarily those led by large firms (especially the car industry and country studies which have particularly stressed the advantages of the Japanese Keiretsu networks), and networks between small and medium sized firms (especially in Italy, with its many industrial districts). This book's focus on the analysis of networks discusses these issues in more detail. In particular, the chapters by Di Tommaso et al., Galassi and Mancinelli and Cottica and Ponti provide insights into the functioning of networks and policy implications thereof.

The relevant unit of analysis in the study of a firm's competitiveness should therefore be the network to which it belongs, rather than the single firm. The objective of the firm is to manage and create knowledge in a network, in order to differentiate, frequently renew its products and to gain the loyalty of its customers.

The large, vertically integrated firms of yesterday primarily relied on the ownership of highly specialised assets (assembly lines, machinery, etc.) in order to gain market power and create value. The ownership of such assets also defined the firms' boundaries. As a result, the key issue was the separation of ownership and control and economists focused their analysis of the firm on this issue. As Chandler (1990) argued, the primary advantage of the modern business enterprise was its scale and scope.

In the new firm, power is distributed differently. In the past, ownership of the firm's resources was concentrated in the hands of shareholders, the owners of the company. The current situation is different since resources are distributed among different stakeholders such as employees, who bring their human capital, and suppliers with innovative or other capacities, etc. Under these conditions, the determinants of market power are no longer cost or scale based, but rather the ability to manage networks. This is the case with Nokia, Microsoft, Gucci, LVMH and a number of automobile manufacturers. At the management level, the governance problem is no longer to ensure that employees work in the company's best interests, but rather to ensure that the integrity of the firm is maintained. When most of the firm's value was embedded in its tangible assets that could be owned, its boundaries were fixed and no problem of integrity arose. Most value now arises

---

5
 The incentive to remain a member of the network depends on the degree of complementarity of activities. The incentive to take part in a network depends on various motivations including the sharing of indivisible factors and services, such as gaining access to a particular skill, competence or service.

6
 Also see Cottica and Ponti (chapter 7).

from assets that cannot be easily appropriated by the firm, such as knowledge or human capital. The new management challenge is therefore to tie the owners of such assets (employees who have specific human capital or hold specific knowledge) to the activities of the firm, by giving them access to some of the firm's resources, although not too much, otherwise the firm loses control. Concretely, as shown by Brown and Hendry (2002), in the case of the introduction of new technologies in a firm, this means making the new requisite skills compatible with existing capabilities. For this purpose, making the skills explicit and integrating them into the firm's business planning system appears to be a successful strategy.

Such investment in complementarity creates unique characteristics for firms which are difficult to imitate and constitute a barrier to entry. Managing a network emerges therefore as a major challenge not only because it leads to the production of successful products or services, but also because a properly managed network is an asset, difficult for competitors to imitate and hence a guarantor of market power. The links between this complementarity and intangible assets are analysed in more detail later. The following section provides evidence of the rise in interest in intangible assets at the country level, and points to the limitations of current indicators.

4. Intangible Assets and Economic Growth

Given the scope of the changes outlined in the previous sections, one could imagine some implications at the macro level. It was argued that intangible assets at the firm level include a wide variety of assets, all those in fact which do not have a physical or financial embodiment. At the country level, it can be argued that the main intangible assets are knowledge, innovation, human capital and social capital (Bianchi and Labory, 2002).

Given the confusion as to the nature and characteristics of intangible assets, there are no perfect indicators. The review by Bianchi and Labory (2003) of the main indicators of a country's performance highlights three characteristics. Firstly, intangible assets are imperfectly measured, in that existing indicators do not capture all their aspects. It is widely asserted for instance that measures of human capital based on an achieved level of education do not include learning during working life, and those countries with a large proportion of early school leavers, who are later trained on the job, are therefore penalised. Another example is that although innovation is often measured by R&D expenditure, not all R&D leads to innovation. Secondly, some intangible assets, social capital in particular, are not measured. Finally, although intangible assets appear to be undervalued, there is strong evidence of their growing importance (OECD, 2003a, b; OECD, 2001a, b; Eurostat, 2001).

Intangible assets have been partially measured using a number of proxies, including R&D spending, employment in ICT, public spending in education, and so on. For instance, estimates prepared by Kendrick, and reproduced by Abramovitz and David (OECD, 1996), show that the share of tangible capital in the total stock of capital in the US economy fell from 65 per cent to 46.5 per cent over the period 1929 to 1990, while the share of intangible capital rose from about 35 per cent to 54 per cent. This is argued to provide evidence that in the context of the emerging knowledge economy, and changes in the nature of competition, firms have not reduced overall capital formation but have rather shifted resources into intangible capital.

OECD measures of investment in tangible versus intangible assets across OECD countries (OECD, 2001b), in terms of percentage of GDP, over the period 1991-98 show that compared to the US, the EU has higher annual average growth rates in investment, but the US has a higher proportion of intangible investments. In Europe, the Scandinavian countries show the highest rates of growth of intangible investments. The case of Finland is noticeable since it shows negative growth of physical capital and a very high growth rate of investments in intangibles, the highest among all reported countries.

To compute these measures, intangible assets are assumed to comprise higher education, software and R&D, presumably measuring respectively the following intangibles: human capital, knowledge and innovation. However, this procedure raises two problems. First, the measures are incomplete: the percentage of the population with higher educational degrees does not measure the whole human capital of a country, since for instance it excludes training during the working life. R&D spending is an input to innovation and does not measure how much a country innovates but how much it invests in innovation. Software does not summarise the whole knowledge base of an economy. Second, other intangible assets are not considered, especially organisational and social capital (see the next two sections).

The result is that intangible assets are underestimated in these measures. Despite these shortcomings, the evidence is that all countries are investing heavily in intangible assets and therefore their importance is growing in the economy.

The OECD also provides evidence of their growing effect on growth. The OECD (2003b) shows that growth is essentially determined by labour productivity, which in turn crucially depends on three factors. Growth can thus be improved by improving first the quality of labour used in the production process; second, the use of capital and especially new capital like ICT; and third, by increasing overall efficiency, i.e. the multi-factor productivity (MFP) by improved managerial practices, organisational change and innovation in the production process. Evidence on the determinants of the MFP is difficult to find because the MFP is a residual. However, a number of studies make progress in this sense. Thus there is growing support for the positive effects of organisational changes on productivity, as reviewed in section 5 below. We must focus our attention on two particular intangible assets which are largely excluded from the statistics reviewed above: the organisational capital and the social capital.

5. Organisational Capital

The consideration of organisational design as a differentiating performance factor has recently experienced renewed interest. This is due to the fact that many firms in many countries are currently undergoing change. The development of databases of firms' organisational designs, based on surveys of managers and employees, has in particular provided new insights into the importance of new organisational practices, their determinants and their effects.

The surveys question how the firm is organised, such as the number of hierarchical levels, the average number of subordinates per head, the extent of teamwork, job rotation, incentive systems, etc. In order to detect change, they query how the organisation is today, and how it has altered. Such surveys provide qualitative data on organisational changes and new work practices and have been analysed by labour and industrial economists. Data are often unrepresentative however of complete industries in a given country, since surveys are confined to particular sectors (e.g. Ichniowski et al, 1997, 1999, focuses on the steel industry) or regions (e.g. Leoni et al, 2003, in a Northern Italian region). Nationally representative databases have nevertheless been compiled in a number of countries, including the US, UK and France.[7]

Studies of the data reveal patterns of change in organisations,[8] characterised by greater communication (both horizontal and vertical), flatter hierarchies, more external interaction, more decentralised work, higher task integration and lower specialisation. Internal labour markets have more complex remuneration systems (profit sharing, pay for skill, etc.), higher selection standards and more training. Industrial relations also benefit from change which seems to establish greater trust between management and workers. Most studies (see Leoni et al., 2000, for a review) of the various data sets find that organisational change initiatives (teamwork, job rotation, flatter hierarchies, pay for performance, etc.) must be implemented together to produce positive productivity effects. Analyses of productivity generally assume that organisational change is incremental to other more common factors (labour and capital) in the production function.[9]

No theoretical rationale for such production function is offered. The only theoretical reference mentioned by some studies is the super-modularity literature (Milgrom and Roberts, 1990, 1995), which states that complementarity between

---

[7] In the US, the National Employer Survey (NES), focusing on the production system and labour organisation, has been conducted several times in the 1990s (Black and Lynch, 1997, 2000). The UK equivalent is the Workplace Industrial Relations Survey (WIRS), based on questionnaires sent to employers, and conducted in the years 1980, 1984, 1990 and 1998. After 1998 a survey of employees was added (see Millward and Forth, 1999, Cully et al., 1999). In France, different surveys have been conducted (see Greenan and Mairesse, 1999), focusing on workplace practices or on wider technological and organisational changes.

[8] Such studies naturally suffer from data problems related to measurement, endogeneity and selectivity (see Leoni et al., 2000 for a technical review). Some of studies nevertheless (e.g. Ichniowski, 1997, 1999, Black and Lynch, 1997, 2000, Greenan and Mairesse, 1999,) control for econometric problems.

[9] Leibenstein (1966, 1975) can be considered the pioneer in such productivity studies, since he seems to have been the first to argue that the productivity differences observed across firms with similar technology might be due to organisational factors. He developed the concept of X-inefficiency, meaning organisational slack.

different change initiatives makes their joint adoption profitable. Complementarity is defined as a case in which the adoption of one initiative raises the marginal profit of adopting another. The problem here is that the theory justifies ex-post why some initiatives should be adopted together, but does not predict the same ex-ante. Analyses of the effects of organisational change on performance generally focus on its impact upon productivity (except for Ichniowski et al. 1997, 1999, who analyse the effects on product quality and on profitability) and wages (with mixed results, see Leoni et al., 2000, for a review). This results in a lack of consideration for the costs of organisational change. Since the studies generally only collect performance data during several years after organisational changes are implemented, long-term effects on performance are not captured. The study by Kato and Morishima (2001) on Japanese data concluded that employee involvement schemes and share option programmes take seven years to have positive effects on performance.

Although data from opinion surveys are not comparable across countries because the questions, and even the management concepts, differ, about a quarter of large firms have nevertheless altered their organisational structures. Rates of change of adoption depend on the size of the firm (larger firms more so), the intensity of competition (international markets exposure), and the sector. The causes, patterns and effects of such organisational innovation (OI) are not clearly understood (Labory, 2000, 2002).

6. Social Capital

Another important intangible which has experienced growing interest among scholars in recent years is social capital. This concept suffers from similar problems as other intangibles, namely the difficulty of definition and, therefore, of measurement.

A useful starting point for a discussion of social capital as an intangible asset might be the work of Coleman (1988, 1990, 1994), who developed a social theory which explains society in the context of individual rational choices. He goes beyond the extreme individualism of neo-classical economic theory by emphasising that social institutions condition such choices (Coleman, 1990: p 300; Coleman, 1994: p 166). Coleman claims that individuals do not act independently, but have interests which depend on the actions of other individuals, and that they therefore develop relationships to pursue these interests. In this way, interaction structures arise composed of authority, trust, and norms of reciprocity. These structures represent a resource for action and thereby constitute social capital.

Consequently the notion of social capital is intrinsic to social interaction structures between individuals and it is this feature that makes it intangible. Social capital, like other forms of capital, is productive in that it allows individuals to reach otherwise unattainable objectives (see also chapter 4 on the productive nature of social capital).

At the collective level, social capital consists of the structural and normative characteristics of a given social system, namely its organisations, norms and institutions. It can take various forms such as trust, communication across social relationships, reciprocal relations which facilitate the development of trust, and the norms which define the form, content and limits of exchange.

Social capital has four main characteristics. Firstly, its public good aspect makes it *not excludable* since it is not a private property, and *not rival*, since an individual benefiting from it does not reduce others' usage and benefits. Secondly, social capital is highly *specific* to the society in question, i.e. to the social interaction structure. Its third characteristic is that it only has *value in use*, i.e. when individuals of a particular group or society actually use it in their productive activities. This is due to its origins in the structure of interpersonal relationships. Hence the value of social capital is exhibited through the performance of economic agents. It is, finally, *dynamic,* since it emanates from, and changes with, aspects of social relationship structures such as membership, activity, members' interests, communication style, etc. Its dynamic nature implies that social capital can be both an asset and a liability. For example, relationships in Tuscan industrial districts based on tacit knowledge exchange, trust and strong member ties created social capital in the 1960s and 1970s since these mutual bonds favoured the district's positive performance. This situation later turned into a liability when the district had to open to foreign markets in order to maintain its competitive position.

According to Coleman, although social capital cannot exist without a structure of relationships (an organisation, a network), it is not in itself comprised of the structure. Social capital is rather the usage of relationships in economic activities.

Coleman's analysis is very useful because it raises a number of points on the concept. An important point is that social capital does not arise unless individuals discover mutual interests in building relationships with each other. Only a complementarity of interests and activities can therefore give rise to relationships and social capital. This implies a complementarity of assets in that physical assets must be suitable for particular activities and must facilitate relationships. Human assets such as the ability to recognise the complementarity of interests and activities, or ability to build relationships, must also be present.

Another important point is that social capital is intimately linked to networks: it arises out of networks and also allows networks to better function, by reducing communication and co-ordination costs. However, the way social capital influences the creation and development of networks has to be better understood, especially in order to improve policy (see section 7 below and chapter 3). Therefore, the research of the next chapters has focused on these two aspects, networks and social capital.

This definition uncertainty implies that the concept of social capital has been reduced to only a few aspects in order to make the concept more conducive to measures. Thus most theoretical studies consider social capital as trust or a reputation for co-operative behaviour and is shown to favour economic performance (for instance, Annen, 2003). Empirically speaking, social capital has been measured using survey data (e.g. the World Values Survey used by Knack and Keefer, 1997) and focused around associative activities (Putnam, 1993), trust and civic norms (Knack and Keefer, 1997). Putnam (1993), in the case of the Italian regions, finds social capital to have a positive effect as defined by the impact of associative activities on growth. Neither the empirical results of Knack and Keefer (1997,) nor those of Olson (1982), support this hypothesis however, since being a member of an association does not mean contributing to its social capital. One can be a member without taking part in the social activities of the association. More importantly, associative activities do not cover the whole of the social interaction structure and do not take into account the active role of network participants.

Hence the aim of the research of this book of analysing more deeply the interplay between social capital and networks. Given that social capital stems from a social interaction structure, it might be useful to more deeply examine networks in order to gain insights into the social capital they use and/or create. Analysing networks implies examining interaction structures, and hence looking at the origins of social capital. This is also what Annen (2003) suggests at the theoretical level. He models inclusiveness, i.e. the size and heterogeneity of a network, as a general factor contributing to social capital.

In this theoretical perspective, Kranton and Minehart's (1998) general framework for analysing network structures might be useful. Cottica and Ponti (in chapter 7) extend the framework via an analysis that captures the dynamic nature of social capital. Galassi and Mancinelli (chapter 5) stress that a mixed-public good framework should be adopted in order to better understand how social capital is formed, and its effects. In this way they consider social capital as having both private and social benefits.

The analysis of networks also needs strengthening from an empirical point of view. Chapter 3 shows that although networks have long been advocated by EU innovation and knowledge diffusion policy as yielding positive effects in this field, the way networks function and are successfully created is still not well understood. Many European public authorities have created innovative networks (clusters) in recent years with mixed results precisely because of this lack of understanding. How are the common language and norms of behaviour, trust and co-operative behaviours built through time? Cottica and Ponti mention some historical studies, of the Italian districts for example, which stress that norms of behaviour and knowledge from agricultural production favoured the development of district-like relationships when farmers left the countryside and started to work in industry. These are very specific conditions that are extremely difficult to repeat and may not in any case be suitable in other contexts. Is social capital so specific that no policy can be designed to favour its creation?

The analysis of the economic importance of intangible assets yields important research and policy implications. More research is needed on networks, and in particular on the way complementarity is created. In our opinion, the social capital that keeps together a network and favours its success is vital in building the complementarity between the various members of the network. Policy action favouring networks should therefore pay attention to the social capital that allows this complementarity to develop.

7. Outline of the Book

Intangible assets, primarily knowledge and human capital are created by combining a number of complementary activities such as R&D, education, motivation, organisation, and relationships. It is difficult to predict ex ante the optimal combination that produces innovation, entrepreneurship and growth. Such properties might imply therefore that an appropriate policy is one which creates linkages between economic actors. The conditions for linkages to develop have however to be determined and put in place. Such circumstances for suitable linkages, networks, and therefore intangible assets, to develop might include the existence of proper incentives such as equal bargaining power and the existence of complementary activities which facilitate the co-ordination of activities and the exchange of knowledge. Sanctions against opportunistic behaviour are also possible. Together these elements imply the need for an adequate level of social capital. This is especially true concerning innovation, i.e. knowledge creation, which is increasingly performed in networks both within and outside the firm.

Hence the growing importance of intangible assets in contemporary economies provides a justification for the shift in industrial (competitiveness and innovation) policy from direct, rather sectoral intervention to correct market failures to the creation of the conditions for the market failures (knowledge not enough diffused, lack of entrepreneurship, and so on) to be resolved. In other words, the shift has been from 'government' to 'governance' as argued by Labory in chapter 3 regarding EU innovation and knowledge diffusion policy.[10]

What we argue in this book is that for such 'governance' policy to become more effective what is needed is a better understanding of the way networks function, how they are created and how they develop, and in particular the role of an important private and collective intangible asset, social capital.

Relationships are influenced by the institutional frameworks that determine the norms and values behind social capital. A particular example is provided by intellectual property rights legislation, which limits access to knowledge not only to those actors directly interested, but to all actors whose activities are complementary. Control, rather than ownership, is probably more important however for intangibles since others barriers to entry exist such as the capability to build, maintain and develop networks. Indeed the earlier discussion in this chapter showed that as the organisation of production expands beyond a firm's legal boundaries, what matters more than direct ownership is the control of certain key assets. Insights will be provided at various parts of the book about the workings of networks, social capital and the complementarities that social capital enables in networks.

Chapter 3 analyses the extent to which EU innovation and knowledge diffusion policy has recently focused on networks between innovative agents without considering social capital. The emphasis of policy has shifted from incentives to innovate to providing a framework for the diffusion of innovation (spillovers), for

---

[10] Many scholars have in fact made this argument; for instance, Borras (2003).

which networks represent a key policy tool. Building links between the various actors of the innovation process is fundamental. Although the EU has taken many measures to favour knowledge diffusion, progress on this front is difficult to evaluate. The ever present gap between the US and the EU in terms of innovation shows that more effective policy action is required. A better understanding of the functioning of innovation networks is needed. For this purpose, clarity on the characteristics of the intangible assets (especially social capital) at work in successful innovation networks would be useful.

Chapter 4 argues that location matters for networks to develop because proximity is correlated with higher levels of social capital. A review of geographical clustering theory and the literature on intangible assets raises issues related to the geography of intangibles. Considering the spatial implications of different types of intangible assets, and more interestingly, the inherent characteristics of intangibles, it is possible to argue that spatial proximity remains of great importance in spite of claims during the internet revolution of the 'death of distance' and the 'end of geography'. The networking of relationships both internal and external to a cluster is a determinant factor for competitiveness. Rather than a group of firms to be analysed individually, the cluster should be considered as an independent actor able to generate intangible assets such as trust and mutual understanding (social capital), learning, the creation and communication of tacit knowledge, as well as collective knowledge and innovation.

Chapter 5 studies the nature of social capital arguing that it should be considered as a productive asset. The only difference between the physical and social capital is that the public good characteristic of social capital is stronger than that of physical capital. Social capital can be regarded as the public element of certain intangible assets, without which no firm can function. The chapter also outlines factors that positively influence a firm's accumulation of social capital. It concludes that social capital is in fact the public value of intangible assets, the capitalised future income streams made possible by the reduction in transaction costs when mutual engagement is the favoured form of interpersonal (and inter-firm) contact. It is both the trust upon which clusters and industrial districts are born, and the outcome of their existence. The challenge of analysing social capital as an intangible asset is that it acts as both an input and an output in a complex series of wealth creating relations.

Chapter 6 examines how public intervention can encourage relationship building, with examples covering university and business initiatives, and the role of public agencies in diffusing knowledge. An appreciation of social capital is vital for the definition of effective policies that favour networks. Although relationships between universities and businesses depend somewhat on public incentives for their creation, the norms, cultures and values of members of the institutions, or their social capital, is equally if not more important. Public entities such as space agencies can therefore favour both the creation and diffusion of knowledge, through encouraging the development of social capital between the members of the networks they create.

Chapter 7 analyses the dynamics of networks. It shows in an evolutionary model the conditions under which innovative networks improve welfare. It also examines the efficiency and stability conditions of such a model. This evolutionary approach improves upon the existing literature since it better captures dynamics than the traditional game-theory framework. The authors show that vertical networks, whereby a supplier of innovation (e.g. a R&D lab) sells to a manufacturing firm (e.g. pharmaceutical company), can improve welfare. They focus on intangible assets which can be sold such as patents or innovations embedded in manufacturing equipment. Other intangible assets such as social capital, human capital or reputation, which are not easily measured and priced, are not able to be included in this theoretical framework.

The last two chapters show some of the results of research performed by other PRISM teams which has been complementary to the research presented in chapters 2 to 7. Chapter 8 presents the problems related to reporting on intangible assets at firm level. It shows that the various new reporting methods that have been developed include not only human capital and knowledge capital, but also social capital. Firms have therefore been aware of the importance of this asset, especially given the diffusion of networks.

Chapter 9 focuses on the relationships between businesses and financial institutions in an analysis of reporting on intangibles to provide better information to these institutions. It highlights findings from research into how providers of finance can better understand their clients' intangibles. Areas are identified where European policy makers should act to encourage the development of scaleable methods to more effectively provide innovation capital to European SMEs, achievable through a more widespread understanding of intangibles

Overall the book takes a multidisciplinary approach in order to provide insights into the links between the micro (firms) and macro (the economy) levels.[11] Whilst most of the chapters are written by economists, the last chapters belong to managerial literature. The recent attention given to intangible assets highlights the need for an analytical framework which prioritises the organisation of production and thereby overcomes challenges to more interpretative models that consider production as a black box. Such a framework should propose a vision in which production competencies such as knowledge, skills, dexterity and judgement are once more the drivers of an organisation designed to compete in a specific market, in which firms act with a view to increasing market power relative to other operators who share the same motivation to compete in terms of innovation.

Although the division of labour in production is based on specialisation and complementarity, rapid change requires continuous interaction outside the firm. This continuous knowledge exchange requires trust because allowing access to one's knowledge implies allowing access to one's secrets in exchange for future development. In other words, allowing access to one's own knowledge means allowing access to the knowledge embodied in the 'work done' in order to stay in the game for future 'work to be done'. The value of a social organisation emerges in that the more firms wish to be mobile and adaptive, the more their social context

---

[11] This has been an important contribution of the PRISM network as argued by Eustace in chapter 1.

must be stable and based on shared values. The exploitation and valuation of such social capital is also crucial to understand strategies of localisation in the new geography of intangibles, as termed by Di Tommaso, Paci and Schweitzer.

Socially stable countries for instance can have decentralised production since all agents are constrained by a common sense of belonging. In contrast, countries in which the social system is fragmented incite firms to internalise all their functions in the absence of outsource possibilities. In the first case, individual agents can focus on a specific activity since they believe that other agents will not only produce complementary goods but also exchange knowledge. In the second case it is not possible to share with other agents. Developed country firms therefore transfer aspects of their standardised production (pre-defined parts or components, i.e. 'work done') to developing countries or to countries in transition, and they keep in house their research and development, design and prototypes (i.e. 'work to be done') because this is the strategic core of the firm.

References

Abernethy, M. and Wyatt, A. (2003), 'Intangible Assets. An Overview', chapter 1, in *Study on the Measurement of Intangible Assets and Associated Reporting Practices*, Report to the European Commission, DG Enterprise,
http://europa.eu.int/comm/research/era/3pct/index_en.html.

Annen, K. (2003), 'Social Capital, Inclusive Networks, and Economic performance', *Journal of Economic Behaviour and Organisation*, 50, 449-63.

Aoki, M. (1988), *Information, Incentives and Bargaining Structures in the Japanese Economy*, Cambridge University Press, Cambridge and New York.

Asanuma, B. (1989), 'Manufacturer-supplier relations in Japan and the concept of relation specific skill', *Journal of the Japanese and International Economies*, 3, 1-30.

Bagwell, K. and Ramey, G. (1990), 'Capacity, Entry, and Forward Induction', Mimeo, May.

Bain, J. (1956), *Barriers to New Competition*, Harvard University Press, Cambridge MA.

Bianchi, P. and Labory, S. (2002), 'The Economics of Intangible Assets', University of Ferrara, Working Paper n. 16/2002.

Bianchi, P. and Labory, S. (2003), 'Macroeconomic Indicators and Policies for Intangible Assets: Measurement Problem or More Fundamental Economic Change?', chapter 2, in *Study on the Measurement of Intangible Assets and Associated Reporting Practices*, Report to the European Commission, DG Enterprise,
http://europa.eu.int/comm/research/era/3pct/index_en.html.

Black, S. and Lynch, L. (1997), 'How to Compete: the Impact of Workplace Practices and Information Technology on Productivity', *NBER Working Paper Series*, n. 6120.

Black, S. and Lynch, L. (2000), 'What's Driving the New Economy: The Benefits of Workplace Innovation', *NBER Working Paper Series*, n. 7479.

Bonanno, G. (1988), 'Entry Deterrence with Uncertain Entry and Uncertain Observability of Commitment', *International Journal of Industrial Organisation*, 6(3), 351-62.

Borras, S. (2003), *The Innovation Policy of the European Union*, Edward Elgar, Cheltenham, UK.

Boyer, R., Charron, E., Jurgens, U. and Tolliday, S. (eds) (1998), *Between Imitation and Innovation. The Transfer of Productive Models in the International Automobile Industry*, Oxford University Press, Oxford.

Brown, J. and Hendry, C. (2002), 'A Case Study on Measuring Skills in Technology Leadership', PRISM project, http://EU intangibles.net

Chandler, A. (1990), *Scale and Scope. The Dynamics of Industrial Capitalism*, Harvard University Press, Cambridge MA.

Clark, K.B. and Fujimoto, T. (1991), *Product Development Performance*, Harvard Business School Press, Boston.

Coleman, J.S. (1988), 'Social Capital in the Creation of Human Capital', *American Journal of Sociology*, 94, 95-120.

Coleman, J.S. (1990), *Foundation of Social Theory*, The Belknap Press of Harvard University Press, Cambridge MA.

Coleman, J.S. (1994), 'A Rational Choice Perspective on Economic Sociology', in N.J. Smelser and R. Swelberg (eds), *The Handbook of Economic Sociology*, Princeton University Press, Princeton, 166-180.

Cully, M., Woodland, S. and O'Reilly, A. (1999), *Britain at Work, As Depicted by the 1998 Workplace Employee Relations Survey*, London, Routledge.

De Banville, E. and Chanaron, J.-J. (1991), *Vers un Système Automobile Européen*, Economica, Paris.

Dixit, A. (1980), 'The Role of Investment in Entry Deterrence', *Economic Journal*, 90 (March), 95-106.

Eaton, B.C. and Lipsey, R.G. (1978), 'Freedom of Entry and The Existence of Pure Profits', *Economic Journal*, 88 (September), 455-69.

European Commission (2000a), *Innovation in a Knowledge-driven Economy*, Communication from the Commission to the Council and the European Parliament, COM(2000)567 final - 20.09.2000.

European Commission (2000b), *Benchmarking Enterprise Policy. First Results from the Scoreboard*, Commission Staff Working Document, SEC (2000) 1841, Bruxelles.

European Commission (2001a), *Statistic on Science and Technology in Europe*, Bruxelles.

European Commission (2001b), *European Competitiveness Report*, Luxembourg.

Eurostat (2001), *Measuring the New Economy*, Luxembourg.

Fransman, M. (1999), *Visions of Innovation. The Firm and Japan*, Oxford University Press, Oxford.

Greenan, N. and Mairesse, J. (1999), 'Organisational Change in French Manufacturing: what do we learn from firm representatives and from their employees?', NBER Working Paper n. 7287, August.

Henderson, R. and Cockburn, I. (1996), 'Scale, Scope, and Spillovers: the Determinants of Research Productivity in Drug Discovery', *Rand Journal of Economics*, 27(1), 32-59.

Ichniowski, C. and Shaw, K. (1999), 'The Effects of HRM Systems on Economic Performance: An International Comparison of U.S. and Japan', *Management Science*, 45(5), 704-21.

Ichniowski, C., Shaw, K. and Prennushi, G. (1997), 'The Effects of HRM Systems on Productivity: A Study of Steel Finishing Lines', *American Economic Review*, 87, 291-313.

Innocenti, A. and Labory, S. (2002), 'The Advantages of Outsourcing in Terms of Information Management', University of Siena, Working Paper n. 470.

Kato, T. and Morishima, M. (2001), 'The Productivity Effects of Participatory Employment Practices in Japan', paper presented at the International Conference on Organisational Design, Management Styles and Firm Performance, Bergamo, 22-23 June.

Knack, J. and Keefer, J. (1997), 'Does Social Capital Have an Economic Payoff? A Cross-Country Investigation', *Quarterly Journal of Economics*, November, 1251-87.

Kranton, R. and Minehart, D. (1998), 'A theory of Buyer-Seller Networks', *American Economic Review*, 1, 570-601.

Kreiner, K. and Mouritsen, J. (2002), 'Knowledge Management as Technology: Making knowledge manageable', forthcoming in B. Czarniawska and G. Sevon (eds), *The Northern Lights*.

Leibenstein, H. (1966), 'Allocative efficiency vs. "X-efficiency"', *American Economic Review*, 56(3), 392-415.

Leibenstein, H. (1975), 'Aspects of the X-efficiency Theory of the Firm', *Bell Journal of Economics*, 6(2), 580-606.

Labory, S. (1997), 'Firm Structure and Market Structure: a Case Study of the Car Industry', Working Paper n. 97/8, European University Institute, Florence, Italy.

Labory, S. (2000), 'Indirect Effects of Organisational Innovations', paper presented at the EAEPE Conference, Berlin, 2-5 November 2000, mimeo.

Labory, S. (2002), 'A Firm's Internal Organisation and its Implications for Market Performance', *Economia Politica*, 2, 259-76.

Leoni, R., Cristini, A. and Labory, S. (2000), Sistemi di Gestione delle Risorse Umane (GRU) e Performance d'Impresa: una rassegna critica della letteratura, Quaderni di lavoro, dipartimento di Scienze Economiche, Università di Bergamo, n.11.

Leoni, R., Cristini, A., Labory, S. and Gaj, A. (2003), 'Flat Hierarchical Structure, Bundle of New Work Practices and Firm Performance', *Rivista Italiana degli Economisti*, August.

Lev, B. (2000), *Intangibles. Management, Measurement, and Reporting*, Stern School of Business, New York University, December.

Michie, J. and Sheehan, M. (1999), 'HRM Practices, R&D Expenditure and Innovative Investment: Evidence from the UK's 1990 Workplace Industrial Relations Survey', *Industrial and Corporate Change*, 8(2), 211-33.

Milgrom, P. and Roberts, J. (1990), 'The Economics of Modern Manufacturing: Technology, Strategy and Organisation', *American Economic Review*, 80, 511-28.

Milgrom, P. and Roberts, J. (1995), 'Complementarities and Firms: Strategy, Structure and Organisational Change in Manufacturing', *Journal of Accounting and Economics*, 19, 179-208.

Millward, J. and Forth, J. (1999), *All Change at Work? British employment relations 1980-98, portrayed by the Workplace Industrial Relations Survey*, London, Routledge.

OECD (1996), *Employment and Growth in the Knowledge-Based Economy*, Paris.

OECD (2000), *Recent Growth Trends in the OECD Countries*. OECD Economic Outlook, No.67: Paris.

OECD (2001a), *Beyond the Hype. The OECD Growth Project*, OECD, Paris.

OECD (2001b), *Intangible Investments, Growth and Policy*, STI Directorate, DSTI/IND(2001)5 (September).

OECD (2003a), *The Policy Agenda for Growth. An Overview of the Sources of Economic Growth in OECD Countries*, OECD, Paris.

OECD (2003b), *The Sources of Economic Growth in OECD Countries*, OECD, Paris.

Olson, M. (1982), *The Rise and Decline of Nations*, Yale University Press, New Haven, CT.

Putnam, R. (1993), *Making Democracy Work*, Princeton University Press, Princeton.

Smith, A. (1976), *An Enquiry into the Wealth of Nations*, reprinted in 1960 by J.M. Dent & Sons Ltd., London (two volumes).

Chapter 3

EU Policies for Innovation and Knowledge Diffusion

Sandrine Labory

The scope of this chapter is an analysis of EU policy and the reorientation required to accelerate the circulation and commercialisation of innovation and knowledge within Europe, taking into account leading-edge policy throughout the global economy. The focus is on policy towards knowledge creation and diffusion, and as such, includes a review of existing EU innovation and knowledge diffusion policies, of their effects (using evidence from the literature), a comparison with other major industrialised countries (the US in particular), and some policy implications in light of the reflections provided in chapter 2.

I outline the fundamental trade-off of research and development (R&D) policy. Namely that providing incentives to innovate requires the appropriation of the returns from innovation and the diffusion of knowledge concerning the innovation. The wider this diffusion of knowledge however, the less the gains from innovation to each individual concerned. The policy traditionally recommended by economists assumed that knowledge could be reduced to information, that is, codified or explicit knowledge. Information can be transmitted at almost no cost and the use of information by some individuals does not preclude its use by others: hence information has the characteristics of a public good. Diffusion therefore poses no problem. Policy should focus on providing the incentives to innovate, via subsidies, a property rights and protection system, and so on. Recent developments in economics have stressed however that knowledge is not only composed of information; it also comprises tacit knowledge, i.e. know-how and competence. The latter kind of knowledge is not easily transmissible, essentially because its acquisition incurs learning costs (trying out, observing, adapting the existing knowledge base, etc.). This is discussed in more detail later. What is important here is that such literature has had a large influence on policy making and has contributed to a shift in policy emphasis, from one side of the trade-off to the other, namely from a focus on incentives to innovate to a focus on diffusion. The main idea of policy is now to create an environment favourable to innovation and knowledge diffusion. For this purpose, networks should be developed within the economy, and in particular the relationships between firms and universities or other knowledge institutions need to be intensified.

This chapter shows that while the shift in policy emphasis has helped uncover some previously neglected problems in innovative activities, it has also led to a lack of precise policy recommendations. It seems that *all* actions that favour collaborative relationships have to be adopted, policy makers choosing from a sort of 'shopping list' of actions. Although networks need to be developed, their adequate type, size and institutional context does not appear to be discussed much. In addition, understanding the motivation to take part in networks seems to be neglected, although it is essential for their creation in the first place. In other words, we need to specify the incentives to take part in innovative activities, and in particular the possibility of appropriating returns from innovation arising in a collaborative network.

Intangibles can bring new insights to this debate. I also discuss the nature and effects of intangibles and show that they might be the key determinants of the nature of those networks most appropriate to innovation and knowledge diffusion. A particular point regards the social capital associated with networks.

1. The Basic Policy Problem

The fundamental policy problem regarding innovation stems from the presence of research externalities, i.e. the fact that innovative knowledge created by an individual or company can be freely captured and used by others. In economic terms, this implies that private returns to innovation are lower than social returns.

Firms have three main ways of mitigating this problem. First, they can try to make knowledge difficult to imitate by avoiding over-codification or communication with other individuals or firms. This solution may be difficult to implement however due to industrial spying for example. Second, firms can try to 'internalise externalities', by making the new knowledge available in industrial associations, by signing collaborative R&D agreements, and by acquiring or merging with other firms that may use their knowledge. Although such solutions allow a firm to capture all the returns from its innovative knowledge, they are quite costly, in particular due to the costs of internal co-ordination which rises the more players become involved. Third, the firm can try to be a first mover in the likely applications of its new knowledge, and thus gain a 'first-mover advantage'.

Although all the above actions help protect innovation from appropriation, they hinder the diffusion of the new knowledge throughout the economy – meaning that there's a fundamental trade-off between providing the incentives to innovate and ensuring diffusion.

Traditional public policy solutions to problems posed by such research externalities have included:

- Setting-up markets for knowledge, especially through granting intellectual property rights (IPR) over the new knowledge.
- Subsidies: given that knowledge can be easily appropriated and become a public good, incentives to innovate can be maintained if R&D activities are

subsidised. The problem with subsidies is the difficulty for policy makers to assert that firms would not have performed R&D activities in the absence of subsidies. There is information asymmetry since firms can easily hide some information in order to get maximum subsidies.

- Public production of new knowledge: innovative activities are performed in public research centres or other institutions, new knowledge from which is made available to firms. The problem with such a solution is that it may lead to a duplication of research efforts, as when different levels of government (regional, national or European) set the same research topics. Also, the research priorities might be guided more by political votes or lobbyists rather than by welfare motives.
- R&D collaboration: the government can favour R&D collaboration at the pre-competitive phases of research.

R&D collaboration has been one of the main instruments used by the European Commission. The economic literature on R&D joint ventures is huge[1] and discusses the conditions for research ventures to increase society's welfare. One important shortcoming is that although research joint ventures are shown to be optimal for certain levels of spillovers (externalities) between firms, no study has yet managed to analyse such spillover parameters in depth, and shown precisely their determinants.

In the prevailing models of industrial organisation,[2] spillovers refer to involuntary leakage and voluntary exchange of useful technological information during incremental innovative activities. Two major types of innovation exist. *Fundamental* innovations can create major technological discontinuities, such as the invention of the steam machine or electricity. Discontinuities are relatively rare and may both destroy or enhance the competence of the existing firms in the industry (Tushman and Anderson, 1996). Since incumbents have to change skills, abilities and knowledge in order to adapt the new technology, new entrants are often able to play an important role in the diffusion of the new technologies. Gambardella et al. (2000) show that the diffusion of biotechnologies in the pharmaceutical industry has been eased by the arrival of specialised new entrants, while incumbents had to change their research methods and knowledge base and did so primarily through agreements with or via the acquisition of the new entrants. *Incremental* innovation (improvements in existing products or processes) is more frequent and generally extends the life cycle of existing technologies. Contrary to discontinuities, incremental innovation does not result in drastic changes in industry structure, and instead creates concentration, changes in the relative positions of the different players and number of firms in the industry for example.

Traditional analysis and policy recommendations rely on two major hypotheses: that all knowledge can be reduced to information, i.e. can be codified

---

[1] Starting from the late 1980s: d'Aspremont and Jacquemin (1988, 1990); Katz and Ordover (1990), Martin (1991), Shapiro and Willig (1990).

[2] See De Bondt (1996) for a review.

and transmitted at zero cost, and that all interactions between agents take place on competitive markets.

Both assumptions can be criticised. The first assumption is restrictive in that much knowledge cannot be codified because it is tacit. A typical example of tacit knowledge is knowing how to ride a bicycle: although you know how to ride, it is difficult to explain all the mechanisms enabling equilibrium and movement. The relaxation of the first assumption leads to the possibility of increasing returns to knowledge. Several economists have provided evidence in favour of this: Machlup (1982) argues that the more one invents the more likely one will be of inventing again, and is confirmed by Scotchmer (1991). In fact, returns to knowledge creation can be either decreasing or increasing. Doubling the number of researchers for example does not necessarily lead to a doubling of innovation. Appropriately combining human capital and organisational assets (both intangibles) can however increase the probability of discovery: doubling the number of researchers and organising them to work in different teams dealing with different activities has for instance been shown to increase the probability of discovery (see Nonaka and Takeuchi, 1998, who underline the importance of such variety for creativity in innovative activities).

Another important point is that the acquisition of knowledge is costly: acquiring and mastering new knowledge requires investments in learning, trying out, understanding, etc. The cost of acquisition of new knowledge increases with the distance between the new knowledge and the existing knowledge base. For instance, a long-established pharmaceutical company incurs high costs in acquiring new biotechnology knowledge since its previous knowledge base was focused on different research techniques (Gambardella et al., 2000). The nature of technology has been widely studied, and a number of features can be outlined. First, technology is complex and is the result of cumulative learning. Thus home grown R&D is not a perfect substitute for buying foreign technologies because firms' own research activities allow them to develop the capabilities to assimilate outside technologies. Another important result from the literature is that firms spend more time developing (designing, building and testing prototypes) than they do researching (developing scientific laws and models). The consequence of these points on the nature of technology is that technological knowledge is not easily transferable: one of the conditions for technological knowledge to diffuse is that firms build the capabilities to assimilate such knowledge.

The evidence from empirical research on spillovers confirms the hypothesis of the existence of cost in knowledge acquisition. Thus more intra-industry spillovers occur in industries with high technological opportunities and with similar products and manufacturing processes (Eliasson, 1994; Jaffe, 1986). Inter-industry spillovers tend to be fewer than intra-industry spillovers (Bernstein, 1988). Such observations have to be qualified however by the fact that the measures of spillovers are imperfect and probably underestimate their true values (Patel and Pavitt, 1995).

As a result, knowledge is an impure public good,[3] the diffusion of which requires learning and transaction costs and can be hindered by barriers to knowledge access. The private returns are not always less than the social returns. When the first hypothesis (all knowledge can be reduced to information) is relaxed, policy recommendations change. The role of policy is to focus on the organisation of knowledge distribution system and to increase the 'distributive power' of the innovation system (Foray, 1994). In addition, innovation and diffusion are not totally distinct, and policies for innovation and the diffusion of knowledge cannot be independently defined (Cohen and Levinthal, 1989).

The second hypothesis (all interactions between agents take place on competitive markets) is also restrictive, since it is quite obvious that not all do and that some agents may indeed negotiate off-market bilateral contracts. Externalities may arise from conversations between individuals during various social events. Hence the role of social capital in spillovers. Social capital comprises the set of market, power and co-operative relationships developed between actors (individuals, firms, institutions) which share a similar culture. Regional economists refer to the territorial dimension of activities, where the territory and the space are not only physical but also include the space of relationships between actors (called 'milieu innovateur' by some authors: Aydalot, 1986; Carmagni, 1991; Maillat et al, 1993; or 'industrial atmosphere' defined by Marshall, 1890). Cultural proximity, in terms of a sense of belonging, a capacity of interactions between individuals, and the sharing of common norms, determines the social capital, which translates into collective learning through different channels, including high mobility on the local labour market, stable and profitable relationships between local actors, and spin-offs.

Given the above considerations, the social capital determines the extent of the diffusion of knowledge and collective learning. The set of relationships that generates the social capital might then be the key to understanding spillovers. The economic literature to date lacks a discussion of the identification of spillovers, and in particular of the channels through which they are realised, and focuses instead on firm size and R&D expenditure as the major determinants of innovation. The social capital constructed within a given economy (a region, country, or set of countries) or firm (both internal and external) might however be the fundamental determinant of both innovation[4] and knowledge diffusion. And although many economists have stressed the importance of proximity in favouring knowledge diffusion, the focus has mainly been on geographical proximity (Acs and Audretsch, 1990; Audretsch and Feldman, 1996; Anselin et al., 1997, 2000; also see chapter 4).

---

[3] A pure public good is both non-rival (the consumption by one individual of the public good does not reduce the amount of the good left to other individuals) and non-excludable (it is impossible to prevent some individuals from accessing the good). Knowledge is an impure public good in that learning costs imply that it can be excludable.

[4] Or at least that of collective learning that results in knowledge creation and hence innovation.

Under the new hypotheses that knowledge is a broader concept than information and that interaction between individuals that can take place outside of markets, the policy recommendations change and should aim to:

- favour the emergence of collective interactions in the production and diffusion of knowledge (rather than create markets); and
- manage ex ante and ex post co-ordination problems. Ex ante, the problem is to elaborate collective goods (ex ante division of research labour). Ex post, the problem is to make sure that the new knowledge is complementary to other projects in society, so that the probability of exploiting positive externalities is high.

In economics, the school of thought which relaxes the two restrictive assumptions above is called the 'evolutionary theory' which stresses the importance of networks between individuals and institutions to favour knowledge creation and exchange. Such literature has developed the concept of national innovation systems (NIS), which can be claimed to have contributed to the shift of emphasis of EU policies in the 1990s. I discuss the advantages and limitations of NIS in more detail in the next sections (also see chapter 5).

2. The Main Instruments of EU Innovation and Knowledge Diffusion Policy

Bianchi (1995) describes the change in emphasis of European industrial policies at the beginning of the 1990s. Instead of directly affecting the *actual decisions* of agents (the firm, industry, etc.) regarding entrepreneurship or innovation, policies now aim at providing favourable conditions to affect agents' *incentives* to make the appropriate decisions. For example, two actions for R&D collaboration were implemented, aiming firstly to lower relationship transaction costs (information search, co-ordination, etc.) by providing for example forums where firms can meet, and secondly at constructing collective intangible assets through a series of framework programmes to build a common knowledge base.

The EU has therefore developed the following policies to exploit its research infrastructure:

- relationships between universities and industry (e.g. ESPRIT);
- publicly funded research labs;
- support to industrial technological development: public subsidies to private R&D can affect innovation through three channels: complementing private spending (increase R&D spending), catalysing inter-firm collaboration and targeting specific technologies;
- favouring competition. Economists argue that in the absence of competition to provide incentives to innovate, monopolies tend to exploit their incumbent advantages with little dynamism. In the EU, the main problem in this respect is the tendency of national governments to continue favouring national firms and

thus preventing the real unification of the European market (the 'mutual recognition principle' for example is not applied in many sectors such as pharmaceuticals).

The Framework Programmes (FPs) now represent the bulk of EU innovation policy. Such programmes have four-year life cycles and define the community's research and development priorities. In the main they have focused on futuristic technologies (materials, information and communications) and those related to natural resources (environment, life sciences, biotechnologies, and energy).[5] Pelkmans (1997) argues however that the institutional infrastructure for these programmes is highly inefficient. It may take for example up to three years to decide on direction due to Member States' unwillingness to effectively transfer competencies. Whatever the case may be, the objective of FPs is to favour cross border collaboration to exploit spillovers and to contribute to the development of the European Internal Market.

There are two main drivers for defining a common technology policy at the EU level. First, the subsidiarity principle, which implies that the presence of crossborder externalities and scale economies beyond national borders justifies a policy at European level, together with the evidence that co-ordinating individual Member States' policies represents neither a feasible nor perfect alternative. Regarding innovation, such conditions are fulfilled, especially the cross-border externalities. Second, EU technology policy should contribute to the establishment of the Internal Market and to the main EC objectives, such as cohesion, sustainable development, the competitiveness of European industry and its citizens' welfare.

A recent project designed by the European Commission is the European Research Area (ERA) (European Commission, 2000). Its primary objective is to examine the structural weaknesses of European research and propose supporting measures, especially through the 6th research Framework Programme (2002-2006). Since a main weakness appears to be the fragmentation of research efforts in the EU, the ERA project aims at favouring the co-ordination of RTD (research, Technology and Development) policies at the regional, national and European levels and at encouraging mobility to work throughout the EU. The 6th FP is in fact the main tool supporting the ERA's creation. Its main objectives are to:

- integrate research in order to maximise the impact of efforts made in the priority research areas defined by the FP;
- provide a structure for the ERA to promote and strengthen co-operation and synergies between and within the national and regional programmes on human resources and mobility;
- strengthen the ERA's foundations to stimulate and support co-ordination programmes and common actions among Member States and European

---

5
I do not review here all the programmes adopted by the European Commission since its foundation and instead focus on main recent policies and their evaluation.

organisations, and to develop a common knowledge base for a coherent implementation of policies.

The instruments proposed to meet these objectives are the realisation of integrated projects, the building of networks of excellence and the realisation of joint projects between the European Commission and its Member States. In reality the ERA project appears to provide a new home for previously stated objectives and proposed actions. The European Commission has been stressing for a long time the importance of joining national R&D efforts to avoid duplication and to make the whole worth more than the sum of the parts.

Table 3.1 Main aspects of the ERA

Integrating European Research	
Priority thematic areas	**Anticipating needs**
Genomic and biotechnology for health	Policy support
Information society technologies	Frontier research, unexpected developments
Nanotechnologies, intelligent materials, new production processes	Specific SME activities
Aeronautics and space	Specific international co-operation activities
Food safety and health risks	
Sustainable development and climate change	
Citizens and governance in the knowledge society	
Structuring the ERA	**Strengthening the foundations of the ERA**
Research and innovation	Co-ordination of research activities
Human resources and mobility	Development of research and innovation policies
Research infrastructure	
Science and society	

Source: European Commission (2000).

Establishing a favourable environment in Europe for innovation is defined as 'encouraging technology transfer, ensuring venture capital availability, helping to protect property rights and developing human resources' (Buigues et al., 2000, p.325). Although apparently all good ideas, it is difficult to find in the literature any explanation concerning how the protection of property rights is compatible with knowledge transfer, what are the trade-offs, whether financial capital other than venture capital is available, and to what extent human resources are underdeveloped in the EU. Hence the policy appears as a 'shopping list' of actions that can be taken to favour innovation and knowledge diffusion.

US and Japanese policies differ from Europe. Although Japanese government sponsored research joint ventures continue to be developed, the recent aim has been to create a 'technological superstructure' for a large group of high technology sectors. The MITI provides a long-term view on industry and identifies an industrial strategy that is helpful in providing a systemic view for the overall impact of the various measures. The US has only recently established specific programmes to promote co-operative R&D. I next compare the relative performance of the EU, the US and Japan.

3. The Innovative Performance of the EU

To assess progress in innovation (and competitiveness in general) at the European and national levels, 'benchmarking' exercises and innovation scoreboards have been introduced. I do not review here the findings of the last scoreboards but I focus discussion on the main indicators and the continuing gap between the EU and the US in terms of innovative performance.

Due to its complex nature, the measurement of technological activity and innovation is imperfect and as such its two main measures, R&D expenditure and patenting activities, are heavily criticised.

The main criticisms of R&D expenditure as a suitable metric are that it:

- underestimates the technological activities related to production: R&D is classified according to the principle activities of the firm, not to *all* activities, whilst innovation occurs not only in R&D departments, but also for example in the production department through learning by doing;
- captures imperfectly the technological activities of small firms, which do not have formal R&D labs and accounting measures;
- underestimates technologies related to information processing such as software; and
- measures the inputs instead of the outputs of innovative activities.

As to patents, the main criticisms of such a metric are:

- Time lag issues: if patenting occurs early in the innovation process, they are a poor measure of its output (Pakes and Griliches, 1984).
- Persistent variations across sectors and countries in R&D productivity, as measured by patents granted per unit of R&D spent. These variations are mainly due to imperfections in measuring R&D, inter-sectoral differences in the usage of patents to protect innovations. For instance, patents are much more important in the pharmaceutical industry than in the car industry, where other means are used to protect innovation (first mover advantage, focus on process innovation, etc.). Procedures and criteria for granting patents also differ widely across countries.

The sources, speed and division of technological activities differ largely across economic sectors and as such much work has been done on cross sector technological differences and interdependencies (Scherer, 1982; Geroski, 1991), the main results of which are:

- more than 75 per cent of the development of new technologies is concentrated within machinery and instruments, electrical and electronic, chemicals, transport and pharmaceutical;
- in all core sectors the focus is on product innovations to be later adopted in end-user sectors;
- the main user sectors are textile, food, paper and printing;
- inter-sectoral differences in productivity growth are best explained by the usage and application of technology rather than by its creation.

Such studies remain at the aggregate level and do not explain how sectoral linkages appear, develop, or evolve over time. Firm-level studies have shown that although smaller firms develop individual technologies, larger firms develop and integrate multiple technologies (the diversity of technologies in the firm increases with firm size). A country with a relatively lower score for a particular criterion does not necessarily need to prioritise policy to catch up. Fewer science and technology graduates might be compensated, for example, by more intensive on-the-job training. Although Europe lodges fewer patent applications, this might mean that Europe needs emphasis on the commercial applications of innovations rather than further R&D activities.

The scoreboards therefore include a wide variety of indicators, ranging from human resources (average level of education of the workforce, percentage of employees in high tech sectors), innovative performance (R&D expenditure, patenting activity), and the diffusion of ICT in the economy. Overall, the scoreboards have been repeatedly concluding on the gap between innovative performance of the EU and that of the US, the US leading. This has led to the call in the Lisbon European summit of 2002 to make all possible efforts to reduce the gap. Some scholars (for instance, Gambardella et al., 2000) argue that what is missing in the EU is not the creation of knowledge but the ability to transform innovation into commercial success. In other words, some Europeans produce ideas, but they do not have the opportunity to transform their ideas into successful products. The problem could be one of property rights (patenting being difficult) or of relationships (they are not linked to actors that could help in the commercialisation), or both. In fact, the literature tends to point to both factors. Regarding the second factor, a deeper look at the case of the relationships between a creator of ideas (a research institution like the university) and those who commercialise ideas (business) might be useful.

4. The Case of University-Business Relationships[6]

Analyses of European technological performance in the 1990s have often used the expression 'European paradox' (European Commission, 1995). Although Europe has a considerable amount of R&D and no serious technology gaps, European firms appear to suffer from an inadequate ability to convert their inventions into commercial success, especially in high technology sectors such as electronics and information technology. The European Commission was aware of this problem and examined numerous policy measures with a view to increasing the technological competitiveness of European firms. Most of the new measures were inscribed into the conceptual framework of both the National Innovation System (NIS) (Nelson, 1993; Lundvall, 1992) and the knowledge economy (Smith, 2000; MERIT, 2000).

The concept of NIS emphasises the need for interactions between the agents of innovation, particularly governments, universities and firms. This interaction is particularly stressed by the 'triple helix' approach that may be considered as an evolution of the NIS approach (Etzkowitz and Leydesdorff, 2000). Although firms play a leading role in innovation in the NIS, the historical existence of different kinds of interactions between the three institutions is more important in the triple helix approach. Although governments have been in principle the main actors, it has been shown that the actual tendency is an equal interaction between the three agents. The knowledge economy framework arrives at the same conclusion, though at a more abstract level, focusing on the circulation of knowledge, whose speed and effectiveness are key in a contemporary economy increasingly based on intangible goods and in which knowledge is the 'intangible asset' *par excellence.*

Several European documents consequently published in the 1990s (EC, 1995; Jones-Evans, 1998) have stressed the need to reinforce linkages between universities and industry and, coherent with this purpose, many European technology policies were elaborated to meet this aim. Although of course the focus was on universities, other institutions 'produce' knowledge and research, for example, some large public research institutions and agencies specifically created to facilitate knowledge transfer.

Two main linkages exist between universities and industry. First, universities are the main source of human capital, even though further training is often necessary for new graduates, and the formal education they provide is the basis for the absorptive capacities of technological development by firms. Second, the research conducted by university departments is usually a source of technological improvement, whose commercial exploitation is subsequently realised by firms. A number of authors[7] who have more deeply examined the relationship between science and technology stress however a fundamental difference in terms of objectives between universities and business, namely that business research is usually oriented towards shorter term goals. This does not mean that basic research

---

[6] This paragraph has been written in collaboration with Roberto Iorio.

[7] Rosenberg (1982) is a classical contribution on this point.

performed by universities should be put aside, but that the complementarity of university and business research is not so straightforward.

These two kinds of relationship, however, cannot be considered as proper 'linkages' since they do not imply a direct contact between universities and industry. Educated people may be hired after they have left university whilst the results of scientific research are published in books and reviews, for which firms may incur learning costs. Such linkages are in fact market relationships which pose the problem that they exclude certain types of knowledge flows. As stressed in the first section of this chapter, certain kinds of knowledge are not marketable in which case direct linkages are the only effective ways to acquire the knowledge.

Making a list of the possible direct linkages between two institutions is not an easy exercise, due to the numerous informal relationships involved, whilst measuring them is even more difficult. For this reason, the main linkages identified and focused upon to date have been those related to explicit R&D collaboration and personal contacts, via for example consultants or entrepreneurs who come from university and remain in contact with their departments (and have set up a spin-off). The Framework Programmes of the European Commission have aimed at reinforcing such linkages, especially through R&D co-operative projects. Geuna (1999) studied the determinants of the participation of the Higher Education Institutions (almost exclusively universities) to the Framework's projects and concluded that a university's relatively higher scientific productivity positively influences both the probability of joining an EU-funded project and the number of times it participates. Other empirical studies, especially concerning Austria (Schibany and Schartinger, 2001) and Italy (Alessandrini and Sterlacchini, 1995) conclude that industries with high internal R&D, and therefore especially large firms, are more inclined to collaborate with universities and be more satisfied with the outcome. Collaboration therefore between universities and industry appears, in the European situation or at least in many European countries, like an elitist phenomenon.

This represents an important and probably fundamental difference between the EU and the United States. The American system of collaboration between universities and firms is characterised by the presence of some leading universities such as the MIT which was born with this specific purpose. Nevertheless, such a system appears to have contributed to the diffusion of industry-sponsored research and to the transfer of technology to commercial applications. In Japan, a country perhaps considered second in 'world technology competition', some tight and frequent personal relationships exist that tie university researchers with individual firms, even though such linkages encounter bureaucratic obstacles. In the EU, there appears to be a sort of reciprocal scepticism towards collaboration, especially in the Mediterranean area. Probably influenced by a more humanistic background, universities define themselves and are perceived by firms as 'pure research' institutions, whose nature is inadequate to, or would be improperly transformed by, a focus on applied research. This results in an uneasy difference in mentalities. European universities appear relatively more reluctant to collaborate; the above-mentioned analyses of Italian and Austrian situations show that firms propose collaboration much more frequently than universities do. Also when public incentives induce collaboration, the lack of an adequate mentality produces negative effects: an empirical study on the dynamics of network formation within the BRITE-EURAM program, for the Second and Third FP (respectively 1990-94 and 1994-98) reveals the prevalence of a competitive behaviour, less socially efficient than a co-operative one, and the existence of trade-offs between the short-term productivity of research and the long-run cohesion of technological capabilities.

Therefore, one problem in Europe is one of 'mentalities' that are not prone to collaboration, especially on the part of the universities which are reluctant to collaborate with business. In other words, one problem is that of social capital. In the US, common interests have induced both universities and industry to co-operate, thus overcoming some initial difficulties and perplexity, expressed for instance in the student protests during the 1970s. American universities moreover appear to propose collaboration, contrary to the European case. Such a situation is not however without problems. In particular, universities face a trade-off between independence and business funding, and run the risk of favouring scientific faculties to the expense of other faculties. Business is concerned about the long-term orientation of university research. Some problems also arise regarding the diffusion of research results: universities aim for a wide diffusion of the results, through publications, while businesses are more prone to patent research and to obtaining exclusive property rights, and hence restricting the diffusion of the new knowledge. This problem is being tackled in the US, while the EU is still at too early a stage of university-business collaboration to be confronted with it (Alessandrini and Sterlacchini, 1995).

This problem shows the two-sided coin of creating networks: not only must the social capital of the different actors that one wish to relate be compatible, but also the conditions for the social capital to adjust and become compatible must be provided: legislation on property rights appears to be a fundamental aspect of this question, as shown for instance by the essential role of the Bayh-Dole Act in the US in favouring university-business relationships (Link, Scott and Siegel, 2003).

5. Assessment: From 'Government' to 'Governance'

The swing in emphasis of EU RTD policy from a prescriptive to more enabling focus can be called a shift from 'government' to 'governance'. Policy has moved away from clearly defining each level and area of competence and targeting public intervention at specific players, towards a blurred definition where levels and areas interact, and through which policy aims to provide the right environment rather than act directly on agents. In terms of RTD policy, 'government' was the policy of subsidy and support to specific industries, whilst 'governance' is now the idea of providing the favourable environment for innovation and its commercialisation.

Few empirical studies have evaluated the EU RTD programmes, many of which have supported generic technologies (Sematech in the US, ESPRIT, BRITE, RACE, etc.) and research collaboration to reduce costs, spread risks, avoid duplication and exploit economies of scale in R&D. Apart from impact studies carried out at national level, few detailed studies have assessed the effects of these programmes. Caloghirou, Ioannides and Vonortas (2003) for example looked at EU research joint ventures and highlighted differences between countries but did not estimate their impact upon the economy. They uncovered large differences between the policies of individual EU Member States. Policy approaches have ranged from indifference to the issue until recently (Ireland), rapidly decreasing attention (UK), lukewarm policies (Greece, Italy), and firmly established programmes to assist co-operative industrial RTD (France, Spain). The level, type and technological focus of the various programmes have varied widely. The EC's policies appear to have played the role of catalyst and co-ordinator seen by Member States as complementary to their own policies.

Research collaboration has focused at a pre-competitive stage, especially in Europe which still lags behind in terms of its ability to transform innovation into commercial success. In Japan by contrast, the specific focus on collaboration to increase technological diffusion appears to have been successful, with three conditions seemingly contributing to this success: the complementarity of participants' technologies, transfers of personnel between participants, and early stage research collaboration followed by strong competition during commercialisation.

The reasons for meagre returns in Europe from bringing successful products to market have long been recognised. A 1993 EC White Paper argued that the main problems were inadequate links between universities and business, a lack of risk capital, insufficient emphasis on R&D within corporate strategy, difficulties of researchers in starting new businesses, and weak market research.

Despite this lack of innovation output, the Framework Programmes have had positive effects on knowledge creation and networking.[8] Luukkonen's (2002) analysis of networks set up within the FP in Finland found that in B2B relationships, firms collaborate mainly with suppliers or clients which implies that vertical collaboration is most frequent. In addition, 64 per cent of the projects with Finnish participants involved firms collaborating with either universities or public research centres. Overall 70 per cent of the companies involved in a FP project collaborated with a university, and 75 per cent with a public research centre. Spillovers are found to be predominantly intra-sectoral rather than inter-sectoral, and the research indicates that the FPs may have reinforced the oligopolistic tendency of the European IT market.

This points to a number of problems with networking:

- Although collaboration is positive for spillovers, it facilitates collusion since if firms' collaboration works out, they might secretly expand co-ordination to the market phase (Luukkonen, 2002, points to such a possibility). This is less true when collaborating firms are small and more numerous since it is less easy to collude in the market, and more difficult to co-ordinate the participants.

---

[8] See Georghiou et al., 1993 (UK); Larédo, 1995 (France); Reger and Kuhlmann, 1995 (Germany); Ohler et al., 1997; (Austria) and Luukkonen and Hälikkä, 2000 (Finland).

- Additionality arises when the collaborative project would have taken place even without EC funding and is difficult to spot. (Evidence is mixed however, as shown by Luukkonen, 2002.)

Overall, the results of the FPs and therefore EU RTD policy are mixed. From the negative point of view, European competitiveness is still lagging behind the US and Japan. The EU situation is however mixed, with some Member States having a good innovative performance (Finland, Sweden) and others not (Portugal, Greece). The relative lack of transformation of innovation into commercial products within Europe still represents a major challenge. More positively, despite its overall lack of competitiveness, the EU is still in the technology race. EU programmes have helped create cross-border networks between firms and between firms and universities or other public research centres. Vavakova (1995) and Lucchini (1998) argue that the FPs have provided stable financial support for networking, reduced competition among researchers and between the public and private sector researchers, and allowed access to complementary skills.

The above discussion points to a number of issues, whose solutions might lead to substantial improvements in EU RTD policy. Although networking undoubtedly has positive effects, the conditions for success do not appear to have been widely debated. The economic theory behind 'networking' policy is composed of two branches: that of strategic collaboration (Katsoulacos and Ulph, 1996) and that of evolutionary theory and the concept of national systems of innovation (NIS). The latter argues that since innovation and technological change result from knowledge flows and collective learning in interactions between individuals and organisations, an important policy for innovation is to favour networking. This idea could also have influenced the new policy emphasis for creating environments that favour certain objectives rather than direct actions. Neither approach to networking however analyses the suitability of various types of networks for particular situations.

In addition, since NIS is a concept and not a theory, this implies a lack of understanding about different types of networks and the conditions under which they function. Systems might not be best characterised as national or supranational but rather as being dependent on other variables such as the sector and type of knowledge base. Since IT is an international industry for example, talking about national or even European systems of innovation is difficult: firms are multinationals and may exploit spillovers worldwide. Innovation in the fashion sector may on the other hand be more related to regional characteristics since the local culture and know-how determines the type and quality of the product, meaning that the innovation system in this case is more regional.

As well as network type and the balance of its constituents, network size is an important parameter to consider. Too small a network might not sufficiently extract knowledge from spillovers and lead to firms' collusion beyond the pre-competitive research stage. Too large a network may lead to a loss of knowledge through the numerous communication flows that have to be established.

Property rights and their distribution among actors in the innovation process might also be essential to determine networking success. If universities cannot obtain patents, they will not be motivated to move to more applied research and to collaborate with businesses.[9] If smaller firms cannot collaborate with universities in more applied projects, they will not undertake R&D which will increasingly take place mainly in large firms having the requisite resources. In Europe there is much fragmentation of research efforts and a lack of exploitation of complementarities between countries, regions and actors at various levels and in various sectors. What the evaluation of EU RTD policy shows is that although networking is necessary, the types, size and focus of networks should be analysed in more depth.

The EC benchmarking exercise might be useful in this respect, not in terms of identifying best practice networking for widespread adoption, but rather for categorising the general characteristics of networking in each country in terms of innovation, culture, university systems, and competitive industrial sectors and so on. One could subsequently evaluate potential for innovation in some sectors, identify priority areas for supporting policies (for instance, put more resources where the country already has a comparative advantage), and spot the potential for cross-fertilisation at the European level. Finland for example is very innovative in the knowledge-based sectors, while Italy is very innovative in design and fashion at the product development stage: the combination of the two might lead to durable competitive advantages thanks to innovative products and new market creation.

Despite this potential, EU innovation policies, with a focus on creating favourable environments for business and innovation, consequently end up being a list of recommended actions with little guidance on implementation and how to actually 'produce' innovation. The key question seems to be 'how do networks function?' A reflection on the nature and effects of intangibles will be useful for clarifying this.

6. Innovation is Complementary to Other Intangible Assets

The discussion in the first part of this chapter emphasised that innovation is a complex process that results from the exchange, accumulation and collective generation of knowledge. To better understand the lack of innovative competitiveness within the EU, a first step is to relate innovation to other intangible assets.

An examination of some channels and obstacles for knowledge can provide valuable context for intangible assets within our discussion. For example, consider human capital and entrepreneurial ability. The traditional literature of R&D spillovers in economics mentioned above does not take on board the role of entrepreneurs in transferring technological information. Baumol (1993) stressed however that an entrepreneur may play a fundamental role in identifying where others' inventions can be profitably introduced, and a role in taking the risk of adapting the exported techniques to the geographic and market conditions of the new location. Other channels for innovation include licensing technology, patent

---

[9] This appears to be the case in the European pharmaceutical industry (see Bianchi and Labory, 2002).

disclosure, publications or technical meetings, conversations with employees of innovating firms (possibly in the context of informal networks), hiring the employees of the original innovator, and reverse engineering (Mansfield, 1985). Even the process itself of R&D involves spillovers since one aspect of such activity is the collection of information and knowledge from outside the firm.

Accompanying these additional channels for innovation is organisational rigidity, a quite neglected obstacle to the adoption of new knowledge. The useful employment of a spillover knowledge is in itself a challenge for the management of innovation. In the pharmaceutical industry for instance, Henderson (1994) shows that the research firms' productivity is higher when they are able to take advantage of knowledge generated in all areas of their organisation. As stressed by De Bondt (1996: p.4), the development of

> a sustainable advantage may require the use of adequate knowledge management structures (e.g. pooling knowledge in semi-permanent project teams, more space in offices so that learning by walking around is stimulated, generalist training, rotation, incentive structures), or more generally, a 'learning organisation', that is an organisation skilled at creating, acquiring and transferring knowledge, and at modifying its behaviour to reflect new knowledge and insights.

Additional channels appear when one considers all possible forms of R&D collaboration which can range from strategic co-operation or alliances without cross-participation, through joint ventures, full co-operation and mergers. Although mergers do not appear to have been extensively covered in economics, they can encompass different functional activities, such as R&D, marketing, production and information systems.

Although economists have examined intangible assets such as innovation, knowledge, human capital and organisation, they have done so rather separately. In reality, one might argue that all intangible assets combine to create a firm's value. Innovation (a new knowledge) has little value unless transformed into a product that is sold on the market. In other words, the organisation of production, commercial activities and employees (with their human capital) all contribute to the value created through innovation. A firm's organisational design does not have value unless combined with human and tangible capital such as machines and equipment. Hence it might be argued that firms' growing emphasis on intangibles in their reporting is due to a strategy of developing complementarities between intangible and tangible resources to augment value creation. Whereas in the past such complementarities were fixed (in particular product definition, technology, organisational structure, job and skills definition, etc.) they are now strategic variables.

Intangible assets raise two major problems. Firstly, their existence means that other factors of production and innovation beyond the cost of labour and (mainly) physical capital must be taken into account; for example, knowledge and human capital, and organisational design which influences the way individuals interact, and therefore whether they can collectively create knowledge or contribute to the diffusion of existing knowledge or competencies within the organisation.

Secondly, intangibles are both input factors and outputted results or assets in the production process meaning that their combination is much more than the sum of their parts.

The fact that intangible assets are simultaneously assets and generators of assets can be explained by examining their nature in more depth. All intangibles are related to knowledge. An individual's human capital depends to a large extent on how he accumulates knowledge. Innovation is in itself knowledge creation. The organisation of a firm or of its activities primarily means distributing knowledge to different units, each specialising in one type of knowledge relevant to the total productive activities of the firm, and organising knowledge exchange between such units. Intangible assets cannot however be reduced to knowledge only since they are also capabilities, i.e. abilities, competencies to set up and solve problems, to communicate with others, and so on. Knowledge without capabilities produces little value, since at the level of the firm, it does not produce the right product for the consumer and hence success for the firm on the market.

As stressed in chapter 2, such capabilities in fact constitute what Adam Smith (1776) called the 'work to be done'. Smith explained such a relationship using the example of a public mourning which suddenly raises the demand for black cloth, the result being that 'the market is under-stocked with commodities, not with labour, with work done, nor with work to be done' (Smith, 1776, p.52). In fact, when demand changes what is important is the work to be done (i.e. the intermediate goods or commodities), not the work done. The work to be done represents the capability to adjust production to demand fluctuations, and to undertake a productive function to produce a good. The work done represents what has been achieved and the firm's accumulated knowledge, totally or partially embodied in the firm's products, past innovations, and its organisational and tangible capital. The work to be done represents the firm's potential given these existing assets and its ability to adapt to changes.

At the level of a country, such 'work to be done' or capability to adapt to change and develop may be defined as comprising the same elements:

- Human capital is the knowledge, skills, experience and abilities of a country's citizens, such as innovative capacity, creativity, know-how, professional experience, motivation, satisfaction, learning capacity, and entrepreneurship.
- Structural capital is the pool of knowledge that stays in the country independent of the flows in and out of citizens, for example culture, institutions, norms, values, rules, knowledge diffused at school, laws and regulations, property rights systems.
- Social capital consists of the resources related to networking in the country such as infrastructures, language, political power.

A fundamental rationale for networking therefore appears: the need to combine tangible and intangible capital to create the proper 'work to be done'. In addition, the difficulties of networking become apparent in that the compatibility of the three types of capital is essential for networking to function.

7. Conclusions

Most innovation policies recognise that innovation is not a linear process linking new knowledge to new products or processes. It is a rather complex process resulting from multifaceted interactions and networking among various people and private and public organisations. Policies therefore aim to build environments favourable to the creation of such networks. Which networks are most conducive to innovation, how, and why, does not appear to be properly understood.

As argued above, a major European weakness appears to be the low capability for transforming ideas into commercial success. Europe is more oriented towards basic research, while the US is more oriented towards its commercial applications. Such European weakness could be the result of the lack of motivation of scientists to transform ideas into commercialised products, which in turn could result from the lack of linkages between scientists, innovators and businesses. It could be that scientists fear to get an insufficient share of the cake, that they work in a culture not focused on making money, or that there exists a lack of social prestige for scientists to make money from innovations. In short, the problem could be double: on the one hand, a property right framework not conducive to exploiting relationships with business; on the other hand, a social capital not conducive to commercialising ideas.

Such issues should be analysed in more depth; in particular, a deeper analysis of the social capital that conditions the forming and development of networks should be performed. An analysis of the differences in the social capital of universities in Europe and in the US would certainly be useful.

Another aspect that would be worth studying in more depth is the variety in nature and configuration of networks. Concerning networks between universities and firms, this chapter has shown that the links can vary from the hiring of new university graduates by firms to explicit agreements for joint R&D activities. The cultural context also matters: in other words, the social capital. For instance, without a climate of trust between universities and business, no linkages will be built. The power of influence held by the different actors in the network also determines success in terms of knowledge exchange and creation: if an actor, say a large firm, is dominant in a network also comprising SMEs, then the kind of knowledge exchanged and its diffusion is likely to be biased towards the interest of the dominant player, that is, knowledge primarily useful for the large firm and unidirectional knowledge flows in its direction.

Hence there are economies of scale in networking but also barriers to effective networking. One issue concerns network size. Should it cover the whole economy or one industry? Or should it be confined to a local area, such as a high tech cluster? Are we sure the knowledge generated by the cluster will generate benefits for the whole economy, and not only to the local area? The conditions for a network to be successful depend on:

- size: if it is too big, it will be difficult for actors to set up links with all other actors, so knowledge might not diffuse so well; if it is too small, knowledge diffusion will take place but knowledge creation might be limited, due to the lack of variety of the actors;
- actors' motivation: if actors can benefit from the network, they will take part in it. One important aspect here is intellectual property rights: if defined in such a manner that actors tend to keep most knowledge for themselves, the network will not be useful;
- distribution of power among actors: as stressed above, domination by one actor may bias knowledge exchange and creation. It might however be necessary if dominant actors are needed to properly commercially exploit innovative results;
- social capital: if actors share the same social capital or have different but compatible social capital (i.e. culture, language, norms and values), relationships and linkages will be eased.

Some network configurations are represented below in Figure 3.1. The first network is highly centralised on a presumably dominant actor. If this is an innovative network, it is probably a case of a large firm taking the property rights and involving a number of other actors in the innovation process.

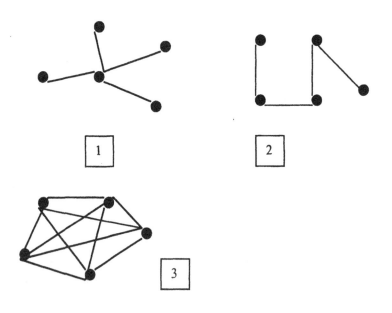

Figure 3.1 Different types of networks

The second network is not centralised, but it is not dense: each actor is related to only one other actor. Knowledge flows in this network are surely not maximum, and the resulting knowledge creation not optimal. The third network is not centralised either but it is very dense. All actors are related to all other actors. Is it too dense? Does it favour rapid and large knowledge creation? To what innovative networks does it correspond in reality?

The following chapters provide insights on both network structure and the social capital necessary for networks to function and to be built in the first place. Overall the aim is not to exhaust research on the topic, but rather to raise a number of issues that have to be deepened in future research.

References

Acs, Z. and Audretsch, D. (1990), *Innovation and Small Firms,* The MIT Press, Cambridge.

Alessandrini, P. and Sterlacchini, A. (1995), 'Ricerca, formazione e rapporti con l'industria: i problemi irrisolti dell'università italiana', *L'industria*, 88, 33-61.

Anselin, L., Varga, A. and Acs, Z. (1997), 'Local Geographic Spillovers between University Research and High Technology Innovation', *Journal of Urban Economics*, 42, 22-48.

Anselin, L., Varga, A. and Acs, Z. (2000), 'Geographic and Sectoral Characteristics of Academic Knowledge Externalities', *Papers in Regional Sciences*, 79(4), 435-43.

d'Aspremont, C. and Jacquemin, A. (1988), 'Co-operative and Non-Co-operative R&D in Duopoly with Spillovers', *American Economic Review*, 78(5), 1133-7.

d'Aspremont, C. and Jacquemin, A. (1990), 'Co-operative and Non-Co-operative R&D in Duopoly with Spillovers: Erratum', *American Economic Review*, 80(3), 641-2.

Audretsch, D. and Feldman, M. (1996), 'R&D Spillovers and the Geography of Innovation and Production', *American Economic Review*, 86(3), 630-40.

Aydalot, P. (ed.) (1986), *Milieux Innovateurs en Europe*, GREMI, Paris.

Baumol, W.J. (1993), *Entrepreneurship, Management, and the Structure of Payoffs*, the MIT Press, Cambridge.

Bernstein, J.I. (1988), 'Cost of Production, Intra- and Interindustry R&D Spillovers: Canadian Evidence', *Canadian Journal of Economics*, 2, 324-47.

Bianchi, P. (1995), *Le Politiche Industriali dell'Unione Europea*, Il Mulino, Bologna.

Bianchi, P. and Labory, S. (2002), 'Intangible Assets in the European Health Industry: the Case of the Pharmaceutical Sector', Working Paper of the University of Ferrara, n. 15/2002.

Buigues P., Jacquemin A. and Marchipont J-F. (eds) (2000), *Competitiveness and the Value of Intangible Assets*, Edwar Elgar, Cheltenham.

Caloghirou, Y., Ioannides, S. and Vonortas, N. (2003), 'Research Joint Ventures: A Critical Survey of Theoretical and Empirical Literature', *Journal of Economic Surveys*, forthcoming.

Carmagni, R. (ed.) (1991), Innovation Networks: Spatial Perspectives, Belhaven-Pinter, London.

Cohen, W. and Levinthal, D. (1989), 'Innovation and Learning: the Two Faces of R&D', Economic Journal, 99, 569-96.

De Bondt, R. (1996), 'Spillovers and Innovative Activities', *International Journal of Industrial Organisation*, 15, 1-28.

Eliasson, G. (1994), *General Purpose Technologies, Industrial Competence and Economic Growth*, Department of Industrial Economics and Management, The Royal Institute of Technology, Stockolm.

Etzkowitz, H. and Leydesdorff, L. (2000), 'The Dynamics of Innovation: from National Systems and "Mode 2" to a Triple Helix of University – Industry – Government Relations', *Research Policy*, 29, 109-123.

European Commission (1995), *Green Paper on Innovation*, Bruxelles.

European Commission (2000), 'Making a Reality of the European Research Area: Guidelines for EU Research Activities (2002-2006)', COM (2000) 612 Final.

Foray, D. (1994), 'Institutions, Incentive Structures and the Nature of Externalities in the Process of Knowledge Creation', Journée 'Forme de co-opération interentreprises et mécanismes de co-ordination socio-économique', December.

Gambardella, A., Orsenigo, L. and Pammolli, F. (2000), *Global Competitiveness in Pharmaceuticals. A European Perspective*, report prepared for the Directorate General Enterprise of the European Commission, Bruxelles.

Garcia-Fontes W. and Geuna, A. (1999), 'The Dynamics of Research Networks in Europe', in Garvin, D.A. (1983), 'Building a Learning Organisation', *Harvard Business Review*, 78-91.

Georghiou, L., Cameron, H., Stein, J.A., Neveda, M., Janes, M., Yates, J., Piper, M., Boden, M. and Senker, J. (1993), *The Impact of European Community Policies for Research and Technological Development upon Science and Technology in the United Kingdom*, HMSO, London.

Geroski, P. (1991), *Market Dynamics and Entry*, Blackwell, London.

Geuna, A. (1999), 'Patterns of University Research in Europe', in Gambardella, A. and Malerba, F. (ed.), *The Organisation of Economic Innovation in Europe*, Cambridge University Press, Cambridge.

Henderson, R. (1994), 'Managing Innovation in the Information Age', *Harvard Business Review*, 1, 100-105.

Jaffe, A. (1986), 'Technological Opportunity and Spillovers of R&D: Evidence from Firms' Patents', *American Economic Review*, 76, 984-1001.

Jones-Evans (proj.coor.) (1998), 'Universities, Technology Transfer and Spin-Off Activities Academic Entrepreneurship in Different European Regions, targeted socio-economic research project no.1042', Final Report, University of Glamorgan Business School.

Katsoulacos, Y. and Ulph, D. (1996), 'Endogenous Innovation Spillovers and Technology Policy', Centre for Economic Policy Research, Discussion Paper: 1407, May 1996, pages 36.

Katz, M. and Ordover, J. (1990), 'R&D Co-operation and Competition', *Brooking Papers on Economic Activities*, Microeconomics, pp.137-203.

Larédo, P. (1995), 'The Impact of Community Research Programmes in France', final report prepared for the European Commission, Ecole des Mines, Paris.

Link, A.N., Scott, J.T. and Siegel, D.S. (2003), 'The Economics of Property Rights at Universities: an overview of the special issue', *International Journal of Industrial Organisation*, 21, 1217-25.

Lucchini, N. (1998), 'European Technology Policy and R&D Consortia: The Case of Semiconductors', *International Journal of Technology Management*, 15(6/7), 542-53.

Lundvall, B.A. (ed.) (1992), *National Systems of Innovation: Towards a Theory of Innovation and Interactive Learning*, Pinter Publishers, London.

Luukkonen, T. (2002), 'Networking Impacts of the EU Framework Programmes', Publication of the database 'Circa-Circa', University of Ferrara.

Luukkonen, T. and Hälikkä, S. (2000), *Knowledge Creation and Knowledge Diffusion Networks: Impacts in Finland of the EU Fourth Framework Programme for Research and Development*, Tekes, Publication of the Finnish Secretariat for EU R&D 1/2000, Helsinki.

Machlup, J. (1982), 'Knowledge: its Creation, Distribution and Economic Significance', in *The Branches of Learning*, Princeton University Press, Princeton.

Maillat, D., Quévit, M. and Senn, L. (1993), *Réseaux d'Innovation et Milieux Innovateurs: un Pari pour le Développement Régional*, EDES, Neuchâtel.

Mansfield, E. (1985), 'How Rapidly Does New Industrial Technology Leak Out?', *Journal of Industrial Economics*, 34, 217-23.

Marshall, A. (1890), *Principles of Economics*, edition Macmillan London, Overston Bristol, Kykuto Shoten Tokio (Guillebad, C.W. ed.), 1961.

Martin, S. (1991), 'Private and Social Incentives to Form R&D Joint Ventures', *EUI Working Papers*, n. 91/35.

MERIT (2000), *Innovation Policy in a Knowledge-Based Economy*, EUR 17023, Commission of the European Communities, Luxembourg.

Nelson, R. (ed.) (1993), *National Innovation Systems: a Comparative Analysis*, Oxford University Press, Oxford-New York.

Nonaka, I. and Takeuchi, H. (1998), 'A Theory of the Firm's Knowledge-Creation Dynamics', in Chandler Jr., A.D., Hagstrom, P. and Solvell, O. (eds), *The Dynamic Firm: the Role of Technology, Strategy, Organization and Regions*, Oxford University Press, Oxford-New York.

Ohler, F., Jörg, L., Polt, W., Guy, K., Hutschenreiter, G., Husz, M., Sieber, A., Gluske, H. and Patsios, S. (1997), 'Evaluation of the Austrian Participation in Community RTD Programmes', Final Report, Seibersdorf, OEFZS, mimeo.

Pakes, A. and Griliches, Z. (1984), 'Patents and R&D at the Firm Level: A First Look', in Griliches Z. (ed.), *R&D, Patents and Productivity. NBER Conference Report*, University of Chivago Press, Chicago-London.

Patel, P. and Pavitt, K. (1995), 'Patterns of Technological Activities: their Measurement and Interpretation', in Stoneman, P. (ed.), *Handbook of the Economics of Innovation and Technological Change*, Blackwell, Oxford-Cambridge (Mass.).

Pelkmans, J. (1997), *European Integration: Methods and Economic Analysis*, Addison-Wesley-Longman, Essex.

Reger, G. and Kuhlmann, S. (1995), *European Technology Policy in Germany: The Impact of European Community Policies upon Science and Technology in Germany*, Physica-Verlag, Heidelberg.

Rosenberg, N. (1982), *Inside the Black Box: Technology and Economics*, Cambridge University Press, Cambridge.

Scherer, F.M. (1982), 'Inter-Industry Technology Flows and Productivity Growth', *Review of Economics and Statistics*, 64(4), 627-34.

Schibany, A. and Schartinger, D. (2001), 'Interactions between Universities and Enterprises in Austria: an Empirical Analysis at the Micro Sector Levels' in OECD, *Innovative Networks Co-operation in National Innovation Systems*.

Scotchmer, S. (1991), 'Standing on the Shoulders of Giants: Cumulative Research and the Patent Law', *Journal of Economic Perspectives*, 5.

Shapiro, C. and Willig, R. (1990), 'On the Antitrust Treatment of Production Joint Ventures', *Journal of Economic Perspectives*, 4(3), 113-30.

Smith, A. (1776), *An Inquiry into the Nature and Causes of the Wealth of the Nations*, edition Library Classics Indianapolis Ind., Indianapolis, 1976.

Smith, K. (2000), 'What is the knowledge-based economy? Knowledge-intensive industries and distributed knowledge base', project on Innovation Policy in a Knowledge-Base Economy, commissioned by the European Commission.

Tushman, M. and Anderson, P. (1996), 'Technological Discontinuities and Organisational Environments', *Administrative Science Quarterly*, 31, 439-86.

Vavakova, B. (1995), 'Building Research-Industry Partnerships through European Programmes', *International Journal of Technology Management*, 10, 567-85.

Chapter 4

Clustering of Intangibles

Marco R. Di Tommaso, Daniele Paci and Stuart O. Schweitzer

The term 'intangible' defines something by a negation, as being 'not-tangible'. This could give the idea that intangibles in economics are treated as residuals. On the contrary, intangible assets have gained such importance as to be acknowledged as the centrepiece of a new paradigm for firms. In the new state of the economy (usually labelled as the *knowledge-based* economy, or the *intangible* economy, as in Foray and Lundvall, 1996, chapter 1) the sources of value and competitiveness for firms, as for regions and nations, have drastically shifted from physical to intangible assets.

These intangibles represent an increasing share of company value and have become the most critical factor for competitiveness. While in 1982 the value of tangible assets reported on the balance sheet of S&P 500 companies represented on average 62 per cent of their market value, by 1998 this figure had declined to just 15 per cent (Daum, 2001).[1]

Therefore, what is needed is a shift in perspective. Rather than considering intangibles as 'exceptions' to be integrated into traditional theoretical frameworks, it is better to re-think traditional concepts and see them in the light of a new rule. This new scenario presents numerous challenges to corporate managers, investors, accounting standard setters, economists and policy makers. One of these challenges consists in understanding how the new rule affects the geographical distribution of productive activities. This is the topic of this article.

Despite a drastic reduction in transportation costs and the fact that many types of exchange no longer involve physical, but rather intangible and intellectual goods, clusters and spatial proximity still have a crucial importance for new generations of firms. The perception that decreasing communication costs may reduce the importance of agglomeration is based on the premise that better

---

[1] The data refers to the value of the so called 'market-to-book ratio', which measures the value of intellectual capital as the difference between the firm's stock market value and book value. The trend of the 'market-to-book ratio' for S&P 500 companies is shown in detail in Lev (2001). Of course, this is a partial result concerning the largest corporations; the impact of intangible assets on smaller firms has not yet been studied. Further evidence on the growing importance of intangible assets is provided by data reported by Bianchi and Labory (2003).

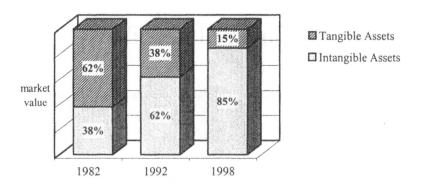

Figure 4.1   Percentage of market value of US companies represented by tangible and intangible assets

communication facilities allow for a decentralisaton of many productive activities and possibly leads to the 'death of distance',[2] and to the decline of clustering. The possibility of distributing information immediately and almost without cost over electronic networks generates the idea that firms are increasingly more able to use worldwide sourcing to lower input costs. However, empirical evidence suggests that clustering and physical proximity are still vitally important in drawing the geography of economic activities. This can be seen both in new manufacturing sectors such as the biotechnology and semiconductor industries and in the service sectors, such as financial, marketing and law consultancy. Examples include Silicon Valley, Bangalore, Boston Route 128, and the City of London.

Existing literature has often considered aspects of the intangible economy from a spatial perspective, analysing the geography of innovative activities (Feldman, 1994), high-technology industrial clusters (Saxenian, 1994a; Maggioni, 2002), the implications of the internet on the location of production (Leamer and Storper, 2001; Feldman, 2002), or the role of knowledge and learning processes (Voyer, 1998; Antonelli, 2000). Rather than focusing on a specific issue, this chapter will attempt to reorganise existing contributions in a systematic framework and to consider the geographical implications of the growing importance of intangible assets as a whole. It will analyse several aspects related to intrinsic features of intangible assets and to new economic trends in order to answer some key questions. Are traditional agglomeration theories, which have been used to explain concentration in traditional industries in the manufacturing sector, still adequate to explain clustering in the intangible economy? What can be added to the growing intangible assets literature by an analysis focused on geography?

---

[2] Cairncross (1997), Bairstow (2001).

1. Intangible Assets: A Growing Literature

It is widely acknowledged nowadays that non-physical assets contribute remarkably to increasing the competitiveness and the value of firms. The enhanced importance of intangibles is generally thought to be a consequence of the complex set of circumstances that has characterised the world economy since the 1970s. These are the globalisation process and the emergence of new competitive productive realities, the discovery and diffusion of new technologies, the growing complexity of the environment in which firms operate and, of course, evolutions in consumer preferences (Maskell and Malmberg, 1999; Asheim, 2001). These aspects relate to the crisis of confidence in the Fordist mass-production system, and the shift away from competition based on price towards a deeper consideration of innovation and quality (Piore and Sabel, 1984; Bianchi, 1991; Lev, 2001; chapter 2 of this book). Moreover, the progressive sophistication of financial products (increasingly disconnected to underlying tangible resources) have made an important contribution to the dematerialisation of production, making it easier to finance expensive intangible assets. All these factors have induced firms to reorganise their production to focus on non-physical assets. In addition, the increasing importance of knowledge and this dematerialisation of the productive process contribute to increased competition. For instance, the possibility of exchanging information across the internet (and hence the diffusion of intangible services) could be seen as a consequence and, at the same time, as a cause of increasing global integration. The literature on intangible assets, however, is still far from being homogeneous and several key questions still remain unanswered.

First, there is no broadly accepted definition of intangible assets. The adjective 'intangible' normally accompanies different concepts, including assets, investments, resources or other phenomena (Canibano and Sanchez, 1998).[3] They can be considered simultaneously as assets and as generators of assets. Moreover, in many cases intangible assets are created by a combination of physical and non-physical assets and since they are often embedded in physical assets, they are even more difficult to identify[4] (Bianchi and Labory, 2002).

The main standard setting bodies usually define intangible assets as identifiable (separable) non-physical and non-monetary sources of probable future economic profits accruing to the firm as a result of past events or transactions.[5] Such

---

[3] As Johanson et al. (1999) noticed, the transformation of the adjective into a noun can be seen as a proof of the existing lack of a generally accepted definition of 'intangibles'.

[4] For instance, human resources are physical or tangible in an obvious sense, but the component that is a source of future benefits within this definition is intangible: skills, ideas, and mental capacities.

[5] Other interpretations are possible. For example, in the UK, the Accounting Standards Board (ASB) has embraced the idea of considering that all intangibles should be understood as part of goodwill, since it is unlikely that they can be sold without selling the whole business. In this case, intangibles are considered as the excess cost of an acquired company over the value of its net tangible assets. Thus, goodwill represents the premium paid for the target's reputation, brand names, or other attributes that enable it to earn an

definitions elaborated for accounting purposes may appear restrictive. When an enterprise has insufficient control over the expected future economic benefits arising from a team of skilled staff and from training, or when intangibles are not clearly identifiable, there might be serious problems in observing that they meet established criteria.

Broader definitions, especially designed for management purposes, have been suggested. Intangibles have been defined as resources that are not visible in the balance sheet, but which contribute to add value to the enterprise (Edvinsson, 1997), or as 'non-physical sources of value (claims to future benefits), generated by innovation (discovery), unique organisational designs, or human resources practices' (Lev, 2001; p.13). As a working definition, a High Level Expert Group (Eustace, 2000; p.31) took intangibles to be 'non-material factors that contribute to enterprise performance in the production of goods or the provision of services, or that are expected to generate future economic benefits to the entities or individuals that control their deployment'. Although these definitions are more useful for the purpose of this article, the risk however is that they are much too broad and comprehensive, become meaningless and cause difficulties in identifying particular components of intangible assets. It is not perfectly clear therefore how intangibles can be classified, although several taxonomies have been recently suggested.

For example, according to Lowendahl (1997), intangibles can be categorised into *competencies* and *relational resources*. The latter refer to reputation, client loyalty, etc. Competencies, defined as the ability to perform a given task, exist at both the individual and organisational level.[6]

Another useful taxonomy of intangible assets is reported by Eustace in chapter 1. The principal intangible constituents of the corporate asset base of most leading companies today can be divided into 'intangible goods' and 'intangible competencies'. The first group is made up of two main sub-classes, *intangible commodities* and *intellectual property*.[7] The second group ('*intangible competencies*') is composed of assets that are generally bundled together and interdependent to such an extent that they are difficult (but not impossible) to isolate and value.

---

excess return on investment, justifying the premium price paid (White et al., 1994).

[6] On the individual level, it includes knowledge, skills, and aptitudes; on the organisational level, competence includes client specific databases, technology, routines, methods, procedures, and organisational culture. Taking the division one step further, it is possible to divide competence and relational categories into two subgroups: individual and collective, depending on whether the employee or the organisation is stressed.

[7] Intangible commodities (e.g. commercial databases and other marketable software with associated long-term royalty annuities) can be bought, sold, stocked, and leased easily and with low transaction costs. Intellectual property, on the other hand, includes patents, copyrights, registered designs, trade secrets and proprietary technology. In this case due diligence costs as well as costs and time of legal search can be significant (Eustace, 2000).

A number of other taxonomies have been proposed, some identifying broad categories, while others tend to be more articulated and detailed.[8] In addition to the difficulty in defining intangibles, an interrelated issue is the remarkable constraints in their measurement. The insufficiency of traditional metrics is therefore at the centre of the debate on intangibles (see chapter 2).

The research into measuring a firm's intangible assets or intellectual capital has produced a plethora of proposed methods and theories over the last few years.[9] Although each of these methods offers different advantages, the management and accounting literature has not yet reached a broad consensus, and imperfections in measuring intangible assets still give rise to problems of information asymmetry and high management costs.

For the purpose of this chapter we will adopt a general definition of intangible assets. We will refer to them as all the possible sources of competitive advantages for firms that have no physical substance. They are both on the input side (e.g. R&D, knowledge) and the output side (e.g. patents, brands) of the production function. Moreover, we consider intangible assets as sources of competitive advantage not just for firms, but also for regions and localities in the globalised economy.

2. Traditional Clustering Theories

An aspect that the literature on intangibles has not yet explored is the impact of intangibles on the geography of production. Analysing whether and how the new and growing importance of intangibles is affecting the traditional theories of clustering and economic geography is a crucial point if one wants to understand them from the point of view of economic theory. The literature on clustering is vast and multifaceted. However, it is possible to identify two main themes, as Schweitzer and Di Tommaso (2003) recently suggested.

The first is that specific factors draw particular firms to a particular locality. In the 'old economy' these factors were the ease of transportation, and the location of supply or product markets or natural resources (Weber, 1909; Lösch, 1940). The earliest industrial agglomerations typically could be understood in terms of the location of natural resources. In the 18th century, economic geography was centred on the effort to find ways to move raw materials from fixed sources to production locations where they could be combined with capital and labour to make final

---

[8] For example Lev (2001) identifies three main groups of intangible assets: innovation-related intangibles, human resources intangibles and organisational intangibles, while Reilly (1992) suggests that there are eight categories of intangible assets: Technology-related (e.g., engineering drawings), Customer-related (e.g., customer lists), Contract-related (e.g., favourable supplier contracts), Data processing-related (e.g., computer software), Human capital-related (e.g., a trained and organised workforce), Marketing-related (e.g., trademarks and trade names), Location-related (e.g., leasehold interests), and Goodwill-related (e.g., going concern value).

[9] For an extensive analysis of the topic, see chapter 8.

products. Because of difficulties in transporting raw materials, industries used to cluster near the sources (Leamer and Storper, 2001). Firm agglomeration can also be explained by the costs of transportation of goods other than raw materials. Production plants have in many cases tended to be located in port cities or, according to the nature of the good, close to rail and more recently in proximity of airports or highway junctions. The easier access to transport drives the agglomeration of firms when transport costs (of raw materials, intermediate goods or final products) are particularly high.[10]

The other theme in the literature focuses on synergies among firms that can be realised by locating near one another. Agglomeration per se offers advantages because of physical proximity. Pioneering papers were focused on the 'market potential', that tends to be higher where firms agglomerate (Harris, 1954), while other studies recognise the importance of competition at the local level (Porter, 1990). In general, although being close to other firms is important, the proximity to other similar, specialised, complementary firms can offer even greater benefits. Clustered firms have access to (a) a local market for skills, which reduces specialised labour search costs, (b) a local specialised supply of raw materials, equipment and services, and (c) technical and market flows of specific knowledge (Marshall,1890; Becattini, 1987; Krugman, 1991). Firms choose a particular location because it is where they can exploit the positive externalities produced by other firms. Firms wish to exploit economies that tend to be characterised by non-rivalry and non-excludability and that are part of a common pool from which any actor can freely draw resources[11] (Feldman 1994; Audretsch and Feldman, 1996; Audretsch, 1998; Cooke, 2001).

Furthermore, clustered firms can enjoy benefits from a reduction of transaction costs (Williamson, 1975), from a reduction of search costs by consumers[12] (Prevezer, 1995), or from the possibility of integrating different complementary functions (Di Tommaso and Rabellotti, 1999). It is important to recognise that although these advantages in general have a cumulative and a self-reinforcing nature (Harris, 1954; Arthur, 1990; Krugman, 1991), diseconomies can be produced by an excessive agglomeration of firms within the same place (Krugman, 1991; Swann et al., 1998).[13]

---

[10] The minimisaton of transportation costs related to the distance from markets and raw materials represents the core of traditional location theories, such as in Weber (1909) and in Von Thünen (1910).

[11] It is usual to refer to these benefits as 'not-pecuniary forms of externalities' (Scitovsky, 1954).

[12] These typologies of clusters have also been termed 'comparison shopping clusters' (Mills, 1992).

[13] Krugman (1991) termed such diseconomies 'centrifugal forces'. According to him they are related to immobile inputs, land rents and negative externalities. Swann et al. (1998), distinguished demand-side disadvantages of spatial concentration (excessive congestion and competition in output markets) from supply-side disadvantages (congestion and competition in input market, e.g. real estate, specialised labour).

However, agglomeration may offer advantages which go beyond those linked to the 'passive' exploitation of other firms' proximity. At least in principle, a cluster of firms is the right environment for the development of strategic relations among firms. In other words, here the assumption is that firms, inspired by what and who they see around them, may show a greater propensity to co-operate (Becattini, 1987; Bellandi, 1996; Cooke, 2001). The forms of co-operation, either vertical or horizontal, may concern aspects such as process and product development, quality control, training, lobbying or marketing. In this case the strategy of the firm suggests choosing a location because of its wish to establish durable relations with other firms. In contrast to passively-acquired external economies linked merely to proximity, the wish of undertaking collective actions[14] with other firms involves active and consciously pursued inter-firm relations (Fountain, 1998; Di Tommaso, 1999). Economies associated with collective actions are the competitive factors of complex realities[15] as in the Italian industrial districts, where small and medium-size firms clustered together have clearly showed the capacity to compete at global level (Bianchi, 1995). Furthermore, the concept of co-operation and networking among firms has been emphasised in the analysis of the success of the Silicon Valley high-tech cluster (Saxenian, 1994a).[16] Traditional literature on clustering and economic geography does not explicitly consider intangible and knowledge assets. Nevertheless, one of the challenges provided to corporate managers, investors, accounting standards setters and policy makers by the advent of the 'intangible economy' refers to the location of activities. What are the spatial implications of the economics of intangibles? Are traditional clustering theories obsolete?

3. The Geography of Intangibles

The increasing importance of intangible assets in comparison with raw materials, physical labour and capital has certainly affected the geographical distribution of economic activities. Following the rhetoric in the popular and business press trumpeting the removal of 'the limitations of geography', most commentators have

---

[14] Collective actions consist of explicit and voluntary co-operative behaviour. Firms involved can gain economies that are substantially different from the traditional economies of proximity because of excludability and compensation mechanisms (Di Tommaso and Rabellotti 1999).

[15] Dunning (1997) used the expression 'alliance capitalism' in order to describe this peculiar tendency of modern economies. In fact, it seems crucial for firm competitiveness to reach a balance between competition and co-operation (Dei Ottati, 1994; Fountain, 1998).

[16] Comparing the cases of Silicon Valley and Boston Route 128, Saxenian (1994a; p.6) concludes that external economies per se do not explain why clusters of specialised technical skill, suppliers and information produced a self-reinforcing dynamic of increasing industrial advance in the Silicon Valley while producing stagnation and decline along 'Route 128'. What is relevant is being part of an industrial system and the capacity to establish regional networks; factors that can be found in the Silicon Valley experience, but not in Route 128.

tended to believe that recent advances in transportation and communication technologies are rapidly making agglomeration economies obsolete (The Economist, 1995; Thurow, 1996; Cairncross 1997).[17] These claims are not new: similar considerations can be found in less recent streams of economic theory. Hall (1900) wrote that the use of modern machinery tends to lower the importance of skilled labour supply and that the more an industry becomes automated, the more its location is likely to become independent of its supply of labour. As an industry expands and becomes more sophisticated, the standardised production of geographically concentrated industries tends to be relocated elsewhere, either closer to consumers or to cheaper input sources (Haig, 1926). But as long as firms in an industry remain innovative, the forces of agglomeration usually remain much stronger than predicted. Economic history has shown us that a general reduction in the transportation costs of both goods and information has always tended to encourage geographical concentration rather than discourage it (Krugman, 1991).[18]

As pointed out in chapter 2, intangible assets can be seen as services and activities mainly concentrated in two different points of the production cycle: before and after manufacturing. The first kind of services (*services before production*) represent every stage of production before manufacture and in some cases consist of services that are prior to the entire production cycle (e.g. education). *Post-production services* determine the control of the market, affecting the commercialisation of outputs. In some cases services aimed at creating and reinforcing customer loyalty can represent a following stage, after the product commercialisation. Even if the production process can take different forms and even if the relative importance of services may vary according to industry and to individual firm, it is unmistakable that these activities represent the real sources of value and competitive advantage for firms.

Analysing the geography of intangibles means examining where these activities take place. It is possible to argue that they are highly clustered in some core regions whether they consist of managerial headquarter functions in large firms or whether they represent the core activities of specialised firms.[19]

When intellectual activities are entirely internalised within major firms, the enhanced importance of intangible assets is reflected by the growth of headquarter functions, which are likely to be located in a small number of key localities around

---

[17] Not only are advances in transportation relevant. Also the increasingly 'weightless' nature of the current economy, where value is extremely high in terms of unit of weight, has substantially eliminated transportation costs as important considerations (Goldfinger, 2000; Schweitzer and Di Tommaso, 2003).

[18] 'The revolution in transport by the introduction of steamships, and above all of railways, has [...] produced as a portentous effect the concentration of population in large towns instead of being scattered in villages or homesteads over the country. The reason for the modern growth of great towns is simple. It is not that cities are much more attractive than before, but that the new means of communication have removed the obstacles to the operation of that attraction' (Devas, 1901; p.100).

[19] Enright (1999; p.1) refers to this process as 'the globalisation of activities and the localisation of competitive advantage'. This means that 'the enduring competitive advantages in a global economy lie increasingly in local things' (Porter, 1998; p.78).

the world (Leamer and Storper, 2001). Recent literature on foreign direct investments and multinational companies (MNCs) has stressed the importance of intangible assets (that are often called *firm-specific assets*) as one of the explanations of the advantageous possibility of extending the production activity across national boundaries (Caves, 1996). It is frequently argued that multinational companies are inherently footloose, which means that they can react almost instantaneously to adverse changes in the host country and shift their production facilities or parts thereof to another country if the present environment changes to their disadvantage (Gilly et al., 1996; Cowling and Sugden, 1999).

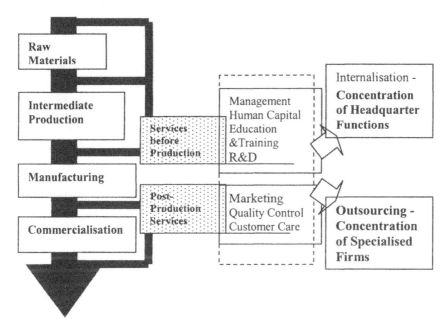

Figure 4.2 Intangibles and the production process

However, production facilities are not located randomly: certain areas, localities and regions offer advantages that MNCs cannot ignore. This advantage traditionally refers to lower costs of inputs (especially of labour) but in the new economy they can be linked to the availability of particular specialised skills or know-how, a favourable environment for learning and innovation, the presence of a strong scientific base (Barry et al., 2001).

However, intangible assets have implications for the spatial distribution of economic activities, which go beyond the location of MNCs. The decline of the Fordist mode of production and the overall tendency towards flexible specialisation and downsizing means that intellectual functions have developed into specialised industries as major firms have externalised these services (Kanter, 1989). These specialised firms, which operate mainly in sectors such as finance, legal work and marketing, tend to cluster tightly together in districts, especially in downtown office buildings (Wall Street, the City of London, etc.).[20] In addition to the outsourcing of services, it is necessary to underline a recent trend in outsourcing manufacturing and R&D activities.[21] Relationships between large firms and subcontractors[22] are changing: in many cases, subcontractors have transformed from 'jobbers' into 'co-makers' and 'co-engineers', by increasing their innovative capacity and organisational skills (Wintjes and Cobbenhagen, 2000). Although the changing nature of subcontracting relationships is widely discussed,[23] while traditional outsourcing of manufacturing activities can in many cases induce firms to seek the lowest cost opportunities worldwide, this new kind of relationship implies high transaction costs due to technological, cultural and institutional distances. These costs can be substantially lowered by physical proximity.

Furthermore, this economic scenario has recently witnessed the emergence of technology-based industries in innovative sectors such as information and communication technology and biotechnology. The geographical distribution of high-tech activities[24] shows a strong clustering tendency mainly driven by the presence of a high-level scientific knowledge base. However, it could be misleading to focus the analysis only on high-technology sectors of the so-called

---

[20] 'Services firms have always exhibited locational patterns similar to manufacturing firms. The more specialised and up-to-date a service activity is, the more likely it is to be concentrated in large cities. The more standardized it becomes, the more it tends to migrate toward customers or inputs' (Desrochers, 2001; p.32). See also Coffey (1992) and Edwards (1998).

[21] Even strategic R&D activities have extensively been outsourced in some research-based industries (most notably in pharmaceuticals; see Pisano, 1990).

[22] Holmes (1986), following Watanabe (1971) and Chaillou (1977), identifies three major types of production subcontracting. In *capacity subcontracting*, only the fabrication of subcontracted components is carried out by the subcontractor with respect to a detailed set of plans and specifications set down by the contractor. In *specialisation (complementary) subcontracting* the decision about the method of production is usually taken by the subcontractor. This case of vertical disintegration of production arises when two firms have (vertically related) complementary assets or technologies. Finally, in *supplier subcontracting*, the subcontractor is an independent supplier with full control over the development, design and the method of production, but who is willing to enter a subcontracting arrangement to supply a dedicated or licensed part to the parent firm.

[23] Many scholars argue that conflictual and hierarchical relationships have not been replaced by collaborative one-to-one forms of partnership. The real shift should be limited to the growing knowledge and technical content of the subcontracting activities and to the fact that subcontracting involves more long-term relationships (Baudry, 1993; Sacchetti and Sugden, 2000).

[24] The definition of 'high-tech industries' is widely discussed: for a comprehensive analysis see Malecki (1997).

'new economy'. This is because there is not a perfectly two-way relationship between technology and intangible assets: while high-tech firms are substantially always intangible assets' firms, the opposite is not true in many cases (Di Tommaso, Paci and Schweitzer, 2003).[25]

The importance of geographical proximity can be seen especially with reference to innovation-related intangibles, such as intellectual property, R&D activities, human capital-related and customer-related intangibles.

Intellectual property intangible assets such as patents, trademarks, copyrights, and trade secrets are, by their nature, mobile across space and the knowledge they incorporate can be spread over long distances. In this sense such assets should, at least in principle, lower the importance of localisation. However there are serious problems of appropriability. As explained in the following section, there are limitations on the effectiveness of patents in protecting new knowledge, which is not always perfectly embodied in legal rights (Geroski, 1995). Localised knowledge spillovers[26] are often indicated as important factors inducing innovative firms to cluster, and technological advance seems to have a cumulative nature within particular areas. The evidence is provided by numerous empirical studies on patent citations: by comparing the address of the new patent with the address of the previous patents cited it is possible to conclude that knowledge fluxes are geographically bounded and that patents usually generate localised spillover effects (Jaffe, 1989; Jaffe et al., 1993; Narin et al., 1997). Starting from these observations, Feldman (1994) concludes that innovation is an increasingly geographical concentrated process because it requires frequent formal and informal relationships among different actors at the local level and between firms and their environment.

Human capital-related assets also seem to have important implications for the geography of production. The increasing dematerialisation of productive processes has certainly determined the emergence of new occupational categories and a different distribution of employment among different kinds of work. The composition of employment is shifting towards more white-collar occupations (Bianchi and Labory, 2003), and 'creative workers' (Lev, 2001), but this is only a partial view of how the labour market is evolving. The economy is experiencing an overall 'upskilling' of workers at all levels and what has really changed is the *knowledge content* of each kind of work even of manual and routine activities.[27]

---

[25] Even if the contributions of new technologies to the progressive dematerialisation of production are not contestable, other aspects must be taken into account: for example, the long lasting trend in consumer behaviour that has determined a shift toward higher relative demand for leisure and related services (Goldfinger, 2000). Firms that derive their value from intangible assets can be found in traditional sectors such as food and beverage (e.g. Coca Cola) or clothing (e.g. Lacoste).

[26] For a comprehensive analysis of knowledge spillovers see Griliches (1995).

[27] Saxenian (1994a) and Scott (1993) showed that the agglomeration of high-technology activity in Silicon Valley and in Southern California is fostered by the presence of a dualistic labour market that includes scientists as well as manual workers such as electronic assemblers.

Skills can be developed through education and training. These activities imply a learning process that requires physical proximity between the 'trainer' and the recipient (Nooteboom, 2000). Once acquired and embodied in an individual, skills could, in principle, be freely transferred according to the mobility of workers that possess them. Labour markets differ according to their geography (Bouman and Verhoef, 1986). Traditionally, a labour market is considered as local for unskilled, semi-skilled and clerical personnel, nationwide for managerial and marketing talent and increasingly world-wide for key technical specialists (Malecki, 1997). However this view has been challenged by recent generations of university spin-off firms. In fact, numerous studies, especially focused on the biotechnology industry, have shown the propensity for scientists to found or to be involved in commercial enterprises near their university, where they usually continue to retain affiliation (Zucker and Darby, 1998; Di Tommaso, Paci and Schweitzer, 2003).

Traditional clustering theories underline that a concentration of similar firms generates a local labour pool which can provide significant economies such as the reduction of costs for seeking qualified personnel (Marshall, 1890; Krugman, 1991). Moreover local mobility of workers is one of the most important means for transmitting know-how and other forms of uncodified knowledge (Saxenian, 1994/b). In addition, according to several important studies, learning and skill acquiring are collective experiences that involve not only workers, but also formal and informal institutions of a particular 'innovative milieu' (Antonelli,1999; Capello, 1999).[28]

Concerning the intangible assets related to organisation, physical proximity can provide opportunities for learning and the rapid adoption of innovative organisational practices. The organisation of firms is becoming more dependent on external factors, leading some authors to write of the 'blurring boundaries of firms' (Florida, 1998; Saxenian, 1994b). Firms require almost continuous interactions with their environment, which is composed of suppliers, customers, competitors and other institutions. Proximity can therefore provide firms significant advantages in terms of organisational learning and change.

Different considerations have to be made with respect to customer-related intangibles.[29] From a spatial perspective, brands appear independent from spatial

---

[28] The concept of 'milieu innovateur' goes beyond mere spatial proximity. 'It refers to a coherent whole in which a territorial production system, a technical culture and protagonists are linked' (Maillat, 1991; p.113). It can be defined as 'the set, or the complex network of mainly informal social relationships on a limited geographical area, often determining a specific external "image" and a specific internal "representation" and sense of belonging, which enhance the local innovative capability through synergetic and collective learning process' (Camagni 1991; p.3). According to Lundvall and Borras (1999; p.73), 'the innovative milieu is the existing regional capacity, in a more institutional sense, that gives rise to the potential for innovation networks to flourish'. On this topic, see also Maillat (1996) and chapter 2.

[29] From a marketing point of view, Guilding and Pike (1990) classify intangible assets into three categories: value creators (advertising, product development and other marketing support), marketing assets (trademarks, brands, entry barriers and information systems), and value manifestations (image, reputation and premium price).

agglomeration. However some locations represent a brand by themselves. This is the case of typical products such as 'Chianti' in Tuscany and 'Parmigiano Reggiano' in Parma. Agro-food firms located in the regions of production of these typical products can gain a competitive advantage just from their location. This can act as a driving force for the clustering of similar firms in those regions. It has to be noted that this is not only the case of local products. In fact, locality can itself become a brand in other context and, for example, in high-technology industries. To be located in Silicon Valley represents a sort of guarantee of a high-tech firm's excellence for customers and investors. Moreover, clustering can give small firms more possibilities to co-operate and undertake joint-marketing activities.

In the light of these preliminary reflections it is possible to say that intangible assets affect the spatial distribution of activities in numerous different ways and the concept of relevant proximity varies according to several factors, such as the nature of the industry, the size of firms, the stage of development of the sector in which firms operate, the extent of the market and the rate of innovation.

Furthermore, it is possible to distinguish the stage of *development* of new intangible assets, which appears to be a phenomenon driven by local proximity and interaction among actors involved, from that of their *diffusion*, which permits long distance relationships among actors.[30] Moreover, the diffusion of intangible assets over long distance, as we will show in the next section, depends heavily on the 'degree of codification' of the exchanged knowledge. Therefore it is necessary to analyse deeper the intrinsic features of these assets, in order to have a complete picture of clustering phenomena in the intangible economy.

4. Intrinsic Features of Intangibles

A general conceptual framework to explain clustering phenomena based on intangible assets can be established by analysing in depth the spatial implications of the inherent attributes of intangibles. It is possible to list five interconnected characteristics, as follows:

- Knowledge content
- Non-rivalry (non-scarcity)
- Partial excludability
- Non-tradability
- Risk and information asymmetries

---

[30] Unfortunately, this distinction is not always clear and it could be misleading. Considering the process of innovation, Kline and Rosenberg (1985) noted that during its diffusion, a new technology is constantly modified and implemented. This led Fleck (1988) to coin the expressions 'innofusion' and 'diffusation'.

Knowledge Content

Intangible assets can be defined by their knowledge content and indeed knowledge is usually listed as a common denominator of the different typologies of intangibles.[31]

In a neo-classical view, firms interact in order to share the risks connected to the production of technological knowledge. These risks are due to the specific attributes of knowledge. According to Arrow (1962), knowledge bears three problems that give rise to market failure: it is a public good, because it is not possible to create a market for knowledge, since the producer cannot fully appropriate it; the process of creation of knowledge is dominated by uncertainty; and there are economies of scale in the production of knowledge.[32]

Recent developments of the Neo-Schumpeterian approach stress the distinction between information and knowledge. Along this line, Burton-Jones (1999) distinguishes *data,* defined as any signal which can be sent by an originator to a recipient, from *information* (defined as data which are intelligible to the recipient) and *knowledge* (the cumulative stock of information and skills derived from the use of information by the recipient). When the recipient is a human being, knowledge thus reflects the processing (thinking or cognition) by the brain of the 'raw materials' supplied in the form of information. This leads to two considerations. The first is that while *information* can be easily codified and has a singular meaning and a unique interpretation, *knowledge* is vague, difficult to codify and often only serendipitously recognised. Therefore, although the marginal cost of transmitting information across geographic space has been rendered invariant by the telecommunications revolution, the marginal cost of transmitting knowledge however rises with distance (Audretsch and Feldman 1996). The second consideration involves the value of information, which depends on the recipient's prior knowledge. If one has no previous knowledge of a particular subject, it is usually difficult, if not impossible, to make sense of data and information related to that subject. Conversely, the more one knows about a subject, the better able he or she is to evaluate and use new data and information about it. This is the argument that traditionally explains the cumulative nature of knowledge and the fact that R&D efforts play a crucial role in capturing, evaluating and utilising knowledge from external sources.[33]

Other taxonomies, focused on the presence of a tacit share of knowledge, have been suggested in the literature. For instance, Foray and Lundvall (1996)

---

[31] Stewart (1997) defined intangible assets as 'organised knowledge that can be used to create wealth'.

[32] The famous 'Arrow problem' (Hodgson, 1999) is based on the fact that knowledge, once acquired, can often be easily reproduced by its buyer, and possibly (apart for restrictions such as patents or licences) sold to others. In addition knowledge, once it is sold, remains in the hands of the seller. Finally knowledge demand and supply are difficult to match, because 'its value for the purchaser is not known until he has the information, but then he has in effect acquired it without cost' (Arrow, 1962: p.616). For a comprehensive analysis of the issue of knowledge as a public good and market failure associated with the production of knowledge, see also Geroski (1995) and OECD (2001).

[33] See, for example, Antonelli (2000) and Breschi (2000).

distinguished *software (*or *ideas*) knowledge, which is codified and stored outside the human brain, from *wetware (*or *skills*) which is knowledge that cannot be dissociated from an individual, since it is stored in our brains, and is comprised of convictions, abilities, talents, etc. The codification and formalisation of knowledge are possible only for ideas, and take the form of a process of reduction and translation of ideas in a standard and compact format, which lowers the costs of storage, transmission and reproduction (David and Foray, 1995). Codified knowledge can be transferred over long distances and across national boundaries at low cost (Foray and Lundvall, 1996). Ideas can thus be used by any number of people simultaneously, and their distribution is usually lower than their production cost. On the other hand, the second kind of knowledge, known also as *tacit*, consists of highly specific pieces of technological know-how acquired of with long processes of learning. Therefore, it cannot be easily transferred, because it has not been stated in an explicit form. The transmission of knowledge, in particular tacit knowledge, needs a process of codification and interpretation, and hence requires frequent contacts and interactions (face-to-face interactions more likely) of agents.[34] The transmission of complex uncodifiable messages, which require understanding and trust, is not likely to be affected by the internet, which allows 'long distance conversations, but not handshakes' (Leamer and Storper, 2001). Although the development of information and communication technologies helped the process of knowledge codification in standard form and allowed its transfer over long distances at a substantially reduced cost (Antonelli, 1999; Burton-Jones, 1999; Breschi, 2000), the share of tacit knowledge has not fallen. Tacit knowledge is in principle both prior to and beyond explicit articulation. Although the boundary between tacit and explicit knowledge may shift, it is possible to recognise that the foundation of all knowledge must remain implicit, because all explicit knowledge is necessarily an emergent property of underlying tacit fundamentals.[35] Codified and tacit knowledge are complementary and co-exist in time, and, more specifically, tacit knowledge remains a key element in the appropriation and effective use of all knowledge, especially during dynamic innovation (Polanyi, 1967; Lundvall and Borras, 1999; Asheim, 2001).

Therefore, in the intangible economy, proximity still matters in transmitting knowledge, both in the case of intentional co-operative behaviours and in the case of knowledge spillovers. The results of many studies indicate that R&D and other knowledge spillovers not only generate externalities, but evidence also suggests that such knowledge spillovers tend to be geographically bounded within the region where the new economic knowledge was created (Jaffe, 1989; Feldman, 1994; Audretsch and Feldman, 1996).

---

[34] To refer to tacit knowledge, Von Hippel (1994) has elaborated the concept of *sticky knowledge*, which indicates the concentration of knowledge across geographical space.

[35] In his classic text on the topic, Polanyi (1967, p.4) reassumes this concept with a naïve but effective example: 'We can know more than we can tell.'

Non-Rivalry (Non-Scarcity)

As Lev (2001) pointed out, physical, human and financial assets are characterised by rivalry since alternative uses compete for the services of these assets. Intangible assets are, on the other hand, non rival which amounts to saying that their opportunity costs are negligible.

This derives mainly from the fact that these assets are generally characterised by large fixed (sunk) costs and negligible marginal costs. As knowledge-based assets they are 'expensive to produce but cheap to reproduce' (Desrochers, 2001; p.25). Moreover, the transmission of these assets cannot be considered an easy process, particularly if they consist of intellectual capital in an uncodified state. In this case know-how can be easily reproduced only by the individuals and the organisations that have developed it, and it is difficult to transfer to others who have no understanding of it. If a firm wants to diffuse its know-how to new employees it must organise expensive training courses to be taken in the firm's offices. When intangible assets have, instead, a codified form (such as patents or trademarks) the concept of non-rivalry can be applied. However the key point is that non-scarcity does not mean ubiquity. Once a firm can use its intangibles simultaneously in every part of the world, it will tend to concentrate its functions of control and management of such assets in a unique headquarters. Rather than force for the dispersion of economic activities, non-rival assets represent a powerful motive for clustering in core regions to gain static and dynamic agglomeration advantages.

Partial Excludability

The well-defined property rights of tangible and financial assets enable owners to effectively exclude others from enjoying the benefits of these assets. In the case of intangible investments, however, the actor that made the investment will rarely be unique in gaining benefits from it.

First of all there is a problem of ownership: the situation of intangible assets is ambiguous. A firm owns its brands or other forms of intellectual capital, but can not own its labour force and its human capital. Other intangible assets, such as a customer base, are completely outside the legal perimeter of the firm. Despite firms' strategies attempting to internalise these sources of value through the development of forms of dependence able to durably link employees and consumers to them,[36] problems of ownership remain substantially unsolved. Therefore, for example, when a firm invests in training its employees, other

---

[36] However, different strategies can be deemed more appropriate. It is reasonable to think that in highly innovative and competitive environments such as in Silicon Valley, firms accept (and even value) the mobility of workers, leaving them free to choose another job in a competing firm, and have the ready-made counter strategy of hiring them after a period during which they have learned important technical information from competitors (Desrochers, 2001).

companies (and society at large) will benefit from such investment when the trained employees change job (Lev, 2001).

Moreover, patents and property rights are not always considered effective methods of protecting new knowledge. There are at least three basic limitations to their effectiveness: the ability of competitors to invent 'around a patent', the fact that some innovations are difficult to patent, and the fact that patents disclose enough information to enable imitators to develop variants of the basic technology patented (Geroski, 1995). These imperfections show up in particular in process innovations, as underlined by the empirical literature (Bianchi and Labory, 2002). In a significant number of cases firms prefer to adopt other informal protecting methods, such as secrecy, lead time, learning curve advantages and marketing efforts (Levin et al., 1987).

Even in the case of intangibles protected by well defined property rights, there are substantial benefits to non owners in the form of spillovers. The extent of these spillovers appears to be local as shown by the previously mentioned literature on patent citations (Jaffe, 1989; Jaffe et al., 1993; Narin et al., 1997; Feldman, 1994).

Non-Tradability

The absence of organised and competitive markets for intangibles is consistent with the traditional literature on the imperfections and the failure of a free market for knowledge and information due to the public good nature of knowledge (Arrow, 1962; Stiglitz, 1985). It is possible to consider failures in the creation of markets for intangibles as a consequence of the inability to write complete contracts with respect to the outcomes of intangibles (Teece, 1998).

The cost structure of many information-related intangibles, which is characterised by large sunk initial investments and marginal production costs, further undermines the operation of the conventional price system for such products.

Moreover, as stated above, in many cases it is not possible to determine a legal ownership of intangible assets and even intellectual property rights cannot always define the boundaries of appropriability for intangible assets.

However, all these impediments do not preclude the existence of markets for intangibles because, as noted by Lev (2001), markets, in principle, exist whenever trade and exchanges take place. What distinguishes intangibles from other assets is the absence of organised, active exchanges with numerous participants and transparent prices. Therefore, because of high transaction costs, exchanges of intangible assets take place mainly by informal contacts made possible by frequent interactions and trust.

Risk and Information Asymmetries

Operations that involve intangible assets are, by their nature, risky and uncertain. The generation of intangible assets through investments in education, R&D and innovation is an uncertain process because of its dynamic nature. In addition, the transmission of intangibles that are protected by property rights is characterised by a high degree of risk. This is due to the information asymmetry associated with intangibles. Problems in recognising and quantifying intangibles give rise to principle-agent tensions among actors involved in the exchange of these assets. Moreover, intangible assets' management represents an extremely uncertain process because of the necessity of 'operating in the dark' (Lev, 2001), without an effective way of measuring and quantifying assets and performances. The 'knowledge-intensive' nature of most intangibles is one of the main determinants of risk: it is more difficult to predict the output of non-physical inputs and for firms to appropriate returns from their products while these products are essentially 'intangibles'. In addition risks are often associated with a 'competence gap' arising from the firm's limited ability to process and understand the available information. The acceptance of this within a marketplace that brings commercial rewards to innovative firms plays a key role in the innovation process (Feldman, 2002). Moreover, the commercial risk of innovation is heightened by the fear of imitation that may limit the extent to which an innovator may obtain a return from innovative efforts (Stoneman, 1995).

These considerations have two effects with respect to firm localisation and agglomeration. The first is that it is reasonable to assume that companies in the intangible economy seek to reduce risks by locating near one another. It is possible to reread the traditional wisdom that agglomeration economies include benefits from the possibility of sharing risks among the clustered firms[37] to highlight the importance of clustering as a mechanism that reduces the uncertainty faced by firms in connection with the development and use of intangibles in a rapidly changing environment (Lundvall, 1988; Camagni, 1991; Saxenian, 1994a). Furthermore, firms seek particularly specialised labour to reduce their competence gap by locating near sources of knowledge (such as research centres and universities) or in clusters where the local concentration of firms in one industry generates a local market for specialised labour.

The second effect of uncertainty is linked to the financing of investments in intangibles. As Von Burg and Kenney (2000) noted, financial backers of new firms and new technologies are traditionally treated as unproblematic. If an innovation is sufficiently attractive, then it is assumed that the financial backing will be available. However, the possibility of financing these activities effectively is limited by their risky nature and by the complexity and difficulties in understanding the content of those processes that need to be financed. Therefore, recent analyses identify a key role of venture capital[38] within regional innovative systems and the geographical proximity between investors and firms. In fact venture capital investments, at least in the US, appear tightly clustered in areas with established concentrations of high-technology business (Smith and Florida, 1998) and hence it is possible to suggest that venture capital and innovative firms have a symbiotic role in the formation of high-tech clusters (Florida and Kenney,

---

[37] 'Reputation spreads quickly within a cluster, helping financial providers to judge who the good entrepreneurs are' (DTI, 1999; p.24).

[38] For a comprehensive analysis of the role of venture capital in the process of technological innovation, see Smith and Florida (1998).

1988). Furthermore, problems of financing intangible assets are enhanced by the large amount of sunk costs that the development of such assets generally requires. In general, the less codified the knowledge underlying intangibles is, the higher the information asymmetries between investors and firms, and thus the greater the importance of face-to-face interactions and social ties between the two actors. Therefore physical proximity has a crucial role in reducing problems associated with market failure for the particular segment of intangible assets investments.

5. Clusters as Generators of Intangibles

The previous section has shown that the peculiarities of intangible assets lead firms to cluster, perhaps compensating for the absence of factors that traditionally underlay agglomeration processes, i.e. fixed natural resources and transportation costs arguments.

The focus on knowledge is not incompatible with the traditional Marshallian theory of industrial agglomeration, and the forces that drive clustering in the intangible economy are not so different from traditional agglomeration economics (Di Tommaso, Paci and Rubini, 2003). Albino and Schiuma (1999) suggest that knowledge is the key factor that underlies all the different interpretative frameworks suggested for industrial districts. Therefore, since knowledge can be considered as a productive factor, industrial districts can be conceptualised as 'cognitive laboratories' (Beccattini and Rullani, 1993; Rullani, 1994).

However, the traditional focus on static external economies can be at least partially replaced by a growing attention to dynamic externalities.[39] The effects of the geographical concentration of firms go beyond the mere increase of static efficiency: they are also important determinants of industrial dynamics and innovation. Learning and innovation are increasingly seen as collective processes that are rarely confined within the boundaries of individual firms (Klein and Rosenberg, 1985; Lundvall, 1988; Feldman, 1994; Saxenian, 1994a; Antonelli, 1999; Boschma, 2001; Capello, 1999). The creation of an 'industrial atmosphere', the presence of specialised services and advanced R&D infrastructures, the possibility of exchanging information and knowledge, and of sharing similar experiences can significantly contribute to the increase of innovation opportunities and to a more rapid diffusion of technological advances (Breschi, 2000; Di Tommaso, Paci and Schweitzer, 2003).[40] Geographical proximity facilitates this kind of social interaction and tacit knowledge transmission, but even if it is a necessary precondition, it is rarely sufficient alone to create and exchange

---

[39] Norton (1999), distinguished *neoclassical* approaches to clusters (based on static spatial externalities), from *post-neoclassical* views (based on dynamic externalities).

[40] This amounts to saying that agglomeration economies act as 'dynamic economies': they do not only lower production costs, but they are also sources of entrepreneurial creativity and innovation (Camagni, 1991).

intangible assets.[41] Also organisational and cultural proximity are crucial elements in these processes (Boschma, 1999). In addition, it is necessary to emphasise the role of networking and interactions among firms at local level (Asheim, 2001; Cooke, 2001; chapter 2, 3 and 7).

With the term 'territorialisation', Storper (1997, p.170) indicates the process of territorial agglomeration where 'economic viability is rooted in assets (including practices and relations) that are not available in many other places and cannot easily or rapidly be created or imitated in places that lack them'. In this sense, geographical proximity can be seen as one of the most important *tangible* assets in the intangible economy.

In the literature, intangible assets have usually been considered as 'firm specific assets', but, as stressed by Porter (1998, p.78), 'what happens *inside* companies is important, but clusters reveal that the immediate business environment *outside* companies play a vital role as well'. Localised creation and utilisation of some non-ubiquitous product and process factors – most notably tacit knowledge – can be viewed as a valuable regional asset. The analysis of collective intangible assets, put forward for instance by Lowendahl (1997), should go beyond the boundaries of individual companies in order to consider clusters of interconnected firms as generators of relevant intangible assets such as trust, understanding and externalities and what in general has been termed 'untraded interdependencies', which can be defined as a 'structured set of technological externalities which can be a *collective asset* of groups of firms/industries within countries/regions' (Dosi, 1988; p.226, emphasis added).

Figure 4.3 shows three levels of analysis with respect to intangible assets. Individual intangible assets consist mainly of competencies, personal skills and capabilities, culture, values and reputation. Firm-specific intangible assets are collective assets that can be exploited by the firm as a whole. These include intellectual property rights, customer loyalty, brands, databases and human capital at the firm level. Cluster-specific or region-specific intangibles are collective assets that belong to a particular set of interconnected firms within the same region. These consist mainly of shared values, norms, mutual trusts, collective knowledge, and all the factors that are usually included in the broad concept of social capital (see chapter 5).[42] Here, one sees the importance of formal and informal institutions that can facilitate localised collective learning through the promotion of co-ordination, co-operation and knowledge exchange.

The organisation of individual intangible assets through formal and informal relationships allows the increase in value of such assets. At each level of analysis

---

[41] 'Spatial clustering alone does not create mutually beneficial interdependencies. An industrial system may be geographically agglomerated and yet have limited capacity for adaptation. This is overwhelmingly a function of organisational structure, not of technology or firm size' (Saxenian, 1994a: p.161).

[42] The notion of social capital is borrowed from sociology (Jacobs, 1961; Bordieu, 1986) and refers to the stock that is created when a group of organisations develops the ability to work together for mutual productive gain (Fountain, 1998). For a comprehensive review of research on this topic, see Lesser (2000).

the value of intangibles is higher than the mere sum of the assets at the previous level considered separately: therefore, as firm-specific intangible assets exceed the mere sum of the individual intangible assets, the value of cluster-specific intangible assets is higher than the sum of the assets of each individual firm belonging to the cluster.

However it is reasonable to underline that this virtuous path does not always take place and collective intangible assets may present an obstacle to the full exploitation of individual assets. The same can be said for clusters that cannot follow innovative trajectories because of a lack of internal co-ordination. Further, agglomeration economies are functional in promoting mainly 'incremental innovation' (Bianchi and Giordani, 1993; Asheim, 1995) through informal 'catching-up learning' (Asheim, 2001) – i.e. learning-by-doing and learning-by-

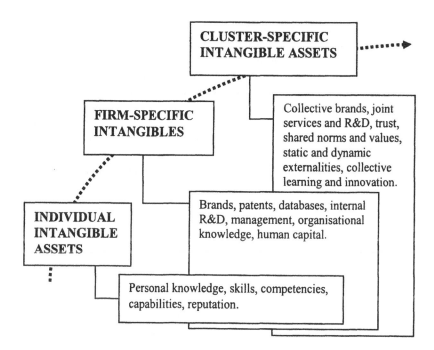

Figure 4.3 Levels of intangibles

using and changing. Organisational inertia due to strong ties can hinder the ability to break path dependency and change technological trajectory through radical innovations and it can also limit the access to new learning sources (Lazerson and Lorenzoni, 1999; Varaldo and Ferrucci, 2001). The continual accumulation of knowledge, in fact, could lock firms into obsolete technological trajectories. In these circumstances, collective learning processes, which are usually barriers to entry to outsiders, may be transformed into barriers to exit for insiders (Bianchi,

1989).[43] Therefore a growing number of scholars recognise the importance of clusters being 'outward looking', stating that it would be desirable to strike a balance between openness to external actors and internal coherence (Maillat, 1991; DTI, 1999; Florida, 1998; Kenney and von Burg, 1999; Norton, 1999; Albino and Schiuma, 1999; Mariotti and Mutinelli, 2001; Varaldo and Ferrucci, 2001).[44]

6. Conclusions

This chapter builds a bridge between two apparently separate worlds: the geography of economic activity and intangible assets. Analytical frameworks of traditional theories of clustering are not made so obsolete, as has been claimed, by the advent of a 'geographically free economy and society'. Physical proximity still has great relevance in shaping the distribution of activities and such frameworks can be used to analyse agglomeration phenomena also in the 'intangible economy'. Nevertheless the focus on the growing importance of intangible assets has important implications for clustering theories. Knowledge, as a common denominator of intangible assets, is now the key productive factor, and its degree of codification is crucial in shaping the geographic distribution of firms. Moreover, traditional external economies can be seen as dynamic economies, fostering innovation. However, the key to success in the intangible economy is linked to the capacity of clustering firms to establish a network of relationships both internal and external to the local cluster. Internal collaboration can create social ties generating trust and promoting learning and innovation through shared experiences. External linkages reduce the risk of lock-in situations that can compromise learning, innovation and creativity. In spite of the important role of place-specific local resources and regional innovation systems, firms in regional clusters are in need of innovative co-operation and interaction with world-class, national and international competence centres and innovation systems in order to stay competitive.

Conversely, the literature on intangibles should take into account the spatial dimension. Geographical proximity plays a key role in the creation and, to some extent, in the transmission of intangibles. Clustered firms can enjoy benefits from the implementation of their collective intangible asset base. Implicit knowledge can be effectively transferred only over short distances, among firms with a similar vision and a common knowledge base. Furthermore, the creation of a local pool of specialised labour can have a positive impact on the quality of a firm's human capital in terms of competencies, skills and experience. Therefore, it is possible to consider clusters as key nodes in the globalised economy. They can act as

---

[43] This is related to what we can term, paraphrasing Granovetter (1973), 'the weakness of strong ties'.

[44] The reaction of the 'Third Italy' industrial districts to the crisis of the traditional sectors in which their firms are specialised represents an interesting case. Recent analyses have shown the emergence of leading firms and multinational corporations within districts. See Albino and Schiuma (1999) for some examples.

generators of important intangibles such as trust, shared values and experiences and collective learning, so that the amount of intangible assets in a geographical cluster results higher than the mere sum of the intangible asset bases of individual firms considered alone.

These preliminary remarks are far from being conclusive. They leave open a wide range of possibilities. It is important to determine the 'relevant' proximity for firms. Do firms seek proximity to other specialised firms? Are these firms likely to be competitors with one another, or collaborators? Do they substitute for one another, or complement each other? Or are they in totally different industries with only a tangential relationship to one another? Do firms in clusters seek the availability of external capital? Do firms seek research centres and technical experts? This depends on the features of the industry, the role firms play in the process of creation, diffusion, acquisition and exploitation of different intangible assets in the form of explicit or uncodified knowledge. Therefore, this article represents a basis for further research on the topic; future industry-specific studies and empirical analyses will improve and complete the interpretative framework proposed.

References

Albino, V. and Schiuma, G. (1999), *New Forms of Knowledge Creation and Diffusion within Industrial Districts*, paper presented at the Conference 'Il Futuro dei Distretti', Vicenza, 4th June.

Antonelli, C. (1999), 'The Evolution of the Industrial Organisaton of the Production of Knowledge', *Cambridge Journal of Economics*, 23, 243-260.

Antonelli, C. (2000), 'Collective Knowledge Communication and Innovation: The Evidence of Technological Districts', *Regional Studies*, 34(6), 535-547.

Arora, A., Gambardella, A. and Pammolli F., Riccaboni M. (2001), *The Nature and the Extent of the Market for Technology in Biopharmaceuticals*, http://www.unisi.it/epris

Arrow, K.J. (1962), 'Economic Welfare and the Allocation of Resources for Invention', in Nelson R.R. (ed.), *The Rate and Direction of Innovative Activity: Economic and social Factors*, Princeton University Press, Princeton.

Arthur, W.B. (1990), 'Positive Feedbacks in the Economy', *Scientific American*, 221, 92-99.

Asheim, B. (1995), 'Industrial Districts as "Learning Regions". A Condition for Prosperity?', STEP Report No. 3.

Asheim, B. (2001), 'Localiced Learning, Innovation and Regional Clusters', from Mariussen A., *Cluster policies - Cluster development?*, Nordregio Report 2001: 2.

Audretsch, D.B. (1998), 'Agglomeration and the Location of Innovative Activity', *Oxford Review of Economic Policy*, 14(2), 18-29.

Audretsch, D.B. and Feldman, M. (1996), 'R&D Spillovers and the Geography of Innovation and Production', *American Economic Review*, 86(3), 630-640.

Bairstow, J. (2001), 'The Death of Distance', in *Laser Focus World*, August, p.248.

Barry, F., Holger, G. and Strobl, E. (2001), *Foreign Direct Investment, Agglomerations and Demonstration Effects: An Empirical Investigation*, http://www.cepr.org/RESEARCH/Networks/FDIMC/Papers/FDI_Barry.doc

Baudry, B. (1993), 'Partenariat et sous-traitance: une approche par la théorie des incitations', *Revue d'Économie Industrielle*, 66, 51-67.

Becattini, G. (a cura di) (1987), *Mercato e forze locali. Il distretto industriale*, Il Mulino, Bologna.

Becattini, G. and Rullani, E. (1993), 'Sistema Locale e Mercato Globale', in Becattini, G., Vaccà, S. (eds), *Prospettive degli studi di Politica industriale in Italia*, Franco Angeli, Milano.

Belkaoui, M.R. (1992), *Accounting Theory*, New York, Academic Press.

Bellandi, M. (1996), 'Innovation and Change in the Marshallian Industrial District', *European Planning Studies*, 4(3), 353-364.

Bianchi, P. (1989), 'Concorrenza dinamica, distretti industriali e interventi locali', in Gobbo F. (ed.), *Distretti e sistemi produttivi alle soglie degli anni Novanta*, Franco Angeli, Milano.

Bianchi, P. (1991), *Produzione e potere di mercato*, Ediesse, Roma.

Bianchi, P. (1995), *Le Politiche Industriali dell'Unione Europea*, Il Mulino, Bologna.

Bianchi, P. and Giordani, M.G. (1993), 'Innovation Policy at the Local and National Levels: The Case of Emilia-Romagna', *European Planning Studies*, 1, 1, 25-41.

Bianchi, P. and Labory, S. (2002), 'The Economics of Intangible Assets', University of Ferrara, Working Paper n. 17/2002.

Bianchi, P. and Labory, S. (2003), 'Macroeconomic Indicators and Policies for Intangible Assets: Measurement Problem or More Fundamental Economic Change?', Chapter 2, in *Study on the Measurement of Intangible Assets and Associated Reporting Practices*, Report to the European Commission, DG Enterprise, http://europa.eu.int/comm/research/era/3pct/index_en.html.

Bontis, N. (1999), 'Managing Organisatonal Knowledge by Diagnosing Intellectual Capital: Framing and Advancing the State of the Field', *International Journal of Technology Management*, 18, 433-462.

Bordieu, P. (1986), 'The Forms of Capital', in Richardson J.C. (ed.), *Handbook of Theory and Research for the Sociology of Education*, Greenwood Press, New York.

Boschma, R. (2001), *Proximity and Innovation*, paper presented at the Third Congress on Proximity 'New Growth and Territory', Paris, 13th-14th December.

Bouman, H. and Verhoef, B. (1986), 'High Technology and Employment: some Information of the Netherlands', in Nijkamp P. (ed.), *Technological Change, Employment and Spatial Dynamics*, Springer-Verlag, Berlin.

Breschi, S. (2000), 'La Geografia delle Innovazioni Tecnologiche', in Malerba F. (ed.), *Economia dell'Innovazione*, Carocci, Roma.

Brooking, A. (1996): *Intellectual Capital: Core Assets for the Third Millennium Enterprise*, Thomson Business Press, London.

Burton-Jones, A. (1999), *Knowledge Capitalism : Business, Work, and Learning in the New Economy*, Oxford University Press, Oxford.

Cairncross, F. (1997), *The Death of Distance: How the Communications Revolutions will Change our Lives*, , Harvard Business School Press, Cambridge MA.

Camagni, R. (1991), 'Introduction: from the Local "Milieu" to Innovation through Co-operation and Networks', in Camagni R. (ed.), *Innovation Networks: Spatial Perspectives*, Belhaven Press, London.

Camagni, R. (1992), *Economia Urbana*, Carocci, Roma.

Canibano, L. and García-Ayuso, M., Sanchez P. (1999), 'Accounting for Intangibles: a Literature Review', *Journal of Accounting Literature*, 19.

Canibano, L. and Sanchez, P. (1998), *Measuring Intangibles to Understand and Improve Innovation Management*, Research proposal. Universidad Autonoma, Madrid, mimeo.

Capello, R. (1999), 'Spatial Transfer of Knowledge in High Technology Milieux: Learning versus Collective Learning Processes', *Regional Studies*, 33, 353-365.

Caves, R. (1996), *Multinational Enterprise and Economic Analysis*, Harvard University Press, Cambridge MA.

Chaillou, B. (1977), 'Definition et typologie de la sous traitance', *Revue Economique*, 28(2), 262-285.

Coffey, W. (1992), 'The Role of Producer Services in Systems of Flexible Production', in Ernste, H., Meier, V. (eds), *Regional Development and Contemporary Industrial Response: Extending Flexible Specialisaton*, Belhaven Press, London.

Connell, J., Schweitzer, S.O. and Schoenberg, F. (2003), 'Factors Underlying High-Technology Industrial Clusters in the United States: the Case of Biotechnology Firms', in Di Tommaso, M.R., Schweitzer, S.O. (eds) (2003), *Promoting High-tech Industries. Can Health Lead the Way?*, Edward Elgar, Cheltenham UK.

Cooke, P. (2001), *Clusters as Key Determinant of Economic Growth: The Example of Biotechnology*, http://www.nordregio.se/files/r0102cooke.pdf

Cowling, K. and Sugden, R. (1999), 'The Wealth of Localities, Regions and Nations; Developing Multinational Economies', *New Political Economy*, 4(3), 361-378.

Daum, J. (2001), *Business Management in the New, New Economy*, presentation for the 'SAP Financials Conference', Basel, Switzerland, 25th 26th June 2001.

David, P. and Foray, D. (1995), 'Accessing and Expanding the Science and Technology Base', *STI Review*, n.16, OECD, Paris.

Dei Ottati, G. (1994), 'Co-operation and Competition in the Industrial District as an Organisatonal Model', *European Planning Studies*, n. 2, 2, 463-483.

Department of Trade and Industry, (UK) (1999), *Biotechnology Clusters*, report no.1888, http://biotechknowledge.com/showlibsp.php3?uid=1

Desrochers, P. (2001), 'Geographical Proximity and the Transmission of Tacit Knowledge', *The Review of Austrian Economics*, 14(1), 25-46.

Devas, C.E. (1901), *Political Economy*, 2nd ed. Longmans, Greens, and Co, London.

Di Tommaso, M.R. (1999), 'Efficienza collettiva, i nodi della politica', *Università di Ferrara, Facoltà di Economia, Quaderni del Dipartimento*, n.13, June.

Di Tommaso, M.R. and Rabellotti, R. (1999), *Efficienza collettiva e cluster di imprese: oltre l'esperienza italiana*, Il Mulino, Bologna.

Di Tommaso, M.R. and Schweitzer, S.O. (eds) (2003), *Promoting High-tech Industries. Can Health Lead the Way?*, Edward Elgar, Cheltenham UK.

Di Tommaso, M.R., Paci, D. and Schweitzer, S.O. (2003), 'The Geography of Intangibles: The Case of the Health Industry', in Di Tommaso M.R., Schweitzer S.O. (eds), *Promoting High-tech Industries. Can Health Lead the Way?*, Edward Elgar, Cheltenham UK.

Di Tommaso, M.R., Paci, D. and Rubini, L. (2003), 'High-tech Clustering: Is Distance Dead?', in Pitelis C., Sugden R., Wilson J.R. (eds), *Clusters and Globalisation: The Development of the Economies*, Edward Elgar, Cheltenham UK.

Dosi, G. (1988), 'The Nature of the Innovative Process', in Dosi, G., Freeman, C., Nelson, R., Silverberg, G., Soete, L. (eds), *Technical Change and Economic Theory*, Pinter, London.

Dunning, J.H. (1997), *Alliance Capitalism and Global Business*, Routledge, London.

Economist, The (1995), 'The Death of Distance', 30 September.

Edvinsson, L. (1997), 'Developing Intellectual Capital at Skandia', *Longe Range Planning*, 30(3), 366-373.

Edvinsson, L. and Malone, M.S. (1997), *Intellectual capital: Realising your company's true value by finding its hidden brainpower*, Harper Business Press, New York.

Edwards, B. (1998), 'Capitals of Capital: Financial Centres Survey', *The Economist*, 347: 8067, May, p.8.

Enright, M. (1999), 'The Globalisaton of Competition and the Localisaton of Competitive Advantage: Policies Towards Regional Clustering', in Hood, N. and Young, S. (eds), *Globalisaton of Multinational Enterprise Activity and Economic Development*, Macmillan, London.

Eustace, C. (2000), *Intangible Economy Impact and Policy Issues*, Report of the European High Level Expert Group on the Intangible Economy, European Commission, Bruxelles.

Feldman, M.P. (1994), *The Geography of Innovation*, Kluwer Academic Publishers, Boston.

Feldman, M.P. (2002), *The Internet Revolution and the Geography of Innovation*, http://www.cs.jhu.edu/~mfeldman/feldman ISSJ Submission.pdf

Fleck, J. (1988), *Innofusion or Diffusation? The Nature of Technological Development in Robotics* ESRC Programme on Information and communication technologies (PICT), Working Paper series, University of Edinburgh.

Florida, R. (1995), 'Towards the Learning Region', *Futures*, 27, 527-536.

Florida, R. (1998), 'Calibrating the Learning Region', in De la Mothe, J., Paquet, G. (eds), *Local and Regional Systems of Innovation*, Kluwer, Boston.

Florida, R. and Kenney, M. (1988), 'Venture Capital, High Technology and Regional Development', *Regional Studies*, 22(1), 33-48.

Foray, D. and Lundvall, B.A. (eds) (1996), *Employment and Growth in the Knowledge-based Economy*, OECD, Paris.

Fountain, J.E. (1998), 'Social Capital: A Key Enabler of Innovation', in Branscomb, L.M., Keller, J.H. (eds), *Investing in Innovation*, MIT Press, Cambridge MA and London.

Geroski, P. (1995), 'Markets for Technology: Knowledge, Innovation and Appropriability', in Stoneman, P. (ed.), *Handbook of the Economics of Innovation and Technological Change*, Blackwell, Oxford.

Gilly, J.P., Colletis, G., Pecqueur, B., Perrat, J. and Zimmermann, J.B (1996), 'Firmes et territoires: entre nomadisme et ancrage', *Espaces et Sociétés*, December.

Goldfinger, C. (2000),'Intangible Economy and Financial Markets', *Communications & Strategies*, 40(4), 59-89.

Granovetter, M. (1973), 'The Strength of Weak Ties', *American Journal of Sociology*, 78(6), 1360-1380.

Griliches, Z. (1995), 'R&D and Productivity: Econometric Results and Measurement Issues', in Stoneman, P. (ed.), *Handbook of the Economics of Innovation and Technological Change*, Blackwell, Oxford UK and Cambridge USA.

Guilding, C. and Pike, R. (1990), 'Intangible Marketing Assets: A Managerial Accounting Perspective', *Accounting and Business Research*, 21(18), 41-49.

Haig, R.M. (1926), 'Toward an Understanding of the Metropolis. II. The Assignment of Activities to Areas in Urban Regions', *The Quarterly Journal of Economics*, 40(1), 402-434.

Hall, S. J. (1900) 'The Localisaton of Industries', *Washington: U.S. Census. (Manufactures*, part 1): CXC-CCXIV.

Hall, R. (1992), 'The Strategic Analysis of Intangible Resources', *Strategic Management Journal*, 13(2), 135-144.

Harris, C.D. (1954), 'The Market as a Factor in the Location of Production', *Annals of the Association of American Geographers*, 44, 315-348.

Hayek, F.A. (1945), 'The Use of Knowledge in Society', *American Economic Review*, 5, 519-530.

Hodgson, G.M. (1999), *Economics and Utopia*, Oxford University Press, Oxford.

Holmes, J. (1986), 'The Organisaton and Locational Structure of Production Subcontracting', in Scott A.J., Storper M. (eds), *Production, Work, and Territory: The Geographical Anatomy of Industrial Capitalism.*, Allen & Unwin, Boston, London and Sydney.

Hope, J. and Hope, T. (1998), *Competing in the Third wave: the Ten Key Management Issues of the Information Age*, Harvard Business School, Boston.

International Accounting Standards Committee - IASC (1998), International Accounting Standard n.38: *Intangible assets*. London: IASC.

Jacobs, J. (1961), *The Death and Life of Great American Cities*, Random House, New York.

Jaffe, A. (1989), 'Real effects of Academic Research', *American Economic Review*, 79 (5), 957-970.

Jaffe, A.B., Trajtenberg, M. and Henderson, R. (1993), 'Geographic Localisaton of Knowledge Spillovers as Evidenced by Patent Citations', *Quarterly Journal of Economics*, 63(3), 577-598.

Johanson, U., Mårtensson, M. and Skoog, M. (1999), 'Measuring and Managing Intangibles: Eleven Swedish Qualitative Exploratory Case Studies, paper presented at the international symposium 'Measuring and Reporting Intellectual Capital, Experience, Issues and Prospects', Amsterdam, 9th-10th June.

Kanter, R. M. (1989), *When Giants Learn to Dance*, Simon and Schuster, New York.

Kenney, M. (1986), *Biotechnology: The University-Industrial Complex*, Yale University Press, New Haven.

Kenney, M. (2001), Regional Clusters, Venture Capital and Entrepreneurship: What can the Social Sciences tell us about Silicon Valley?, http://hcd.ucdavis.edu/Faculty/Kenney/vita/Reg.htm

Kenney, M. and von Burg, U. (1999), 'Technology, Entrepreneurship, and Path Dependence: Industrial Clustering in Silicon Valley and Route 128', *Industrial and Corporate Change*, 8(1), 67-103.

Klein, S., Rosenberg, N. (1985), 'An Overview of the Process of Innovation', in Landau R., Rosenberg N., *The Positive Sum Strategy: Harnessing Technology for Economic Growth*, National Academy Press, Washington DC.

Krugman, P. (1991), *Geography and Trade*, MIT Press, Cambridge MA.

Lazerson, M.H. and Lorenzoni, G. (1999), 'The Firms that Feed Industrial Districts: A Return to the Italian Source', *Industrial and Corporate Change*, 8(2), 235-266.

Leamer, E.E. and Storper, M. (2001), The Economic Geography of the Internet Age, *NBER Working Paper*, No. W8450,

Lesser, E.L. (2000), *Knowledge and Social Capital*, Butterworth-Heinemann, Boston.

Lev, B. (2001), *Intangibles – Management, Measurement and Reporting*, Brooking Institution, New York.

Levin, R., Cohen, W. and Mowery, D. (1987), 'R&D Appropriability, Opportunity and Market Structure: New Evidence on Some Schumpeterian Hypotheses', *American Economic Review*, Papers and Proceedings 75, 20-24.

Lösch, A. (1940), *The Economics of Location*, Jena, Fisher.

Lowendahl, B. (1997), *Strategic Management of Professional Service Firm*, Handelshojskolens Forlag, Copenhagen.

Lundvall, B. Ä. (1988), 'Innovation as an Interactive Process: from User-producer Interaction to the National System of Innovation', in Dosi, G., Nelson, R, Silverberg, G, Freeman, C., Soete, L. (eds) (1988), *Technical Change and Economic Theory*, Pinter, London.

Lundvall, B. Ä. and Borras, S. (1999), *The Globalising Learning Economy: Implications for Innovation Policy*. Office for Official Publications of the European Communities, Luxembourg.

Maggioni, M. (2002), *Clustering Dynamics and the Location of High-tech Firms*, Physica-Verlag, Heidelberg.

Maillat, D. (1991), 'The Innovative Process and the Role of the Milieu', in Bergman, E., Maier, G., Tödtling, F. (eds) (1991), *Regions Reconsidered*, Mansell, London and New York.

Maillat, D. (1996), 'From the Industrial District to the Innovative Milieu: Contribution to an Analysis of Territorialised Productive Organisatons', *IRER Working Papers*, No.9606b.

Malecki, E.J. (1997), *Technology and Economic Development: The Dynamics of Local, Regional and National Competitiveness*, 2nd ed, Longman, Harlow.

Mariotti, S. and Mutinelli, M. (2001), 'La formazione dei gruppi multinazionali nei distretti: interpretazioni generali ed evidenze empiriche per il caso della meccanica italiana', in Brioschi, F., Cainelli, G. (2001), *Diffusione e Caratteristiche dei Gruppi di Piccole e Medie Imprese nelle Aree Distrettuali*, Giuffrè Editore, Milano.

Marshall, A. (1890), *Principles of Economics*, London, Macmillan; Italian version (1977), *Principi di Economia*, UTET, Torino.

Maskell, P. and Malmberg, A. (1999), 'Localised learning and industrial competitiveness', *Cambridge Journal of Economics*, 23, 167-185.

Mills, E.S. (1992), 'Sectoral Clustering and Metropolitan Development', in Mills, E.S., McDonald, J.F. (eds), *Sources of Metropolitan Growth*, New Brunswick, Center for Urban Policy Research, 3-18.

Napier, C. and Power, M. (1992), 'Professional Research, Lobbying and Intangibles: A Review Essay', *Accounting and Business Research*, 23(89), 85-95.

Narin, F., Hamilton, K.S. and Olivastro, D. (1997), 'The Increasing Linkage between U.S. Technology and Public Science', *Research Policy*, 26, 317-330.

Nooteboom, B. (2000), *Learning and Innovation in Organisations and Economies*, Oxford University Press, Oxford.

Norton, R.D. (1999), 'The Geography of the New Economy', in Jackson, R.W., *The Web Book of Regional Science*, Regional Research Institute, West Virginia University, http://www.rri.wvu.edu/regscbooks.htm

OECD (2001), *OECD Science, Technology and Industry Scoreboard. Towards a knowledge-based economy*, OECD, Paris.

Petrash, G. (1996), 'Dow's Journey to a Knowledge Value Management Culture', *European Management Journal*, 14(4), 365-373.

Piore, M. and Sabel, C. (1984), *The Second Industrial Divide*, Basic Books, New York.

Pisano, G.P. (1990), 'The R&D Boundaries of the Firm: An Empirical Analysis', *Administrative Science Quarterly*, 35(1), 153-176.

Polanyi, M. (1967), *The Tacit Dimension*, Routledge and Kegan Paul, London.

Porter, M. (1990), *The Competitive Advantage of Nations*, Free Press, New York.

Porter, M. (1998), 'Clusters and the New Economics of Competition', *Harvard Business Review*, November-December, 77-90.

Porter, M. (2000), 'Location, Competition, and Economic Development: Local Clusters in a Global Economy', *Economic Development Quarterly*, 14(1), 15-34.

Prevezer, M. (1995), 'The Dynamics of Industrial Clustering in Biotechnology', *Small Business Economics*, 9, 255-271.

Reilly, R. (1992), 'Interstate Intangible Transfer Programs', *CPA Journal*, 62(8), 34-40.

Roos, R. and Roos, J. (1997), 'Measuring your Company's Intellectual Performance', *Longe Range Planning*, 30(3), 413-426.

Rullani, E. (1994), 'Il Valore della Conoscenza', *Economia e Politica Industriale*, 82, 47-74.

Rullani, E. and Romano, L. (eds) (1998), *Il postfordismo: idee per il capitalismo prossimo venturo*, ETAS libri, Milano.

Sacchetti, S. and Sugden, R. (2000), 'La natura e l'impatto dei network industriali di subfornitura', Quaderni del Dipartimento, Facoltà di Economia, Università di Ferrara, n.4, Marzo 2000.

Saxenian, A.L. (1994a), *Regional Advantage: Cultural and Competition in Silicon Valley and Route 128*, Harvard University Press, Cambridge MA.

Saxenian, A.L. (1994b), 'Regional Systems of Innovation and the Blurred Firm', in De la Mothe, J., Paquet, G. (eds), *Local and Regional Systems of Innovation*, Kluwer, Boston.

Schweitzer, S.O. (1997), *Pharmaceutical Economics and Policy*, Oxford University Press, New York.

Schweitzer, S.O. and Di Tommaso, M.R., (2003), 'Why do Biotechnology Firms Cluster? Some Possible Explanations', in Sugden, R., Cheng, R.H., Meadows, G.R. (eds), *Urban and Regional Prosperity in a Globalising, New Economy*, Edward Elgar, Cheltenham.

Scitovsky, T. (1954), 'Two concepts of external economies', *Journal of Political Economy*, LXII, 2, 70-82.

Scott, A.J. (1993), *Technopolis: High-Technology Industry and Regional Development in Southern California*, University of California Press, Berkeley and Los Angeles.

Skandia (1995) *Value Creating Processes*, Supplement to 1995 Skandia Annual Report.

Smith, D.F. and Florida, R. (1998), 'Venture Capital's Role in Regional Innovation Systems: Historical Perspective and Recent Evidence', in Acs, Z.J. (ed.), *Regional Innovation, Knowledge and Global Change*, Pinter, London.

Stewart, T.A. (1997), *Intellectual Capital: The Wealth of Organisations,* Doubleday/ Currency, New York.

Stiglitz, J. (1985), 'Information and Economic Analysis: a Perspective', *Economic Journal*, 95, 21-41.

Stoneman, P. (ed.) (1995), *Handbook of the Economics of Innovation and Technological Change*, Blackwell, Oxford.

Storper, M. (1997), *The Regional World. Territorial Development in a Global Economy,* The Guilford Press, London.

Sveiby, K.E. (1997), *The New Organisatonal Wealth. Managing & Measuring Knowledge-Based Assets*, Berrett-Koehler Publishers Inc, San Francisco.

Swann, G.M., Prevezer, M. and Stout, D. (1998), *The Dynamics of Industrial Clustering: International Comparisons in Computing and Biotechnology*, Oxford University Press, Oxford.

Teece, D.J. (1998), 'Capturing Value from Knowledge Assets: The New Economy, Markets for Know-How, and Intangible Assets', *California Management Review*, 40/3, 55-79.

Thurow, L. (1996), *The Future of Capitalism*, William Morrow, New York.

Varaldo, R. and Ferrucci, L. (2001), 'Cambiamenti Istituzionali nell'Impresa Distrettuale: Meccanismi Inerziali e Logiche di Evoluzione', in Brioschi, F., Cainelli, G. (eds), *Diffusione e Caratteristiche dei Gruppi di Piccole e Medie Imprese nelle Aree Distrettuali*, Giuffrè Editore, Milano.

Von Burg, U. and Kenney, M. (2000), 'Venture Capital and the Birth of the Local Area Networking Industry', *Research Policy*, 29, 1135-1155.

Von Hippel, E. (1994), 'Sticky Information and the Locus of Problem Solving: Implications for Innovation', *Management Science*, 40, 429-439.

Von Thunen, J.H. (1910), *Der isolierte Staat in Beziehung auf Landwirtschaft und Nationaloekonomie*, Jena, Fisher; English version (1966), *Isolated State*, Pergamon press, Oxford and New York.

Voyer, R. (1998), 'Knowledge-based Industrial Clustering: International Comparisons', in De la Mothe, J., Paquet, G. (eds) (1998), *Local and Regional Systems of Innovation*, Kluwer, Boston.

Watanabe, S. (1971), 'Subcontracting, Industrialisation and Employment Creation', *International Labour Review*, 104, 51-76.

Weber, A. (1909), *Theory of the Location of Industries*, University of Chicago Press, Chicago.

White, G.I., Sondhi, A.C. and Fried, D. (1994), *The Analysis and Uses of Financial Statements*, John Wiley and Sons, New York.

Williamson, O. E., (1975), *Markets and Hierarchies*, Free Press, New York.

Wintjies, R. and Cobbenhagen, J. (2000), 'Knowledge Intensive Industrial Clustering around Océ', MERIT Working Paper, University of Maastricht.

Zucker, L.G. and Darby, M.R. (1998), 'Intellectual Human Capital and the Birth of U.S. Biotechnology Enterprises', *American Economic Review*, 88 (1), 290-306.

Zucker, L.G. and Darby, M.R., Armstrong, J. (1998), 'Geographically Localised Knowledge: Spillovers or Markets?', *Economic Inquiry*, XXXVI, 65-86.

Chapter 5

Why is Social Capital a 'Capital'? Public Goods, Co-operative Efforts and the Accumulation of Intangible Assets

Francesco Galassi and Susanna Mancinelli

Given the idea of this PRISM research team of the University of Ferrara that social capital is a key intangible asset that should be more explicitly considered for policy to become more effective, this chapter aims at providing more insights precisely on this intangible asset. We argue that social capital (SC) is a productive asset just as is physical capital, an approach which underscores that an increase in trust-based relations on average reduces transaction costs, just as an increase in physical capital ought to reduce average production costs. In turn this means that several characteristics normally associated with physical capital are also shared by SC. In both cases, a productive asset is created by foregoing a current benefit in return for a probable future benefit. We can therefore analyse SC with the same approach we normally use for physical assets. SC is however essentially a public good, in that it resides in the willingness of individual decision makers to engage co-operatively with each other. This is the aspect of SC that establishes it firmly as a form of collective intangible, and in this context we adopt a mixed-public good framework, since income streams deriving from SC are not totally appropriable for private use, and we likewise suggest that SC be considered the public component of mixed-public capital. As an example, consider a network of firms investing in R&D and creating voluntary agreements aimed at achieving environmental targets for reduced pollution, increased recycling, etc. In this case voluntary agreements are the public component of the mixed-public R&D.

This chapter aims to identify and analyse the conditions under which incentives exist for a dynamic increase of SC, taking into account that the public component of a mixed-public good creates certain distortions in private decisions leading to SC accumulation. These decisions, and their distortions, arise from the nature of benefits yielded to firms, the structure of internal and external costs and the individual firms' expectations.

1. Physical Capital: A Brief Review

The role of physical capital, defined as tools, machines and buildings involved in the production of commodities, is quite well understood. We can say briefly that most economists would agree that physical capital has three characteristics. First, physical capital is created by refraining from consuming a portion of current income and thus generating savings to undertake initial investment. Likewise physical capital is maintained in operation by devoting a portion of current income streams to the replacement of broken or worn out parts. Second, physical capital is created (that is, investment is undertaken) in direct proportion to expected benefits. This is precisely because a decision to invest implies giving up a current (certain) benefit in return for a future (uncertain) one. As the perceived benefits to be gained by reducing current consumption increase, so does the proportion of income that individuals are willing to set aside for investment. Conversely, as the probability that expected benefits will materialise declines, so does the proportion of income diverted from consumption to investment. The two opposing principles of uncertainty and benefits are extremely important for understanding how physical capital is created. We will argue below (sections 2 and 3) that the same applies to social capital.

The third characteristic of physical capital is its effect on production costs. An increase in physical capital (either *more* machines or *better* machines for example) should reduce the average unit output cost. This is of course the objective when individuals save and invest for higher returns, since if introducing a machine to a production process lowers unit output costs, the difference saved constitutes the investor's return, provided of course there is a market ready to absorb the product. We will return on this point below.

Two important considerations need to be made here. First, you will have noticed we said that increasing physical capital 'should' reduce costs. That is, until a particular machine has actually been put into operation, it will not be known whether it actually does reduce costs. That is what we meant earlier when we said that the creation of physical capital involves an element of uncertainty. Investors gather information about the functioning of the new machine and form expectations concerning its likely contribution to lower costs. This constitutes their expectation of benefits from their investment, that is, from the sacrifice they make today by refraining from consuming a certain portion of their income. But it needs to be stressed that these expectations may be incorrect, and that external factors may intervene to cause even the most carefully calculated savings/investment decision to yield much lower than expected benefits or even increased costs. Since this cannot be known in advance, all savings/investment decisions have an element of 'guessing', or of applying past experience to the current problem and extrapolating past observations to likely future occurrences. As will be discussed below, the formation of expectations plays a central role in SC.

The second consideration concerning the effect of physical capital is that economists usually believe that as capital increases, each additional unit (each new machine, say) will produce less than the previous one. This is known as the 'Law of Diminishing Marginal Returns' and it is used to explain why investment is not infinite: at a certain point, the extra cost savings from the additional machine will fall below the benefits foregone.[1] At this point, investment stops. As we will see, this too is relevant to our discussion of SC.

We can derive from the above some straightforward but important implications concerning investment and the growth of the stock of physical capital. First, anything that reduces the *expected* net benefits derived from increasing physical capital will reduce the rate at which investment is undertaken. Thus any increase in uncertainty over the performance of the machinery to be used or over the claims that will be made on the stream of income the machine generates (e.g. taxes), will increase the probability that the benefits obtained from investment will not match the current sacrifice in consumption. In that case, investment will not take place, it not being worthwhile to reduce current benefits in expectation of future benefits. Secondly, and consequently, the process by which individuals form expectations about likely future events is crucial: if individuals form expectations by observing their surroundings and extending their experiences into the future, it is easy to see that the process of capital formation can take one of two characteristics. In one case, a high level of investment implies a ready market for products which in turn means that most investments return enough to justify the sacrifice from current incomes. Thus individuals find it worthwhile to save and invest, and the sum of millions of such decisions justifies this. A virtuous circle is set and kept in motion.

On the other hand, if most investment decisions do not work out, individuals will not invest or save, except the minimum necessary to keep whatever capital they have in working order. Expectations as to the benefits from denying current consumption for the sake of future benefits will be pessimistic, and because few decisions are made to invest and expand, few such decisions succeed. The circle is in this case vicious, and society is stuck on a low income/low growth situation. This is of course the reason why dynamic economies such as the USA tend to grow faster than poor economies, and when poor economies do catch up (e.g. South Korea) they achieve this by means of establishing clear property rights that increase the certainty of successful investing and favour savings and accumulation to achieve this.

In conclusion, this section has argued that we can understand physical capital, one of the traditional factors of production, as the response to a set of incentives which encourage current sacrifices for future benefits. While we have seen this as an exclusively private process, which was necessary given the limit on our discussion, there are obviously significant public good aspects involved in the formation of physical capital. This does not reduce the basic thrust of our analysis, however. Most importantly, this discussion gives us a frame of reference to approach the accumulation of social capital.

---

[1] The foregone benefit is obviously equal to the interest rate.

2. Social Capital: An Intangible Productive Asset

The concept of social capital (SC) is troublesome, involving innumerable attempts at a coherent definition. We will not examine them here (see Guttman, 2001; Dasgupta and Serageldin, 1999; and Portes, 1998) beyond saying that the broadest possible agreement appears to be that SC consists of the set of norms that govern social behaviour, and that these norms are in the main unwritten but tacitly understood. There is no need to stress that such a catch-all assertion raises more questions than it answers, and in particular (as Durlauf, 1999, pointed out) that the social cohesion and conformity implicit in such a definition are not necessarily morally desirable or socially benevolent. However, discussing yet again what SC is, and what it is not, would not constitute a productive exercise here. We prefer instead to take an extremely pragmatic approach and focus instead on the forces that augment or diminish SC.

To do this, however, we need a working definition. Our definition does not attempt to identify what SC *is*, asking instead what it *does*. We will begin by drawing an explicit analogy with physical capital: the effect of physical capital, we said, is to reduce production costs, which in turn acts as the incentive to create physical capital in the first place. Likewise, the effect of SC is to reduce the transaction costs which exist since individuals cannot easily or constantly observe others' intentions or actions. Just as increasing physical capital permits lower production costs, so increasing SC leads to lower transaction costs.

The savings made possible by SC take the form of reduced monitoring costs resulting from mutual trust. 'Trust' of course is an ambiguous word to be defined in greater detail later. At present it is enough to point out that not *all* transaction costs can be eliminated thanks to trust; no matter how much the parties involved in a transaction trust each other, problems remain, for example of measurement, legal title, and enforcement. Some savings are nevertheless obtainable thanks to trust-based relations, and to the extent that such savings reduce entry costs into transactions, they have the same effect as increases in physical capital on output costs.

For example, writing contracts that cover all contingencies in a relationship is extremely difficult and therefore expensive. If the parties can leave some 'gaps' in their contracts, since they share an understanding (a 'gentlemen's agreement') as to how they will behave in unforeseen circumstances, this will have two cost reduction effects. First, it will be easier and cheaper to negotiate the original agreement, and secondly, if an unforeseen eventuality does arise it can be dealt with without costly re-negotiations. At its extreme, in family-run firms or clusters of firms for example, no contracts are written at all, precisely because there is a clear internal ethos which prescribes mutual rights and obligations in virtually all situations. Needless to say, these organisations are extremely flexible.

In the absence of a certain level of trust, contracting parties are compelled to protect their allocations of costs and benefits from ulterior motives through more complex and rigid contracts; a costly activity which may simply discourage potentially beneficial transactions from taking place at all. Low SC therefore requires more resources for transactions through the establishment of the requisite guarantees and protection, just as relatively low physical capital requires a greater amount of effort to produce equivalent units of output.

To continue with our analogy, we turn now to the question of foregoing current benefits for future rewards, in other words, the mechanism that brings about the construction of physical capital. Any alteration of the relative inducements of this trade-off will affect the rate at which the physical capital stock grows. The same can be said about SC, since in any transaction, party A will have to make a commitment (in time, money or some other resource) before party B can do likewise. Once A's commitment is made, B then has the opportunity to defect, capturing a benefit without committing resources. In this case the greater overall benefit jointly obtainable from co-operation remains unrealised, and while B is better off, A is worse off.

It follows that A will make a commitment only if his expectations of B's actions are such that there's a high probability that B will not defect, that is, that B will carry through with his share of the investment (committing time and resources to the joint project) so that a joint product will result to be shared at the end. The higher A's monitoring of B to ensure B's co-operation, the smaller A's net benefit from the joint action. At a certain level of monitoring, no net benefits will accrue to A at all, and the joint action will simply not take place. It follows that when individuals generally expect others to defect (i.e. trust is low) they will refrain from engaging in joint projects because the net benefits will be low, and possibly negative. The level of trust that individuals have to place in others in order to engage in a joint project has been rigorously defined and estimated elsewhere (Galassi, 2001).

Like physical capital, SC therefore arises when the expected balance of payoffs offers the right inducements. The reasoning is not circular, if properly understood: each individual takes a certain view of the probability of defection of others with whom he is engaged, and the sum of these probabilities may be said to constitute a measure of trust in society. Any given player takes that value as given, just as any seller in a perfectly competitive market takes the price as given, but the sum of individual actions yields a social equilibrium, which may be one of high or low trust. What matters here is this. Notice that the steps in the construction of SC are quite similar to those of physical capital: an original commitment (a diversion of resources from current consumption to a project that may yield future benefits) is made if the probability of a certain return is above a minimal 'threshold' level. Once again, because A cannot observe B's intentions (just as an investor in physical capital cannot totally observe the markets or the future functioning of a new machine), expectations play a central role in the decision. This defines trust, in our view, and the functioning of SC. Trust is the expectation that the other party in the transaction will not defect. If expectations are formed by observing and extrapolating events, then just as for physical capital we can imagine two situations. In the first, individuals trust each other (SC is high) and are willing to engage in transactions which require that they commit resources. Because most of these transactions work out (that is, produce a joint benefit), large numbers of people share in the benefit of co-operative action. Co-operation is thus seen to pay off, so individuals will be willing to enter into more joint projects and few defections will take place. Few resources have to be devoted to monitoring the other party, and the social equilibrium is one of co-operative engagement and accumulation.

In contrast, just as in the physical capital case, if trust is low, few joint projects will be undertaken and those that do will require significant monitoring. Net benefits will be low and the inducements to engage in co-operation will be correspondingly scarce. Defecting will then be an attractive option, and expectations will form that co-operation is not worthwhile and, if absolutely necessary, has to be buttressed with significant amounts of strict monitoring. Few joint action benefits will then be realised and the social equilibrium will be one of stagnation (see François and Zabojnik, 2002, for a formalised discussion of the external shocks that can transform a co-operative outcome to a situation of low trust equilibrium). All these phenomena are discussed in greater detail in section 3 below.

There remains one last point to stress to complete our analogy between physical and social capital. The benefits generated by an increase in physical capital are mainly privately captured, although obviously there are spillovers and externalities. The construction of SC differs in this case in that what is created is essentially a public good. SC is, therefore, an intangible asset in the sense that it does not consist of physical objects, but rather of interpersonal or inter-institutional relations based on established mutual trust. Because the benefits of this type of relation are not wholly internalisable by individuals or firms acting in the market, we are in effect dealing with the purest form of collective intangible. This intangible has to be created, just as for tangible assets, but differs fundamentally in its spread of income streams, which as we said are mostly public. Hence, the benefits from a successful co-operative action will only partly accrue to the individuals concerned, because the demonstration that there are high payoffs to co-operation is in itself a benefit of successful co-operation. Of course, a successful co-operative action will lower the cost for the individuals involved to engage in further co-operation. This offers an insight into the formation of industrial clusters (repeated successful co-operative interaction) and the already mentioned high trust equilibriums that we will discuss in greater detail below. The point is simply that the public goods aspect of SC is stronger than for physical capital.

Of course, one consideration is that there are externalities in the construction of physical capital as well. But whereas physical capital can be protected by patent and copyright laws, no such possibility exists for SC. Noting that physical capital also produces externalities does not weaken the argument we are presenting that physical capital and SC can be analysed with the same tools. If anything, this strengthens our comparison.

This section has suggested that the same criteria can be used to analyse physical and social capital. In both cases, the accumulation of productive assets will be undertaken if current foregone income is invested for sufficient returns to justify diverting income flow from immediate consumption. In both cases the asset is maintained by additional 'sacrifices', that is, additional diversions of current income streams over time (replacement of worn or broken parts for physical capital, ongoing co-operation for SC, see below). In both cases the current decision is made on a probabilistic assessment of future events: for both physical and social capital extrapolating from past experience to form expectations as to the future state of the world is essential to successful accumulation. Nevertheless while the analogy is useful, it is important not to push it too far. Since SC, unlike physical capital, is not a privately owned productive asset, there are important consequences for its creation and accumulation. To these differences we now turn.

3. The Mixed-Public Good Framework

We have shown above that social capital is similar to physical assets in that it consists of an abstention from current consumption for the purpose of generating future income streams. However, we have focused on private benefits, excluding one side of the coin. In fact, SC has an essentially public good dimension, which generates income streams not wholly subject to private capture. It is therefore an intangible productive asset with an unavoidable public dimension. Within this context, following the work by Mancinelli and Mazzanti (2002), this section will shift the analysis of social capital more explicitly towards a mixed-public good approach, in which interrelations between economic agents are investigated in a dynamic scenario where both market and non-market benefits are jointly relevant. We will show that the sum of mutual trust-based relationships which reduce transaction costs (as outlined in section 2) form a productive asset that, though intangible, contributes in fundamental ways to the establishment of industrial clusters and to the flexible and versatile productive relations that characterise the post industrial economy.

First of all, let us be clear about what is meant by 'mixed-public good'. In the economic literature,[2] a mixed-public good, or impure public good, is a good which jointly gives private and public benefits. A typical example is that of an individual who, by being inoculated against an infectious disease, confers both a private benefit on himself and a public benefit by reducing the risk of spreading the disease through the community. In this case inoculation is the mixed-public good.

In this chapter, firms are economic agents and social capital is the public component of a mixed-public capital. As an example, we may think about a network of firms which invests in R&D and create voluntary agreements aimed at achieving environmental targets for reduced pollution, increased recycling, etc. Voluntary agreements are the public component of the mixed-public capital R&D and can be considered the SC in which each firm chooses to invest.[3] SC in this

---

[2] See Cornes and Sandler (1986).

[3] Each time a firm invests in R&D it decides to invest both in a private component of capital (for instance technological amelioration appropriable by the firm) and in a public component of capital (the co-operative agreements among firms).

example is consistent with the main aspects usually highlighted in the literature, those of 'trust' and 'ease of co-operation'.[4]

Our intention is to highlight trust and co-operation and in doing so to focus on the voluntary nature of actions and on incentive schemes to support investment decisions in an environment where both market and non-market returns are present.

The following situation is typically faced by firms: a firm can invest in standard technology and incremental innovations not requiring co-operative efforts within a network (the firm internalises investments and associated returns); this can be termed 'Business-As-Usual' (BAU) scenarios. The firm may otherwise invest in R&D involving radical innovations representing structural breaks from BAU or involving skills, knowledge and competencies which it only partially owns. This form of innovation, as mentioned above, requires a radical co-operative effort, and investment in an impure public good. Each unit of investment in the impure or mixed-public good produces some private benefits and some public benefits. The opportunity cost of the 'radical co-operative innovative' capital is, in the short run, the value of the returns from investing in BAU options.

The framework as presented above may characterise different real-world situations where inter-firm co-operation is the key to successful performance of a network. This can also be referred to, without opening up a debate over taxonomy, as either a 'cluster' or a 'district' of firms. What matters is that firms at some point need to join their efforts to achieve benefits which derive from, and build on, public-like forms of investments.

The need to establish voluntary co-operative schemes to achieve goals specific to the network, but appropriable by participants, characterises most forms of voluntary agreements, inter-firm intra-district co-operation and inter-firm inter-district co-operation, whose relevance as engines for innovation and regional growth has increased over the last decades, following both the reduced role of the state as 'regulator' (top down approach) and the reshaping of governance and business strategies within the post-Fordist society. Socio-economic changes occurring in the post-Fordist era shifted the focus of interest from man-made forms of capital to human, environmental and social capital assets (Gerelli, 1999). Furthermore, market and non-market 'horizontal' networks of firms play a major role with respect to 'vertical' and hierarchical relationships, bringing about a new scenario described by a cultural change in local and national production. Finally,

---

[4] Paldam (2000) specifically provides the following definitions, revolving around the notion of trust, co-operation and network:

Definition 1 of Ease of co-operation: 'Social capital is the ability of a person belonging to a population to work voluntarily together with others (belonging to the same population), for a common purpose in groups and organisations.'

Definition 2 of Trust: 'Social capital is the quantity of trust a person (belonging to a population) has in other members of the same population.'

Moreover, Paldam assesses: 'It would appear that trust is primary to most co-operation. However, by working together people further build trust, so the two concepts have some interactive simultaneity. Trust and the ease of voluntary co-operation are thus two interlinked concepts.' (Paldam, 2000, p.636)

intentional (multilateral) externalities replace standard Marshallian 'unintentional' externalities in explaining growth and innovation processes. Although positive network externalities are realised, unlike unintentional exogenous spillovers, the voluntary and intentional production of joint social benefits is costly. Therefore, incentives matter.

Thus, the role of 'intentional co-operative strategies' emerges as very relevant in the demand for a new way of thinking to institutions, rooting out new rules, with respect to those relevant in the Fordist era, endogenously created and bottom-up driven. Those bottom-up coalitions share the risks of investing in community specific knowledge (vs. firm specific assets). Moreover, coalitions should usually rely on informal rules and non-coercive incentives for sustaining *effective and efficient* agreements.

The public element of the welfare function of a firm participating in a network agreement is, in our framework, the stock of SC on which the decision behind the actions relies. SC is nonetheless strictly entangled to private components of welfare (it is not a pure 'independent' public good).[5]

The scenario is common to most situations characterising the post Fordist, post Keynesian era, where the hierarchical nature of economic activities has been (partially) replaced by horizontal-market-network-structures and the role of the state as a third party enforcer has decreased in importance, leaving more space to voluntary schemes. This entails a stronger co-operative effort for producing beneficial private-public elements.[6] As Oughton and Whittam (1997, p.4) sharply point out:

> It is evident that the relative decline in the significance of internal economies of scale in production and the associated movement away from large scale production toward flexible small production has been one of the factors associated with the change in the size distribution of firms (...) at the same time there are clear signs that external economies of scale are playing an increasingly important role in some regional economies (...).

Co-operation between firms may generate gains via the establishment of collective external economies. Moreover, it is important to underline the voluntary element of the agreements in co-operation and production: SC is *self-enforcing, self-financing*, in opposition to *third-party enforcement frameworks*.

---

[5] Piselli (2001) and Bagnasco (2001) incorrectly define SC as a public good. Nonetheless, they seem aware of the mixed nature of SC. Piselli, following Coleman (1988), points out that SC, as a situational and dynamic good, is a necessary *by-product* of other activities, but whose property rights are not assignable to agents outside the common effort they pursue. Further, if we omit the possibility of externalities generated by SC toward outsiders of the network, the returns are not purely public, since only insiders (investors) benefit from it.

[6] Thus, the value of SC (as meant here) increases. Although it is evident that SC is not a sufficient condition for development and innovation, it is surely a necessary pre-condition.

In the situation described above, social capital is the public component of a mixed-public capital which consequently accumulates or declines depending on the structure of individual incentives (benefits and costs). Moreover, SC is subject to decay as a renewable "collective resource". In fact, decay depends on endogenous factors such as easy-riding (non-consistent actions of investment between agents) and also on exogenous factors.[7] Depreciation occurs due to a lack of strategic investment in co-operation in any period of time. In other words, depreciation derives from 'non use' rather than excessive use, as for many forms of collective man-made capital. Depreciation reflects the fact that much SC investment is community-network specific.

In this framework the steps of voluntary co-operation among firms may be represented as follows:[8] firms initially voluntarily share the production costs of a good or service, of private and/or public nature, expecting to receive some proportion of the benefits.[9]

At a second stage, the firms, which have previously formed a network, weigh up the private and public benefits arising from the co-operation. Returning to our example, each firm invests in two kinds of capital. The first one has private characteristics only (it has no effects on the other firms inside the network). The second one, on the contrary, has the characteristic of a mixed-public good: it has both a private component (which has no effects on the other firms) and a public component (which has effects on the other firms). We can think of the investment in private capital as investment in what we have previously termed BAU (business as usual) capital stock, and of the investment in the 'mixed-public' capital as investment in R&D involving radical innovations. In this case we can consider technological amelioration appropriable by the firm only as the private component, and the already mentioned formation of voluntary agreements among firms to achieve environmental targets as the public component. Hence, the public component is SC in the meaning of 'co-operation' and 'trust'.

It is then possible to assert that whenever a firm invests in one unit of R&D, its investment is partly the creation of a private asset and partly the creation of social capital, the two components being complements. Since each firm's choice about SC has effects both on its own benefits and on other firms' benefits, a contribution by one firm of an extra unit of the mixed-public capital (R&D) has three effects: (i) an increase in the firm's private benefit due to the private component (ii) an increase in the firm's private benefit due to the public component (SC); (iii) an increase in the total amount of the public component, SC, available to any firm.

---

[7] The point is emphasised by Piselli (2001), who stresses that SC is created by interactive and dynamic strategies, and is mined by individual behaviour and exogenous factors. Investment flows are thus necessary for maintaining the stock.

[8] For an analytical treatment of what follows see Mancinelli and Mazzanti (2002).

[9] Notice that in this framework the analysis about SC concentrates on situations where an economic relationship among agents exists.

This is true for every firm inside the network, so that each firm's benefits depend also[10] on all other firms' choices about SC.

Since social capital is considered a public-collective good, the possibility of sub-optimal provision must be considered. Each firm which chooses its own contribution to SC aims only to maximise its own benefits, net of costs, without internalising the benefits created by its choice to the other firms of the network. The investment of the individual firm in SC may hence be less than the optimal social level of investment.

This is consistent with the well-known free rider problem, in which one individual relies on the public good supplied by another. When a free-rider problem exists the reaction of one party to another's supply of a public good[11] is negative, in that the first party relies on the public good provided by the other without reciprocity.

4. Further Extensions

In order to analyse the incentives for a dynamic positive accumulation of SC, we will specifically consider some elements which concern (i) the relationship of complementarity between the private and public components of the mixed-public good, (ii) the role of increasing returns to scale in the firms' benefit functions and (iii) the firms' expectations.

The first issue is the *relationship of complementarity* between the private and public components of the mixed-public good (R&D). Complementarity theoretically enhances the probability of achieving a socially optimum outcome, affecting the sign and slopes of reaction curves.[12] The way through which complementarity may improve the free-rider problem may be illustrated as follows. Intuitively, since the two components of the mixed-public capital are complements for each firm, an increase of one firm's investment in the public component (SC) may induce the other to increase its own investment in the complementary private component (technological amelioration appropriable to that firm only) and, hence, on the mixed-public capital (R&D). In this way, through the extra investment in R&D, the second firm necessarily determines an increase of its investment in SC too. Hence its reaction curve may have a positive slope, with evident positive implications for the free-rider problem. This means that each firm inside the network reacts positively to the other firms' investment in SC. None rely on the others' contributions to SC, but, on the contrary, through the relationship of complementarity between the private and the public components of R&D, the

---

10
  Besides, of course, their choices about the private component and the social capital.
11
  The so-called reaction curve.
12
  In this case, the reaction curve compares an individual firm's choice about SC with other firms' choices. It is generally characterised by a negative slope, to indicate the free-rider problem that is the firm's reliance on the SC provision of the other firms.

investment in SC by each firm is mutually reinforcing. This leads to an individual firm's choice of equilibrium SC closer to the optimal social choice.

Secondly, we must consider the effects on investment choices in SC when increasing returns to scale are assumed in the firms' benefit functions. Nowadays the problem of the sub-optimality of individual choices in co-operation is generally analysed in context of decreasing returns to scale of the net benefit function, namely in situations in which costs associated to some actions (i.e. the investment in SC) increase more rapidly than the associated benefits. On the other hand, it has been shown (Sandler, 1992) that increasing returns to scale establish an incentive for joint production and, hence, joint investment by firms. Increasing returns to scale should therefore also increase joint investment by firms in SC. Under this assumption, the costs associated with investment in SC should increase less rapidly than the benefits, and hence no firm would be satisfied with the level of SC invested by the others. Once again the free-rider problem would be irrelevant and the reaction curve of each firm would have positive slope. Moreover we do not think that the assumption of increasing returns to scale in SC investment is such an unwarranted assumption.

Finally we want to consider the case of *non-zero conjectures*. The assumption on which the sub-optimality of the individual choice of public goods is grounded is one of zero conjectures: economic agents expect no reaction by the rest of the community to their own changes in choices of fundamental variables as their contribution to the public good. Such an assumption can be criticised and found empirically inconsistent. On the contrary, if we introduce the assumption of *non-zero conjectures* in our framework on SC, different results may be reached. We can for instance realistically assume that each firm expects that an increase in its own level of investment in SC will induce the other firms to increase theirs, because of the complementarity relationship and increasing returns to scale, or just due to the imitative effects that can exist. Each firm could then be stimulated to invest more in SC, because it would expect that if it invested less it could have negative effects on the other firms' investment decisions, thus generating a process of investment adaptation.

The previous analysis enables us to highlight elements which positively influence firms' accumulation of SC.

The first one is the degree of complementarity between the public and the private component of the mixed-public stock, of which SC represents the public component. From the above discussion it follows that investments in SC by firms increase if they are strictly connected to factors that increase private benefits too. Hence the probability that a firm invests in trust and co-operation with other firms inside a network increases if this sort of investment is associated with another kind of investment which has merely private characteristics, in the sense that it influences only the private benefits of the firm and has no effects on the other firms of the group. In the example made in the above section each firm invests in voluntary agreements with the other firms of the network for achieving environmental targets not because or, at least, not only because this is a 'good thing', but because this increases its own benefits. These agreements in fact allow firms to invest more in technological improvements appropriable just by themselves. Another element which incentivises SC accumulation by firms is the presence of increasing returns to scale. Investments in SC by firms may increase therefore if R&D investments show increasing returns to scale. Finally, firms' expectations about the reactions to their own choices on SC play a relevant role. As we have seen, a firm will be positively influenced to invest in SC if it expects the other firms inside the network to positively react. Therefore a positive environment is a relevant factor to incentive SC accumulation.

5. Conclusions

This chapter has proposed some relevant conclusions in the way to approach the economic analysis to social capital. First of all, it has been suggested that social capital can be analysed with the same criteria normally used for physical capital. It has been shown in fact that SC can be considered a productive asset, just like physical capital, and that economic agents invest in both forms of capital if current foregone income can be invested to obtain the requisite future returns to justify the diversion of such income. Expectations about the future state of the world are essential to the successful accumulation of capital, be it physical or social. The only aspect in which the two forms of capital partially differ is that the public good characteristic of SC is stronger than for physical capital. Consequently, if we are right in arguing that SC is expressed practically as the tendency of agents to engage in sustained co-operative interaction, each decision contributing to the creation of this intangible asset increases the stock of trust upon which agents can draw to reduce transaction costs and further the inter-firm relationships on which clusters of industry rely. We can therefore say that SC is the public element of those intangible assets without which no firm can function.

This is the reason why the second part of the chapter focused on the analysis of social capital in a mixed-public good framework. It has been suggested that SC may be considered the public component of a mixed-public capital stock. The example made was that of a network of firms which invest in R&D and create voluntary agreements aimed at achieving environmental targets for reduced pollution, increased recycling, etc. Voluntary agreements are the public component of the mixed-public capital R&D and can be considered the SC in which each firm chooses to invest. Since SC is considered as a public good, the possibility that an individual relies on the SC invested by others has been considered with the aim of highlighting some elements which positively influence firms' accumulation of SC. Along this line the analysis conducted suggests that a relevant factor is the degree of complementarity between SC and the private component of the mixed-public capital stock: the more this sort of investment is linked to another sort of investment which has merely private characteristics, the higher the probability that a firm invests in trust and co-operation (SC) with other firms inside a network. A second relevant element which positively influences SC accumulation by firms is the presence of increasing returns to scale related to investment in SC. Finally each firm's expectations about the reactions of the other firms to its own choices of SC accumulation play a relevant role. If each firm expects that an increase in its level of investment in SC will have positive effects on the other firms' choices, this will induce an increase in its own levels of investment too, because the opposite choice, to rely on investments made by others, could have negative effects on the other firms' decisions, thus generating a process of investment adaptation.

The analysis conducted in the second part of the chapter reinforces what we initially suggested: that SC is a form of capital and that, as such, it responds to the same incentives as physical capital (the balance of payoffs and agents' expectations). This leaves us with a clear answer to the question of whether SC is the collective value of intangibles, or whether it is the value of non appropriable intangibles. The difference is obvious: the collective value of intangibles includes the *appropriable* aspects of non-physical assets, such as individual skills and knowledge, together with the *individual or private benefits* derived from non-appropriable trust-based relationships. On the other hand, the value of non appropriable intangibles is, properly speaking, the public element of such interpersonal relationships. SC is, therefore, the public value of intangible assets, that is, the capitalised future income streams made possible by the reduction in transaction costs when mutual engagement is the favoured form of interpersonal (and inter-firm) contact. It is, in the end, the trust upon which clusters and industrial districts are born, and at the same time it is the outcome of their existence. This encapsulates the challenge for SC as an intangible asset in that it is simultaneously an input and an output in a complex series of relationships that create wealth.

References

Bagnasco, A. (2001), 'Teoria del capitale sociale e "political economy" comparata', in Bagnasco, A., Piselli, F., Pizzorno, A., Trigilia, C. (eds), *Il Capitale Sociale*, il Mulino, Bologna.

Coleman, J. (1988), 'Social Capital in the Creation of Human Capital', *American Journal of Sociology*, 94, 95-120.

Coleman, J. (1990), *Foundations of Social Theory*, Harvard University Press, Cambridge.

Cornes, R. and Sandler, T. (1986), *The Theory of Externalities, Public Goods, and Club Goods*, Cambridge University Press, Cambridge.

Dasgupta, P. and Serageldin, I. (eds) (1999), *Social Capital. A Multifaceted Perspective*, The World Bank, Washington, D.C.

Durlauf, S.N. (1999), 'The Case "Against" Social Capital', mimeo, Department of Economics, University of Wisconsin.

François, P. and Zabojnik, J. (2002), 'Trust and Development', *Quarterly Journal of Economics*.

Galassi, F.L. (2001), 'Measuring social capital: Culture as an explanation of Italy's economic dualism', *European Review of Economic History*, 5, 29-59.

Gerelli, E. (1999), 'Thinking about the Future: Economic Aspects', paper presented at the seminar *Scenarios: the art of thinking the unthinkable*, University of Pavia, Pavia, mimeo.

Guttman, J.M. (2001), 'Self-enforcing Reciprocity Norms and Intergenerational Transfers: Theory and Evidence', *Journal of Public Economics*, 81(July), 117-52.

Mancinelli, S. and Mazzanti, M. (2002), 'A Microeconomic Approach to Social Capital', Quaderni del Dipartimento di Economia Istituzioni Territorio, n.13, Ferrara, University of Ferrara (http://www.deit.economia.unife.it).

Oughton, C. and Whittam, G., (1997), 'Competition and Co-operation in the Small Firm Sector', *Scottish Journal of Political Economy*, 44(1), 1-30.

Paldam, M. (2000), 'Social Capital: One or Many? Definition and Measurement', *Journal of Economic Surveys*, 14(5), 629-653.

Piselli, F. (2001), 'Capitale sociale: un concetto situazionale e dinamico', in Bagnasco, A., Piselli, F., Pizzorno, A., Trigilia, C. (eds), *Il Capitale Sociale*, il Mulino, Bologna.

Portes, A. (1998), 'Social Capital: its Origins and Application in Modern Sociology', *Annual Review of Sociology*, 15, 1-14.

Sandler, T. (1992), *Collective Action. Theory and Applications*, Wheatsheaf, London.

Chapter 6

Public Intervention to Increase Collaboration between Innovative Agents

Roberto Iorio

This chapter analyses two aspects of public intervention aimed at increasing collaboration between agents of innovation. I first address the case of university-business relationships, and then consider public agencies, as illustrated through the example of space agencies. As argued in chapter 3, public intervention in research and innovation activities has been analysed greatly in neoclassical economics. It is justified in a context of market failure theory which suggests possible solutions to private underinvestment. The evolutionary theory of innovation and the paradigm of national systems of innovation in particular, shed new light on the institutional aspects of this problem underlying the need for collaboration between institutions. Consideration of social capital leads to the conceptualisation of these themes in a new and comprehensive manner, and also reveals new problems. As outlined in chapter 2, the increasing interest of economists in the concept of social capital, whose origins stem from sociology,[1] is probably due to the contemporary economic environment. In a global and rapidly changing economy, networks may be the most effective form of organisation for anticipating and managing change and innovation. Although collaboration is required between private agents and institutions, it requires trust and, to some extent, common habits and mindsets. Effective collaboration requires social capital.

The effectiveness of an entire national system of innovation requires greater collaboration between universities and industry which have different goals and cultures. Can public intervention overcome these barriers? An answer can be constructed through looking at public agencies, and particularly those in the space related domain. Space agencies encourage and establish deep and continuous interactions between agents of innovation. They thereby help in the construction of 'institutional social capital' and the development of the other 'collective intangible assets' required in such a field at the frontier of science. They strive to avoid the inefficiencies stemming from isolated competencies. Lock-in problems may appear, however, when networks constantly involve the same agents and when practices turn into routines. Since public agencies can be less innovative than

---

[1] For a sociological analysis of the concept, see the fundamental study by Coleman (1990); for an economic introduction, see Gambetta, 1998.

mechanistic in their behaviour, we need to evaluate their effectiveness in encouraging and producing innovation.

This chapter addresses these issues in more detail. The first section examines the contemporary needs for networking. It addresses the economic issues related to collaboration between agents of innovation through the concept of social capital. The focus is on collaboration between universities and industry, highlighting the role of personal networks. Section two analyses the potential role played by governments in developing social capital through collaboration between institutions. The cases of university-business relationships and of the usefulness of public agencies are considered. Possible shortcomings of such a policy tool are also pointed out. Section three considers the case of space agencies, public agencies present in almost every advanced country. It firstly highlights the traditional economic reasons for their establishment, and then focuses on the way they favour interaction between agents of innovation. The workings of the Italian Space Agency, the European Space Agency and NASA are compared. Section three concludes with an analysis of certain shortcomings of the space agencies, and highlights the importance of review and evaluation. The concluding section summarises the theoretical basis of the paper, adding the concepts of sunk cost and barriers to entry, and highlighting the importance of openness within a technological community and the role that public agencies can play.

1. The Case of University-Business Relationships

Recent years have seen the emergence of co-operative networks as important players in the new techno-economic paradigm. Faced with a rapidly changing world and increasing global possibilities, the resources of a single firm may no longer be sufficient to survive. Compared with other forms of organisation, networks of firms may be more effective in monitoring and anticipating innovation and change, particularly in an economic environment where specialisation is increasingly more common and of strategic interest.

> In the highly specialised and uncertain environment, networks allow deeper economic specialisation than hierarchies, reduce transaction costs relative to markets, and co-ordination costs relative to hierarchies, and provide the most fertile ground for innovation (Hämäläinen and Schienstock, 2001, p 29).

It should be stressed that networks are not always desirable, not only in the private sector but also in the public sector. Competition must of course be preserved (Garonna and Iannarino, 2000).

The concept of collaboration gives rise to much discussion in economic theory, the risk of 'betrayal' in a network being the classical problem. A member of a network can absorb much information from the network before abandoning its ties and trying to use the information for its own benefit. Game theory (the prisoner dilemma) teaches us that the fear itself of a betrayal by other players may induce non-co-operative behaviour and therefore sub-optimal solutions (Gambetta, 1998). Another and more subtle problem may arise from differences in mindsets and culture, such that, even if each member of the network recognises the possible advantages deriving from collaboration, their inherent differences create very high barriers to working together. Such barriers may be overcome if network members share in common more than their own self-interest. For example, the presence of a social sanction for betraying trust may reduce risk, whilst a shared cultural history may reduce differences.

The concept of social capital, upon which the attention of scholars is increasingly focused, encompasses the two problems described above. Although we will not offer a rigorous definition of social capital, since no universally recognised description exists, we can say that social capital exists if trust in the loyalty of partners is reasonably high and if differences in 'culture' (behaviour, basic ideas, ways of operating) are reasonably low. We can therefore say that the presence of social capital may lower the co-ordination effort that represents the main costs of a network and a barrier to the entry of other members. If trust is low, many measures need to be taken to ensure the stability of networks. A set of rules must exist whose pervasiveness and coerciveness is positively correlated with the threat of deceptive behaviour (chapter 5). Institutions and rules, however, imply co-ordination costs that can be reduced by the presence of social capital. Although obviously correlated to the number of members of a network, these factors do not appear to be the main determinant variables. Considering the nature of social capital, its absence may be a serious drawback in networks of firms that also compete against each other. This is an even worse problem in networks involving institutions that have different goals and mindsets.

The evolutionary school and the National Innovation System theory have analysed the behaviour of institutions involved in innovative processes (universities, other research centres, business, local government) in depth and underlined the importance of their relationships. To apply social capital theory to such economics implies referring to the same conceptual framework. This implies an economic environment where rationality is bounded, utility and profit maximisation are not the only motivations of human behaviour (trust and culture more so) and where individual agents exist as well as organisations with their own rules. In an environment where rationality is bounded, knowledge is a scarce resource whose exchange and dissemination is crucial. Moreover, since knowledge cannot completely be made explicit (a large part remains tacit), it may be shared only through personal contacts. For these two reasons, interactions among agents are of fundamental importance. According to the NIS school, innovation is an interactive process that is favoured by the relationships between innovative agents. NIS particularly emphasises that different results arise from the diverse organisational design and interaction methods of institutions. They highlight the different results generated by alternative modes of interactions between universities, industry and government and the crucial importance of an established and constant interplay between these three main innovative agents.

Technological advance proceeds through the interaction of many actors. Some of the key interactions involved *are* between component and systems producers, upstream and downstream firms, universities and industry, and government agencies and universities and industries (Nelson, 1993). Although the development of this conceptual framework did not precede the existence of contacts between these institutions, it surely increased attention towards these topics and the need to create innovative networks on a global and local level. Many governments have made great efforts to increase such interaction and networks. The USA is probably leading this 'race' and has established many exchanges between universities and industry.[2] The NIS framework is meanwhile becoming the guideline for current European technology policy, directed primarily at encouraging interactions between universities and industry (see chapter 3).

Relationships between universities and industry are not however without difficulties. Because different bodies (or their members) will certainly have different interests, mindsets and goals, their social capital might not be compatible in the sense of not favouring communication. Since the term 'social capital' is used explicitly referring to large communities, it seems that co-operation between institutions is a peculiar problem, where problems of trust are largely the result of different cultures. It is probably useful therefore to use the term 'institutional social capital'. A specific goal of universities is the diffusion of knowledge whereby the results of research are spread through publications, and papers are evaluated through peer review, etc. In short, universities are characterised by the practice of 'open science' (Dasgupta and David, 1994). On the contrary, industrial research is characterised by a strict proprietary regime in which firms desire to patent the results of their research, or to keep it secret, so as to avoid other agents reaping the benefits of their inventions. University research is mainly basic, while industrial research is for the most part applied.

Social habits during research are also different. In the phase that precedes publication, professors organise meetings, seminars and conferences to present their 'intermediate' results in order to improve their research through others' ideas and intellectual contributions. The benefits deriving from these exchanges are certainly superior to the fear that other researchers might 'steal' their ideas (extreme specialisation makes this rather improbable). This practice generates personal contacts and establishes networks that may lead to collaborative research. In industry however, since diffusing intermediate results implies offering an advantage to rivals, there is no reason to do so and no benefit from such a practice. This difference in approaches to research generates different types of personal networks in universities and industry. Balconi, Breschi and Lissoni (2002) find that networks of innovators which include academic scientists are larger and more connected than those that do not.

These considerations about 'social practice' in research lead to a closer analysis of the concept of networks. Some networks may arise through formal agreements and collaborations directed to a precise and pre-defined goal, and some simply through informal personal contacts. Sociologists use the term 'social networks' to refer to the social contacts and acquaintances of individuals. The differences

---

[2] The Bayh-Dole Act in 1984 was an important legislative turning point because it increased the possibility for universities to patent their research.

between formal and informal situations can be quite small however. Personal informal contacts may become the basis for formal collaborations directed to a specific goal, particularly if we refer to professional, rather than generic, friendships (Balconi, Breschi and Lissoni, 2002). A personal acquaintance may provide the required bridge between different institutions to help overcome barriers to collaboration. It is important to understand more deeply such relationships and the structure of social networks, even for the purposes of public intervention.

In a certain sense, the American economy is more dynamic and more capitalistic. American universities are managed in a more entrepreneurial manner than in Europe and are more prone to collaboration with universities, as stressed in chapter 3.

Despite much greater business involvement, US universities do not seem to have lost their autonomy. In 1991, only 4.9 per cent of US university research was funded by firms, compared to 7.7 per cent in Germany, 7.8 per cent in the United Kingdom and only 2.4 per cent in Italy (Alessandrini and Sterlacchini, 1995). This shows that the essential factor for economic success is not the 'privatisation' of the university system and the provision of high amounts of business funding. It is due to high public and private R&D expenditure, a well-functioning education system, and effective and well-regulated linkages between universities and industry, not exclusively based on economic considerations.

The advantages of university-business relationships are numerous. An Austrian study (Schibany and Schartinger, 2001) describes the range of incentives for businesses to collaborate with universities and the benefits that actually accrue. The authors provide evidence that the main role in knowledge transfer is played by human factors, and therefore by tacit knowledge. In fact, the primary motive for collaboration quoted by business is to benefit from the problem-solving capacity of universities. This means that the intellectual competencies and methodologies learnt at university are perceived as even more important than a specialist education. This has a clear policy indication. Universities should keep their education goal of providing a general 'way of reasoning', which should be combined with developing a practical capacity to solve specific problems.

The European Commission is conscious of the risks of too specialist an education (MERIT, 2000). The specific role of university research is also recognised. 68.3 per cent of respondent firms to an EC survey considered the chance to access state-of-the-art science as very important, while 51.3 per cent recognised access to high quality university research as a clear benefit, and a similar proportion claimed to be certain that collaboration would increase their own research capacities. Firms expect to receive ideas for new products and processes from universities, as well as direct support in the development process, and new instruments and techniques. Evidence in Germany (for instance, Schuetze, 2000) in 1993 of ca. 2900 manufacturing firms is that their R&D functions benefited from collaboration with universities. The main finding was that knowledge generated in academia has significant effects on the innovative activities of firms whose technological capacities are expanded to more successfully develop new and improved products. Schuetze (2000) underlines that collaboration with universities in R&D projects reduces risk. Universities may also benefit from co-operation with firms via, for example, greater funding for research, access to new ideas and techniques and potential new research projects and domains. From a social point of view, public attention towards co-operation is justified if the overall effect of co-operation is higher quality research. As stressed in chapter 3, such a condition should be met because R&D collaboration may be considered a proxy for knowledge spillovers whereby an internalisation of externalities should imply a higher level of research.

Other difficulties arising in the relationship between firms and universities relate to their dissimilar natures, differing goals, cultures and organisational design (universities are much more bureaucratic for example). However, these challenges may be turned into advantages if the actors are able to define a clear and favourable framework of rules. After all, even though the two institutions fulfil different functions in the innovation system, an intermingling of the two cultures is highly desirable for reciprocal and social advantage.

It is possible that countries with little contact between firms and universities lack proper incentives. Too restrictive regulations on the mobility of university personnel and a lack of information about activity at other institutions are two examples. Poor communication about the activities of universities, and its implications for industry, emerged in the Austria study, and may have important policy implications. An efficient policy that stimulates co-operation between universities and industry should take into account and try to facilitate the different possible types of interactions highlighted by Schibany and Schartinger and listed hereafter:

- personal mobility in terms of sabbaticals or permanent transfers of university researchers to the enterprise sector;
- spin-off creation of new enterprises;
- lectures by business people at universities;
- the training of business people by university researchers;
- joint supervision of PhDs and Masters' theses;
- joint publications between the university and the enterprise sectors;
- joint research projects;
- financing of research assistants by the enterprise sector.

The spin-off process has emerged as an important source of innovation, leading most EU countries to pursue active policies to promote the establishment and growth of university SMEs. Several initiatives have been taken for this purpose, such as the foundation of science and technology parks, of incubators, university enterprise centres, the mobility of researchers and the financing of technology transfer. However, the EC itself recognises that these schemes do not appear to be as effective as in the US and in fact, the lack of entrepreneurial mentality in universities appears to be the main difference between Europe and the US, even in the spin-off process.

Another point to examine in more depth concerns the different characteristics of firms and universities such as size, sector, and so on. Differences among research and teaching staff should also be considered. Although larger firms have a higher tendency to collaborate with universities, substantial differences still exist between countries. Nordic universities for example have a higher propensity than those in the Mediterranean to develop linkages with high-tech SMEs, partly because of the prevalence of low-tech enterprises in the industrial structure around the Mediterranean. However, being low tech does not necessarily imply an absence of potential spillovers. One policy option to possibly examine is that of trying to enhance the technological level of small firms so that they could benefit from direct linkages with research institutions, especially through personnel mobility rather than through R&D collaboration. Sector analyses shows that both the frequency and the type of linkages vary widely across sectors.

The results of the EC Framework Programmes (Geuna, 1999) show very different propensities to collaborate across countries. It follows that instruments such as benchmarking and adoption of best practices should be applied with caution, taking into consideration the different situations, cultures and also the resources of each country. Although these factors should not be taken too much into account, they are however a natural starting point for analysis because qualitative differences may be a source of richness, particularly in a rapidly changing economic environment. The EC has also recognised the necessity to take local differences into consideration.

It is clear that policy should create an environment favourable to creating and sustaining relationships, rather than directly setting up or imposing them. One of the EC's aims is rightly to be a facilitator of such relationships. The Framework Programmes, public agencies and the Industry Liaison Office (see Jones-Evans, 1998 for an evaluation) are directed towards this goal. These important policy measures run the risk however of being insufficient or even superabundant. Cultural proximity should not be neglected, since relationships develop between individuals who share, at least partly, a common culture, norms and values. In other words, social capital may be an important determinant of the frequency and the nature of linkages. The force of European policy should be directed to stimulate a debate in order to overcome the mental barriers to collaboration. Creating a favourable environment also means overcoming the other difficulties emerging from the above discussion: the lack of reciprocal information, the unsatisfactory definition of property rights, legal barriers and low incentives to co-operate.

2. Social Capital and Public Agencies

Given the increasing importance of networks in the contemporary economy and the difficulties that may arise in networking, a crucial question is whether there is indeed scope for governments to intervene. Although it is well known that the presence of externalities in a network is the classical justification for public intervention, the complexity of the theme implies other considerations. Garonna and Iannarino (2000) argue that research networks are characterised by a market failure that arises even in the case of private investment in R&D. Pure private research is inefficient. Pure public research is impossible to sustain as well as being inefficient, not for economic theoretical reasons but for 'sociological' ones. There is a however a 'third way' that may be more desirable. A combination of the two is necessary, partly through shared funding, but mainly engendered by government stimulation of collaboration and openness, which leverages the autonomy of the actors. An important part of this policy concerns the patent system, which must try to balance the need for disclosure and the need to maintain market incentives.

A crucial success factor for networks is their degree of 'disclosure', a characteristic that should be nurtured by governments. Agents that are initially reluctant to exchange knowledge often fear network breakdowns, and so require public intervention to reduce this risk and increase what we have called social capital. Moreover, if the main difficulty in establishing and maintaining a network is the lack of social capital, public intervention may be justified by the need to enhance it. A reverse causality between social capital, meaning trust and common culture, and networks is also true since not only does social capital favour the development of networks, but also do networks favour the further development of social capital. An established network increases trust and converges habits and work practice. Although the specific purpose of a network is to increase the circulation of codified knowledge, a collateral and highly positive effect is also the increased circulation of tacit knowledge.

Game theory provides insight as to the behaviour of economic agents in co-operation because a much repeated interaction may overcome difficulties deriving from lack of trust. When two or more agents interact a high (infinite) number of times, a 'deceptive' behaviour which may be maximising in a one-shot game becomes less fruitful than a 'loyal' one (see also chapter 7). When different institutions interact, the frequency of their interactions may help them learn each others' mindsets and *modus operandi*.

The re-occurrence of interactions therefore helps the functioning of networks. Frequent interactions bring other advantages beyond increasing trust or co-operative behaviour. They develop a common cognitive frame, help to share language and to recognise each other's knowledge domain (Hämäläinen and Schienstock, 2001). But how can reticent agents become regular co-operators? An external agent may be necessary. Government may be this agent, helping to match together economic actors, offering incentives to overcome challenges and favouring stable co-operation through long-term projects. The European Commission is aware of the need to intervene in this field and, particularly in recent years where this topic has come to the fore, specific policies towards networking have been put into effect.

Regarding linkages between universities and industry, several official documents (see, for example, European Commission, 1995) have emphasised the need for reinforcing collaboration. The debate is still open on the optimal ways to achieve this. Successfully gathering together players with different interests is not easy, since as pointed out in the second chapter, complementarities have to develop to motivate them to join a network.

An established government agency may understand the mindsets and methods of different agents and therefore possess the knowledge and policy instruments to favour matching them up. It may promote long-term and/or repeated collaboration, so that agents learn to co-operate and trust their collaborators. This kind of agency therefore increases existing social capital and helps to keep together tangible and intangible resources, avoiding the risk that such resources are dispersed or not fully used. In this sense the role of a public agency involves all the so-called collective intangible assets, such as social capital, shared knowledge, diffused competence, etc.

Direct transfers of knowledge between open science communities and the proprietary R&D organisations of the private business sector are especially problematic to institutionalise. The coexistence of two reward systems within any single organisation makes the behaviours of the participants difficult to anticipate, and tends to undermine the formation of coherent cultural norms that promote co-operation among members. Specially designed institutions, having a research mission distinctive from that of either traditional academic science or profit oriented labs, may therefore be more effective in maintaining such knowledge transfer. (David, Foray and Steinmueller, 1999, p 313).

In addition, David, Foray and Steinmueller (1999) stress that networks do not always represent a superior organisational form. When co-ordination costs are low, speed of action and decision are essential and may not be guaranteed in networks. In this case, public agencies may favour other organisational forms. Other considerations concern the policy tools available to a funding agency. The social capital perspective helps to position them in a more organic perspective.

The literature on networks and social capital underlines that although it is true that a public agency increases social capital and other collective intangible assets, networks may nevertheless become inefficient if their environment changes dramatically and requires not occasional, but systemic adjustments (Hämäläinen and Schienstock, 2001). Stable networks may for example become faced with lock-in problems if costs of change are particularly high. In this sense, strong social capital may be liable to rigidity and other weaknesses. Since long lasting institutions tend to encourage consolidated behaviours and routines, a public agency may itself encounter lock-in problems. An agency may for instance tend to repeatedly favour the same firms and universities when allocating its funds, and replicate almost automatically its procedures each time. Putting it simply, an agency may lack the necessary flexibility and adaptability to the changing environment. The risk in always favouring the same agents is particularly serious. In doing so the funding agency generates asymmetric power relationships which may generate conflicts to which networks are particularly vulnerable.

There exists another element of rigidity. A public entity by nature tends to grow, or at least exist at constant size, beyond the scope and scale of its *raison d'être*. Therefore although public funding agencies may be the best overall policy instrument to reinforce networks up to a socially optimal level, the dangers highlighted above must be avoided. A system of rewards and punishments could be studied, linked to the results and effectiveness of such agencies. This might stimulate them to actively reach their institutional goals, be dynamic and rapid in adapting their behaviour to the environment, and therefore reduce the structural incentives that lead to routine and self-preservation.

3. Rationale, Actions and Evaluation of Space Agencies

Public Agencies as Instruments to Overcome Market Failures

A concrete example of collaborative networks, within which we can immediately check for the above-mentioned considerations, can be found by studying public agencies specifically dedicated to the support of scientific and technological research, such as the national and supranational space agencies.

The United States, Canada, several European countries and the European Union as a whole all operate agencies[3] whose goals are to favour scientific and technological research in the space sector, to allocate public funds for this purpose and to co-ordinate activities for the research and commercial application of technologies developed in the space ambit.

The previous sections stressed that that public intervention, especially through the specific instrument of a dedicated public agency, is justified by the need to overcome certain 'institutional failures', and by the need to implement collective intangible assets. Other justifications exist, more rooted in traditional theory, particularly referring to the market failure concept (see Arrow, 1962). Other issues concern the peculiarity of the space sector itself.

The space sector is very competitive internationally, especially in terms of the prestige a country obtains when its space sector is innovative and successful. Although competition is nowadays less intense, the space sector remains a very important component of success in the 'technology race' among countries. Several studies (for example, Guerrieri and Milana, 1998) indeed confirm that high technology industries are key drivers of a nation's long-term economic performance.

Another traditional government responsibility, justified at a theoretical level within the concept of market failure, is intervention to create public infrastructure. This concept refers not only to traditional structures, such as transport facilities, but also to immaterial communication structures, such as telecommunications or the even more modern tools of satellite navigation systems. These are the fundamental technological infrastructures upon which a great part of the competitiveness of an advanced economy is based. Aerospace research generates large spillovers in precisely these fields which provide further justification for the particular attention paid by governments to this sector.

One of the main reasons for public intervention into this sector is the series of spillovers it generates into a number of other sectors, such as telecommunications, medicine, and military goods. Note that regarding military goods public intervention is justified not only by spillovers but also by the fact that defence is historically one of the state's tasks.

---

[3]   The European Union does not have its own Space Agency, since the European Space Agency (ESA) is not a EU body. It was established in 1973 and began work in 1975 to combine the aims of the former European Launcher Development Organisation and the European Space Research Organisation, both dating from the early 1960s. ESA has 15 Member states in Europe plus Canada as a Co-operating State.

Space research is both basic and applied, and the distance between the two is constantly reducing. This is due to the fact that scientific research cannot be conducted without the help of suitable technological instruments and that scientific research is the basis for technology itself. Studies conducted on the origins of the universe for example require theoretical models, whilst the observation of cosmic rays is necessary to verify such models, a task in itself that requires advanced technologies. Orbiting a satellite or space shuttles carrying humans clearly requires advanced technological research. The main distinguishing factor of applied research at the heart of space technology is the high degree of knowledge spillovers into other sectors. An important example of spillovers is research on materials, crucial for satellites, and which has proven to be extremely useful for other sectors. The medical sector in particular is one of the many socially important examples.[4]

Marengo and Sterlacchini (1990), in their study of inter-sector technology flows in the United States, the United Kingdom and Italy, confirm that the aerospace sector is a strategic sector in the sense of generating spillovers to a large number of other sectors of the economy, at least in the first two countries (the sector was too small in Italy to be explicitly considered). Although an older but still fundamental study on space activities in the USA (Mansfield, 1969) states that such spillovers alone are not enough to justify large amounts of public expenditure on aerospace activities, the emphasis of commercial application of space research is indeed increasing. EU policy, particularly directed toward SMEs, confirms this. It should also be remembered that private demand for space technologies has been growing significantly. The share of private demand for European space agency output exceeded that of public demand in the year 2000, having represented only 54.6 per cent of public demand in 1996 (Eurospace, 2002).

The above discussion makes the rationale for creating a space agency clear. The next question is what actions should the space agency takes. My comparative analysis of the various space agencies concludes that action is generally twofold. On the one hand, the agency identifies research themes in the space ambit and finances universities and research centres that conduct this research through an appropriate selection process (many space agencies do not have their own research centres). On the other hand, the agency searches out technological research already being conducted in academia and in industry. In fact the government not only plays the role of financier but also of main purchaser, since space technologies are of great public use. Moreover, because of the large spillovers deriving from space activities, a space agency has the fundamental role in facilitating their dissemination throughout the national technological system. For this purpose, it is necessary to nurture collective intangible assets. In this chapter, a particular focus is given to the Italian space agency. The reason is that because the space sector is not very developed in Italy, the work might help understand either how a public agency's action can help in decreasing the competence gap in this sector, or how

---

[4] For a synthetic but complete framework of the possible technological spillovers of space research see Ramaciotti (1999).

inappropriate social capital arises which hinders the development of an economic sector.

Public Agencies as Instruments to Implement Collective Intangible Assets

A primary task of space agencies is to co-ordinate and finance research in the field of space activities, which may be distinguished as either scientific or technological and for which each space agency has distinct programmes. As has been said above, scientific and technological research are rigorously linked. From this interaction it follows that universities and research centres on one hand, and high-tech firms on the other, are the points of reference of a space agency and that the success of space activities largely depends on the ways these actors collaborate.

Let us examine this more closely. In order to understand how space activities are divided between the scientific and technological fields, Table 6.1 depicts the division of funds of a national space agency, in this case the Italian Space Agency (ASI). In the field of scientific research, ASI finances programmes in five distinct areas (with examples):

- sciences of the universe (exploration of the characteristics of the Universe through satellite missions);
- planetary exploration (probes toward Mars);
- earth sciences (physics of the atmosphere, meteorology and geology);
- life sciences (role of gravity in biological processes, behaviour and adaptation of man in space and life on other planets);
- engineering sciences (space systems of telecommunications and micro-electronics).

It is immediately understandable that to develop these scientific programmes, the right advanced technological support is required. In fact some scientific programmes are in reality often supporting basic technology research efforts (*general purpose* technologies).[5] Planetary exploration for example requires advanced telecommunication technologies, robotics and advanced sensors, whose development precedes many very relevant earthly applications in the domains of multimedia communication, distance learning and distance working, etc. Similarly, earth science studies cannot be made without earth observation instruments, the applications of which are absolutely strategic and of great public relevance, such as in monitoring terrain for military and civil protection.

---

[5] ESA differs from the ASI in that it does not include basic technology research in scientific programmes, but in technology ones.

Table 6.1 Division of funds for programmes 1998-2002 (Lire, billions)

Programme type: Research:	Current	Compulsory	New	Total expenditure for programme	Commitment for 2003 and following years
Basic research	69	540	735	1344	0
Space Station	1318	0	40	1358	267
Telecom	220	0	580	800	0
Earth Obs.	379	0	835	1214	70
Launch systems	365	0	430	795	0
R&D	105	100	610	815	0
Education	0	0	20	20	0
General expenses	254	135	15	404	0
TOTAL	2710	775	3265	6750	337

Source: Agenzia Spaziale Italiana (1997)

As the interaction between science and technology is fundamental, it is useful to see how ASI promotes it. Funding is the main channel. In the case of scientific programmes, ASI firstly invites applications for certain research areas, asking participants to present their proposed research projects within the defined scope. The projects are then evaluated and the best ones financed. Basic selection criteria examine the potential verifiability and timeliness (three years) of results. The relevant point, for our analysis, is that programmes that impose synergies with research institutions are given preference. This demonstrates that the ASI encourages synergies between innovative actors and that it therefore adheres to the most recent guidelines concerning innovation policy. However, ASI only funds collaboration and brings together the actors without actually participating in the common activity.

NASA is different in this respect since it actively aims to create true innovative networks. The Commercial Technology Network (NCTN) of NASA acts as a mechanism for enabling technology transfer and commercialisation. This network consists of a series of NASA-affiliated organisations across the United States that provide expertise and services to US enterprises, facilitating the transfer, development and commercialisation of NASA-sponsored technology. It provides rapid access to the federal R&D base and its core is the National Technology Transfer Centre and six Regional Technology Transfer Centres. The federal R&D base involves more than 700 laboratories and centres nationwide which are sponsored by NASA and which co-operate with other agencies. The reach of this network, the number of agents involved, and its territorial diffusion is remarkable.

Hence not only is the dimension (in terms of number of researchers involved and amount of funding) of the American space programme much higher than the Italian one, but also the attention to the diffusion of knowledge appears to be higher: NASA has regional technology transfers that provide information on the technologies to make them visible to any actor (firm) that may find it useful.

It is more relevant here to compare the US situation with the EU as a whole, rather than Italy only. The European Space Agency promotes a wide and articulated technology transfer programme (TTP), particularly directed towards SMEs. Since it is entirely possible that small firms are not aware of all existing technological opportunities, the space agency fills the information gap by means of a catalogue of space technologies that may be used in other sectors. This is obviously just a pre-condition for technology transfer, for which public competition is the chosen method. Firms presenting an innovative project are put in contact with others already working with ESA and are then financed. ESA obtains an economic return by means of royalty payments if it owns the intellectual property of the transferred innovation. Although the explicit ESA networking policy is mainly directed to overcoming information barriers, the chance to adopt already existing technologies implies for firms a reduction of production and product development costs.[6]

The Shortcomings and Problems in Evaluating a Public Agency

We have seen some of the benefits of public agencies in terms of increasing social capital. There remain however several shortcomings of such an instrument of public intervention. One risk is that the size and scope of public agencies becomes unwieldy. ASI, like other national space agencies, simultaneously implements several policies directed towards different objectives. Since many diverse capabilities are needed for these different purposes, much investment in tangible and intangible assets is needed to sustain such an agency. The core competencies and tacit knowledge of a successful public agency represent part of a country's wealth. Since the performance of the Italian high-tech sector has been low relative to other European countries, especially in the space sector,[7] perhaps such

---

[6] Information and data reported in this section are taken from the following web sites: Italian Space Agency: www.asi.it; European Space Agency: www.esa.int; National Aeronautics and Space Administration: www.nasa.gov.

[7] The size of the aerospace sector, which is quite limited for Europe as a whole, is particularly small in Italy. Even though Italy is one of the main contributors to the European Space Agency, its international position in the industrial aerospace sector is quite weak: the contribution of Italian exports to total world exports in high-tech aerospace products is 3.4 per cent for 1990-92, while this figure is 10.8 per cent for the United Kingdom, 11.1 per cent in Germany and 12.0 per cent in France. The USA are world leaders in this respect with 40.1 per cent, whilst the EU 12 as a whole has 42.7 per cent (Guerrieri and Milana, 1998).

competencies are not fully exploited and structural limits reduce the return on investment in tangible and intangible assets.

Lock-in risk, whereby agents lose the flexibility to act as they require in a network, have been mentioned previously. A 1998 BETA study (reported in Bach, Cohendet and Schenk, 2002) showed that activities of the ESA directed at promoting co-operative R&D projects at the European level were failing. Space collaboration networks had turned into space clubs, progressively isolated from their environment. This is partly due to 'structural' reasons since projects are large and inherently costly, implying that only big firms participate and that the number of new participants is limited. This is the reason why all the space agencies are paying an ever increasing attention to high-tech SMEs, whose large number and smaller size may favour the creation of dynamic networks.

Another form of agency inflexibility arises when the same subjects are continuously favoured in the funding and assignation of projects. A public agency may lose its independence and become a pawn for certain powerful economic players. In order to allocate its funds to firms, ASI takes their economic returns into consideration in order to estimate their self-financing capacity for the necessary development activities of a project. There is evidence that funding granted by ASI is to private enterprises that rely on such continuous provision of funds. The causes for this may be the weakness of the space sector in Italy, rather than the ASI. The number of firms operating in this sector is in fact quite limited. Since the Italian market is characterised by the presence of a few big firms and several small firms, there is not great competition for funding large projects. This situation implies a dominant bargaining position for these large firms who do not fear losing further funds and therefore do not make sufficient efforts to self-finance their projects. This may be evidence of the lack of any rigorous evaluation of the social and economic benefits of funding. If funding does not generate a self-enforcing capability inside these firms, the social benefit cannot be considered as positive. Many authors and ASI personnel emphasise the extreme difficulty in making rigorous ex-ante and ex-post evaluations of funding effectiveness. I argue in the last paragraph however that evaluation is both possible and indispensable.

The evaluation of funded projects is a central issue. From the social capital perspective, it is particularly difficult due to the need to consider the effectiveness of public agencies in encouraging collaboration, and their ability to avoid the development of 'excess' social capital exhibited through routines and low reactivity to change. Although instruments such as benchmarking and best practice are valuable, they are somewhat inadequate for examining a rich but complex concept such as social capital. Therefore, if policies to encourage social capital continue to be prioritised, a great effort is needed to find more sophisticated evaluation techniques. As a starting point and sanity check, we could say that a main problem in evaluating the success of promoting university-industry-government relations is still to clarify exactly what has to be measured, and more concretely, what the indicators of policy effectiveness are (Leydesdorff, 2003).

Evaluation is not only a technical, conceptual problem. It also concerns culture and mindset, habit, willingness and resources. This is largely a political problem. There is a natural tendency of bureaucracies to shirk evaluation, particularly economic assessment. The need for efficiency and responsibility within public institutions is however increasing, and even though goals are often social, the economic crisis in the welfare state urges a more rigorous evaluation of the efficiency of the use of public money.

The United States, perhaps paradoxically due to their historic scepticism towards government intervention, have a more ancient tradition in this sense. A significant conceptual effort in the field of technology policy has been made, and has not remained confined to academia. In the EU, although the awareness of the need for a rigorous evaluation of public policies has also greatly increased in recent years, some grey areas still exist.

Regarding the Italian situation, a 1998 law created a committee for the evaluation of technology research (CIVR: Comitato di Indirizzo per la Valutazione della Ricerca). This committee resides in the Ministry of Education, University and Research, as does the ASI. It establishes indicators and principles according to which the activities of the agencies and organisations dedicated to research should be evaluated. It is perhaps significant that the Italian Space Agency did not submit sufficient documentation for an evaluation to the CIVR in 2001. ASI personnel themselves consider the lack of rigorous evaluation as one of the main shortcomings of the agency, and their new chairman thankfully agrees.

4. Conclusions

Interacting agents are confronted with challenges resulting from differences in culture, mindset and lack of trust. In other words, they may face a lack of social capital. This increases the costs of relationships, and may even induce them to sacrifice collaboration, leading to both private and social losses. In contrast, costs sunk into developing relationships may be reduced with sufficient social capital. There is of course another side to this coin in that if agents forming a community or a network develop exclusive mannerisms, or consolidate ways and habits, such a community may become 'esoteric' such that the barriers are raised for agents outside the community. In economic terms, these barriers represent costs for potential new entrants and represent in effect a new concept of barriers to entry.

In 'technological communities', where economic agents and institutions operate in a specific technological field, the social relevance of the openness of such a community depends on the strategic character of the field of study, in the sense of implications and influence on many other sectors of the economy. In this paper we have considered the space sector, characterised by a high strategic character, due to the important spillovers of activities and products developed in this field. Therefore the degree of openness of this technological community is crucial for the whole economic system and it is of fundamental importance that agents operating in this sector co-operate and overcome obstacles deriving from different cultures. But it is even more important that this community remains open, where lock-in phenomena are avoided and where routines do not become so intensive and languages so specific to discourage agents that have the capabilities from entering and operating successfully therein. A public agency may be the policy instrument to maintain low barriers inside the existing community and towards potential members, therefore favouring interactions among agents, creating a climate of trust and collaboration, but avoiding the creation of a closed community. Firstly though, selection should be objective, competition real, and every agent should have a true chance to participate in the projects. Once 'admitted', the circulation of information and accommodating behaviour should be constantly guaranteed. In such a way a public agency becomes something more than an instrument to allocate funds. Rather than identifying competencies, it builds them. By keeping the technological community open to newcomers, abilities that otherwise could be dispersed or not fully exploited are kept together and mutually reinforced. In such a way the competitiveness of the whole economic system is increased and the circulation of knowledge is encouraged and developed. Only in such a way is the full potential of a technological sector exploited.

References

Agenzia Spaziale Italiana (1997), *Piano Spaziale Nazionale 1998-2002. Strategie e linee programmatiche*, Roma.

Alessandrini, P. and Sterlacchini, A. (1995), 'Ricerca, formazione e rapporti con l'industria: i problemi irrisolti dell'università italiana', *L'industria*, 88, 33-61.

Arrow, K.J. (1962), 'Economic Welfare and the Allocation of Resources for Invention', in *The Rate and Direction of Inventive Activity,* National Bureau of Economic Research, Princeton University Press.

Bach, L., Cohendet, P. and Schenk, E. (2002), 'Technological Transfer from the European Space Programs: a Dynamic View and Comparison with Other R&D Projects', *Journal of Technology Transfer*, 27, 321-338.

Balconi, M., Breschi, S. and Lissoni, F. (2002), 'Networks of Inventors and the Location of University Research: an Exploration of Italian Data', *CESPRI working paper*, n.127, March.

Coleman, J. (1990), *Foundations of Social Theory*, The Belknap Press of Harvard University Press, Harvard, Cambridge, MA.

Dasgupta, P. and David, P.A. (1994), 'Toward a New Economics of Science', *Research Policy*, 23 (5), 487-521.

David, P., Foray, D. and Steinmueller, W.E. (1999), 'The Research Network and the New Economics of Science: from Metaphors to Organisational Behaviors', in Gambardella, A. and Malerba, F. (eds), *The Organisation of Economic Innovation in Europe,* Cambridge University Press, Cambridge.

European Commission (1995), *Green Paper on Innovation*, Bruxelles.

Eurospace (2002), 'Eurospace Facts & Figures : the European Space Industry 1996–2000'. http://perso.wanadoo.fr/eurospace/eurospace_facts_and_figures_1996_2000.pdf

Gambetta, D. (1998), 'Possiamo fidarci della fiducia?', in Gambetta, D. (ed.), *Le strategie della fiducia*, Einaudi, Roma.

Garonna, P. and Iannarino, S. (2000), '"Scienza aperta" e politiche pubbliche della ricerca: verso una "terza via"?', in Garonna, P. and Iannarino, S. (eds), *Economia della ricerca*, Il Mulino, Bologna.

Geuna, A. (1999), 'Patterns of University Research in Europe', in Gambardella, A. and Malerba, F. (eds), *The Organisation of Economic Innovation in Europe*, Cambridge University Press, Cambridge.

Guerrieri, P. and Milana, C. (1998), 'High-Technology Industries and International Competition', in Archibugi, D. and Michie, J. (eds), *Trade, Growth and Technical Change*, Cambridge University Press, Cambridge.

Hämäläinen, T.J. and Schienstock, G. (2001), 'The Comparative Advantage of Networks in Economic Organisation: Efficiency and Innovation in Highly Specialised and Uncertain Environments', in *Innovative Networks. Co-operation in National Innovation Systems*, OECD, Paris.

Leydesdorff, P. (2003), 'A Methodological Perspective on the Evaluation of the Promotion of University-Industry-Government Relations', *Small Business Economics*, 20, 201-204.

Mansfield, E. (1969), *The Economics of Technical Change*, Longmans, London.

Marengo, L. and Sterlacchini, A. (1990), 'Intersectoral Technology Flows. Methodological Aspects and Empirical Applications', *Metroeconomica*, 41(1), 19-39.

MERIT (2000), *Innovation Policy in a Knowledge-Based Economy*, EUR 17023, Commission of the European Communities, Luxembourg.

Nelson, R.R. (1993), *National Innovation Systems: a Comparative Analysis*, Oxford University Press, Oxford.

Ramaciotti, L. (1999), 'Il settore aerospaziale: alleanze strategiche e globalizzazione', *L'Industria*, 3, 489-509.

Schibany, A. and Schartinger, D. (2001), 'Interactions between Universities and Enterprises in Austria: an Empirical Analysis at the Micro Sector Levels', in *Innovative Networks. Cooperation in National Innovation Systems*, OECD, Paris.

Schuetze, H.G. (2000), 'Industrial Innovation and the Creation and Dissemination of Knowledge: Implications for University-Industry Relationships', in *Knowledge Management in the Learning Society*, OECD, Paris.

Chapter 7

Dynamic Networks in Innovation-Intensive Industries

Alberto Cottica and Giovanni Ponti

1. Networks as Evolving Intangible Assets

Networks versus *markets* or *hierarchies,* have emerged in recent times as a valuable metaphor to describe business relationships between firms. Economists have long been aware of the existence of competitive advantage stemming from finely tuned co-ordination between buyers and sellers of specialised inputs. The matter has however been treated as a parameter rather than a variable, filed under headings like 'industrial atmosphere' (Marshall, 1916) 'transaction costs' (Coase, 1937), and left out of the core models of theory of the firm.

Network theory, in contrast, assumes that specialised inputs cannot be purchased on the spot market. A buyer in need of a specialised input can either manufacture it in-house or establish a link, i.e. a (costly) time-contingent relationship with one or more suppliers. This approach places the decision to establish links at the very core of the firm's business model, thereby accommodating empirical evidence that, in many industries, firms devote considerable effort and financial resources to choosing and 'breeding' their business partners. In other words, it is generally recognised that something as immaterial and difficult to define as 'co-ordination', 'mutual understanding' or even 'empathy', is a valuable and important source of competitive advantage.

Case studies of successful networks of firms have unfailingly highlighted the role played by time in building links. Uzzi (1997) for example reports that 25 per cent of Fuji Electric's subcontractors in 1983 had been doing business with Fuji for 21 years or more. Likewise, Lazerson (1993) reports that in the garment district of Modena (Italy), the majority of artisans assembling clothing for garments work for at least three clients.

The precise recipe for effective network links capable of accommodating fine-grained technical requirements and significantly lowering transaction costs in a general climate of trust has not yet been discovered. Brusco (1982) makes a case for assigning a role to trade associations, shared labour ethics, and clear political hegemony. These however are all long-term factors, difficult to apply effectively with any one agent, no matter how powerful and well informed, and utterly impossible to recreate in the short term. Many scholars have in fact resorted to long-range historical research to explain the successful performance of locally concentrated networks of firms. In this area of research Italy's *industrial districts* have been a prime source of examples. Bagnasco and Pini (1981), for example, establish a causal link between the nature of arrangements between landowners and farmers in the 19th century and the 'propensity to entrepreneurship' of Italian industrial districts. Their argument is that such agreements, involving farmers making their own decisions, improved their skills of dealing with the market, of evaluating their investments, of bookkeeping, etc., skills which, later on, would be used within the local economies to launch new enterprises. Capecchi (1992) and Poni (1991) highlight the relationship between Bologna's current world leadership in packaging machinery and a history of technological development (and even technology policy, such as invention protection). This spans more than four centuries, beginning with silk production and continuing with the 19th century technical schools. Going even further back, Putnam (1993) notes that the map of industrial development in contemporary Italy correlates with the development of the politically independent free city states in the 14th century. He argues that the free cities provided a context in which actors were encouraged to interact and look for solutions to collective problems, and that the development of such skills might be at the origin of the relative outperformance of northern Italy's economy compared to the south.

This body of literature unambiguously suggests that proximity is neither a necessary nor sufficient condition for the creation of an efficient network, and that the fine fabric of business relationships characterising Silicon Valley for example, cannot be produced as would be a new plant from a green field. Building an effective network requires time and effort from a whole array of agents, and evidence suggests that networks exhibit the characteristics of capital goods. At the same time, network links are obviously immaterial: they are cognitive, relational, cultural, even historical, and certainly not physical. In this sense it seems perfectly appropriate to think of complex and multi-layered networks of business relationships as *intangible assets* for the economy as a whole (just as an array of network links is an intangible asset of each individual firm), and of network link creation as *specific investment* by firms.

Given the above considerations, it is not surprising that issues relating to the 'economics of networks' are also relevant to the 'economics of intangibles' (see chapters 2). Until very recently however, the literature had little to say about the precise nature of the returns from investments in networks. It was generally concluded that network structures would enjoy lower transaction costs, or be conducive to information sharing. The closest thing to a formal analysis available generally followed the line that given the agents' lack of anonymity in a network, and given the network structure's short-term rigidity (consistent with its asset nature), agents are subject to repeated interaction which allows for co-operation (see chapter 4 for more details). A full-fledged theory linking networks, firms' payoffs, industry performance and social welfare, however, was yet to come.

Recent advances in network theory[1] offer a modelling strategy to identify the forces at work and answers questions more relevant to policy concerning for example optimal network size, level of information sharing, and policies to promote the creation of efficient networks.[2]

In this paper we argue that *the nature of networks as intangible assets is connected to their economic efficiency in producing innovation.* We do so by reviewing a stream of literature from two different perspectives. Firstly we look at the empirical research on innovation, with its recurrent theme of vertical disintegration. Secondly we turn to the theory of vertical integration itself, which requires innovation to justify idiosyncratic demand shocks that apparently explain the existence of network industrial structures. We suggest that a recently developed model of bipartite networks, proposed by Kranton and Minehart (2000), may be a useful way of looking at innovation in industries where new technologies and products are normally supplied by third-party suppliers rather than in-house. The model's predictive power, however, is undermined by an excess of equilibria and, perhaps, a lack of realism (innovation for example is always achieved by investing a fixed amount in R&D). Moreover, most of the equilibrium networks in the model turn out to be inefficient.

The empirical literature, in stark contrast, highlights the ability of networks to evolve to more efficient allocations. The reason for this discrepancy may indeed be due to the static nature of Kranton and Minehart's model in which buyers are assumed to take their decisions simultaneously and once and for all. To ameliorate this situation, we look at evolutionary dynamic models of innovation and the theoretical debate therein. Innovation economists, well aware of the difficulties, have tried several solutions for modelling the complex process of invention and discovery in a mathematically simple way. One of the more interesting suggestions comes from a fairly recent body of literature, which looks at economic issues through the lens of cognitive philosophy, and states that given the context of turbulence implied by network models and innovative activity, the notion of· strategy changes. This happens because, in a turbulent (emergent) environment, agents are no longer in a position to list all possible states of the world and compute payoffs. We discuss in section 3 the cognitive notion of strategy, which seems the most realistic to apply to innovation models, and suggest it could reasonably be embedded into evolutionary dynamic models.

In section 4 we construct a model, based on Kranton and Minehart (2000), after which in section 5 we incorporate an evolutionary dynamic approach to the original model. In addition to the fact that our dynamic approach is more realistic in describing innovative activities, our conclusions are realistic insofar as the long-run equilibrium of networks turns out to be efficient.

Finally, section 6 attempts an economic interpretation of this efficiency result. The long-run efficiency of the perturbed evolutionary model adds a new dimension to the view of networks as intangible assets: while network links are assets for

---

[1] See Jackson and Wolinsky (1996) and the literature cited therein.

[2] See the extensive discussions of these issues in chapters 1 and 2.

individual firms, the long-run, efficient equilibrium network configuration can be thought of as an asset for the industry as a whole. Each link's return on investment, unsurprisingly, depends on the overall link pattern, which cannot be controlled by any individual participant and should instead be thought of as a feature of the industrial system.

2. Innovation and Efficiency in Networks

We consider networks here mainly from an innovation economics perspective, where some manufacturing firms in an industry buy innovation (either as patents or embedded in manufacturing equipment) from vertically disintegrated third-party suppliers, rather than produce it in their own R&D labs. Far from being simply a mathematical assumption, vertical networks in the innovation case study literature are a fairly familiar landscape. Following Kranton and Minehart (2000), we model our industry as a bipartite network in which sellers are independent R&D labs and buyers are technology consuming firms. Such a structure can potentially have consequences on economic welfare in (at least) three ways.

First, a network structure may alter the industry's *innovative capabilities*, broadly defined as the rate of innovation output to innovative effort. The reason for this effect is that some of the knowledge mobilised to innovate is 'tacit', i.e. not embodied in any formalised written form.[3] Participants in a network move within an informational space where 'fine-grained' technological (or heuristic) specifications are (relatively) easily available, and where innovation effort is hardly ever duplicated.

This is suggested by rather diverse sources. Lane and Maxfield (1997), approaching business strategy from a cognitive perspective, observe that relationships between technology producers and technology users may become 'generative', providing new insights as to nature and usage of products and leading to very successful innovation patterns. Scott (1999) uses the economic geography toolbox to uncover strong propensity to spatial agglomeration in the US recorded music industry, and explains its role in the innovation process in that industry. Dependent on novelty for its lifeblood, the music industry survives and thrives in agglomerations that function as evolving pools of creative power, constantly shifting registers and cognitive content.

From a more traditional perspective, Russo (1985) and others have observed that technological innovation often occurs at multiple points of encounter between different actors. Pavitt's (1984) influential taxonomy recognised 'specialised suppliers' of technology (where specialisation embodies the notion of a link within a network) as a major source of innovation. In support of Pavitt's hypothesis, Cottica's (1994) study of the packaging industry found that 96 per cent of innovative packaging developed over the 1978-1992 period is invented outside the firms which use it. It may be noted that the notion of networking as an 'intuition

---

[3] See, for example, Becattini (1989).

machine' for knowledge production can be a useful tool for understanding the remarkable innovation performance achieved by some spatial clusters of firms. In this case, *physical proximity* permits an effective sharing of the same, constantly evolving, information space.

Second, case studies have often argued that networks enjoy welfare advantages over vertical integration in that they facilitate *information sharing* in the form of tacit, as opposed to explicit, knowledge transfers. Links connecting firms in a network are by definition information-conducive, which participants use to share newly acquired knowledge, both intentionally and via unintentional 'leakages'. Since full information sharing is always required in the social optimum, as strongly put forward by Katsoulacos and Ulph (2000) among others, this is by no means a secondary issue.[4]

Third, a network structure is likely to influence *incentives to innovate*. This relation is twofold. On the one hand, vertical disintegration implies that the innovator may not appropriate the full social value of the innovation (therefore opening the way for underinvestment). On the other hand, idiosyncratic demand shocks may render networks particularly effective in *risk sharing*, disengaging the success or failure of R&D firms from that of single users of innovation. In vertically disintegrated industries innovative activities can easily be shifted from unsuccessful to successful downstream firms.

While concerns for surplus appropriation by innovators runs through the whole history of innovation economics,[5] the idea that vertical disintegration may yield welfare gains in the presence of demand uncertainty was developed more recently (and outside of innovation theory) as in Piore and Sabel's (1984) work concerning *flexible specialists*, Brusco's (1982) industrial districts, or, earlier, in Richardson (1972).

The desirable properties of networks in 'smoothing out' the effects of firm-specific demand shocks need not be confined to innovation economics. Kranton and Minehart (2000) list a number of industries to which network models may be applied, dividing them into two broad categories consisting firstly of the fashion, culture, and craft industries and secondly of high-tech. In the words of the authors, in these industries '*uncertainty over firms' innovation success and over the demand for new products both translates into idiosyncratic uncertainty in inputs demands*'.

The role of networks as risk-sharing devices is the main focus of this paper. To this aim, we rely on Kranton and Minehart's (1998, 2000) models of vertical networks which concern exchanges in which buyers and sellers, through their links, establish direct relationships and trade goods. These relationships between buyers and sellers are not exclusive however, since buyers may be linked with, and can obtain their input from, different sellers. Buyers make individual valuations about inputs (that reflect demand uncertainty) and they compete on the basis of

---

[4] Clearly, modelling these phenomena requires subtlety. If you use the empirical evidence to simply assume that networks innovate better, you will get a model that predicts more innovation in network industrial structures.

[5] See, for example, Arrow (1962).

these valuations to obtain inputs from sellers with whom they are connected. In Kranton and Minehart (1998), link costs are paid by the buyers, and sellers are passive agents. Under these assumptions, it is shown that all (Pareto) efficient allocations correspond to (network) equilibrium of the underlying non-co-operative game.

Clearly, this framework is not suitable to describe innovative activities. Innovations do require specific investments and moreover it would be too unrealistic to assume so out of a model casting R&D labs as passive agents. In a sequel paper based on the same theoretical framework, Kranton and Minehart (2000) assume that *sellers must invest* in order to produce the specialised goods required by buyers. This situation is stylised by a two-stage game in which, firstly, buyers choose sellers with whom they want to be linked and sellers decide whether to make specific investments. In the second stage, uncertainty about each buyer's valuation for the good is resolved and exchange takes place. This new setting is much better suited to innovation economics: just interpret sellers as independent R&D labs, buyers as technology users, and specific investments as R&D. Unfortunately, Kranton and Minehart's (1998) efficiency result on network equilibria does not hold when specific investments are take into account. It is shown that, if idiosyncratic shocks are sufficiently large, network may be equilibria of the game. However, the number of network equilibria is extremely large (i.e. the model has little predictive power), and these equilibria may not be efficient. Such inefficiency arises because sellers' incentives are not usually aligned with economic welfare.

3. Cognition and Evolution: Feeding Dynamics into Innovation Models

Kranton and Minehart's (2000) model employs standard (static) game theory techniques to compute its results. This is a favoured modelling strategy in innovation economics for obvious reasons of rigour, clarity and mathematical tractability.[6] However, it is not necessarily the best way to model innovation. In a sense, the strategic framework depicted by these models feels 'too narrow', as it does not capture the trial-and-error, false starts and redirection, the lucky stumbling into something completely unexpected, and the inexplicable market rejection of excellent innovative products that seem to accompany any scientific or technological endeavour.

In an attempt to account for these effects, scholars have followed at least three different paths. The first path is to model innovation as a stochastic process. Since firms allocate resources to R&D, the probability of making a discovery is positively correlated with the amount of resources allocated. This does not pose many problems from a mathematical point of view since although the firm's strategic space is still mono-dimensional for R&D investment, it computes its

---

[6] See Beath et al. (1995) for a survey and vindication.

payoffs in expected values rather than deterministically.[7] The second path is more interesting and allows for some kind of multidimensionality in the firm's strategic space. Katsoulacos and Ulph (2000), for example, model innovative activities as a three-stage decision. Firstly they choose one of many possible research paths, either substitutable for each other to lead to the same discovery, or complementary, leading to complementary discoveries.[8] Secondly they decide how much R&D effort to put into the chosen research path. Finally each firm decides whether to share with the other firm the new knowledge produced in the event of a discovery. Even in this case, static game theory, and all its desirable properties, functions, though at the price of breaking up the model's results into several cases. For both these approaches, the agents' strategic space does not include any linking activity, which leaves open the possibility for networks that exist completely independent of the model's outcomes.

A third, and completely different approach, to innovation arises from recent developments in the application of cognitive philosophy to economic analysis. Recent literature, drawing on earlier work by Winograd and Flores (1986), puts forward a convincing case for a cognitive approach to innovation economics. The argument, that echoes the Schumpeterian notion of 'creative destruction', is that the identity of products (or 'artefacts', a broader concept that also encompasses man-made intangibles like organisational arrangements) is not a datum. Rather, it is a convention that agents need to accept in order for products to 'find their place'. This means that people cannot use a product, nor can the market decide its price, until we have agreed upon the nature and the purpose for human consumption of the product's technology. While the issue may be excluded for simplicity within a static setting, cognitive scientists argue that it is inappropriate to exclude it totally from innovation economics, and claim that a new technology cannot be a success in the market until agents have understood it and assigned it a role in their lives. Innovation is in many senses therefore 'an ongoing process of negotiation'.

This argument rings a familiar tone to industrial economists dealing with innovation issues. As is well known, the literature records many examples of innovations that ended up being 'misused' by the market. The internet was conceived as a way of ensuring military communication in case of nuclear attack, and ended up as a complex socio-economic phenomenon; the MP3 compression standard for audio files, created to solve a purely technical problem of memory and bandwidth space, turned upside down the social use of music (and the recorded music business with it); and third generation mobile communication is

---

[7] Also, the innovation production function turns out to be conveniently convex. Some of the models generated by this approach make use of optimal control dynamics, like tournament models (the first firm to successfully innovate takes all of the market). See Beath et al. (1995) for a survey.

[8] Katsoulacos and Ulph's model involves two firms, so all that matters in terms of their results is the nature of the first firm's research path relative to that of the other.

encountering serious problems not for technical shortcomings, but for a lack of applications that users are happy with and will pay for.[9]

The multi-agent nature of this negotiation process engenders what Lane and Maxfield (1997) call a *complex foresight horizon*, in which it is impossible not only to make reliable forecasts, but even to identify with any degree of certainty the relevant players. They use the metaphor of a Bosnian diplomat in early September 1995 trying to bring an end to the bloodshed in his country. He finds it extremely difficult even to tell friend from foe, in a context of suddenly shifting alliances and new players entering the game with unclear interests. They argue that in a world characterised by emergent cognitive ambiguity, such as that of technological change, a strategy becomes something very different from what it conventionally meant. Strategy, under a complex foresight horizon scenario, should include provisions for actively monitoring the world to discover unexpected consequences, adjustment mechanisms to respond to events, and permission for a variety of agents to initiate new, experimental courses of action.

We argue that innovation within such environments fits the cognitive mould better than innovation with greater certainty of outcome, and for two reasons. Firstly, cognitive scientists maintain that control over the innovation process is distributed among agents and that the inventor is in general not capable of predicting and imposing the use of his invention in the market. While this argument seems reasonable for a relatively wide range of product innovations, it is inappropriate for in-house process innovation, where the inventing firm does not negotiate with other parties.[10] In-house usage however represents only a degenerate case in bipartite vertical networks, where the inventor tries from the very beginning to diagnose and interpret (and occasionally create) the needs of the technology user. In consequence, *most if not all innovations in vertical networks can be expected to happen under complex foresight horizon scenarios.*

The second reason for which vertical networks are particularly suited to a cognitive approach is that a strategy suited to a complex foresight scenario would almost always encompass investing in meaningful relationships, through which agents may, through mutual criticism, build and update their interpretation of their

---

[9] Interestingly, the killer application of GSM, the SMS short text message system, was a completely unexpected success. Giussani (2001) quotes several leading technicians involved in the development of the GSM protocol agreeing that no one saw SMS coming. ('There was some excess capacity, so the engineers decided to include it, in case someone could find a use for it (...) It was just an option, something that a company could claim to have available on its network.') In 2000 an estimated 200 billion SMSs have been sent and paid for.

[10] In fact, even this can be disputed. Russo (2000) discusses a radical process innovation, kervit, which took place in the late 1930s in a traditional industry, ceramic tiles, to be used in-house by the inventing firm. The technology anticipated single-firing, which would only much later become an industry standard, but had to be abandoned since the other industry players, through several socially shared incremental innovations, made the more traditional double-firing process more competitive than the innovative one. According to Russo, the difficulty of imitating kervit was one of the reasons for its downfall.

individual situations.[11] In consequence, *most if not all innovations under complex foresight horizon scenarios can be expected to happen in vertical networks.*

To the best of our knowledge the cognitive approach to innovation economics has never been applied to vertical networks as defined in this paper, which aims at merely a first, preliminary attempt to do so. We suggest that the negotiation, trial-and-error, experimentation, and occasional mistakes implied by the cognitive approach to innovation can be embedded into a perturbed evolutionary dynamic model. We therefore assume that Kranton and Minehart's (2000) bipartite network game is played repeatedly by two populations of buyers and sellers. During each period, each player adopts the best reply to the result of the previous period with probability $1 - \varepsilon$. However, we also assign some small probability to the possibility that they may choose some other course of action. Sellers may decide to make specific investments that would not have been profitable in the previous period and subsequently look for a market for their goods (implying an incomplete negotiation on the social use of a new technology), and buyers may decide to alter their link structure with the various sellers (implying the emergence of a new alliance). The noise in the system may be thought of as a very rough way to model decision making under complex foresight horizon scenarios; the survival of the fittest payoff scheme guaranteeing that, once a player happens to a more desirable state than the original one, they will tend to cling to it, while still allowing for tentative deviations.

4. The Static Model

We provide the reader here with a synopsis of Kranton and Minehart's (2000) model upon which our result is based. They consider a game between a set of *buyers* and a set of *sellers* in which buyers demand one indivisible unit of a specialised input and sellers can produce at most one unit of this specialised input.

Each buyer perceives a random valuation for the specialised input, composed of *aggregate* (i.e. common to all buyers) and *idiosyncratic* (i.e. firm-specific) components. While the former captures market conditions common to all firms in the industry, the latter refers to firms' specific demand. This formalisation takes into account *demand uncertainty* in that specialised inputs have different values for different buyers, depending on the demand they face for their own products.

In the game, buyers have to determine the identity of those sellers (if any) with whom they want to establish a relationship (link), important since sellers can sell their input only to buyers with whom they are linked. Other options possible for buyers are to *vertically integrate* (that is, to produce the input they need in-house) or to not invest at all in relationships with specialised sellers (i.e. to rely on the spot market of non-specialised inputs). At the same time, sellers have to decide whether to carry out specific investments to meet buyers' demands. If they do not, the input they produce will be indifferent to non-specialised inputs sold on the spot market.

---

[11] See Lane and Maxfield (1997).

All these decisions are taken *before* market valuations are known. This is because link formation and specific investment decisions are usually long-term, and cannot be contingent upon specific market conditions. After buyers and sellers make their (simultaneous) decisions, market valuations for buyers are determined and game payoffs are distributed.

When buyers decide to buy an input through a network, their expected payoffs are determined not only by the behaviour of other agents but also by the pricing mechanism (i.e. how gains from trade are distributed between buyers and sellers). Following Kranton and Minehart (2000), we shall assume that gain sharing is determined by the *competitive rule*. This rule mimics the outcome of a sequence of simultaneous ascending bid auctions, and works roughly as follows. Once a network is formed, buyers bid in the auctions of their linked sellers. The price rises simultaneously in all auctions until, for some subset of sellers, demand equals supply, at which point this subset of the auctions ends at this price. The process continues for the remaining auctions until market clears.

Kranton and Minehart (2000) observe that, under the competitive rule, a buyer obtaining an input earns the difference between their valuation and the valuation of the next best (linked) buyer. Therefore, if a buyer participates in a network, they efficiently choose the number of links according to the investments of the other buyers. In contrast, for a seller, the mechanism of a second-price auction implies that investment incentives are not aligned with economic welfare, since sellers obtain as revenues the valuation of the next best (linked) buyer. This simply reflects the 'appropriation problem' we considered in section 1.

Kranton and Minehart's (2000) equilibrium results can be summarised as follows:

- If the expected value of the aggregate shock is sufficiently low, then the vertically integrated structure is always an equilibrium of the game. If the reverse occurs, then a no-investment scenario is equilibrium. Vertical integration (no investment) structures are the only equilibrium outcomes when they are (Pareto) efficient (Proposition 4).
- With the competitive rule, whatever the dispersion of the aggregate shock, there are always appropriate values for link and specific investment costs for which the game has network equilibria (Proposition 7).

Intuitively, a network is in equilibrium when participation costs are sufficiently small and investment costs sufficiently large to induce buyers to invest in networks rather than to vertically integrate. To ensure that sellers have the necessary incentives, investment costs however cannot be too high.

It can also be shown that not only do network equilibria exist, but these equilibrium structures *always* yield greater welfare than vertical integration or no investment (Proposition 5). Consistent with the literature cited above, networks' efficiency increases with demand uncertainty (Proposition 2). Network equilibria however may not always be efficient.

We provide the reader with a simple example of Kranton and Minehart's (2000) equilibrium results. Figure 7.1 shows an efficient (equilibrium) network with 4 buyers and 2 sellers.

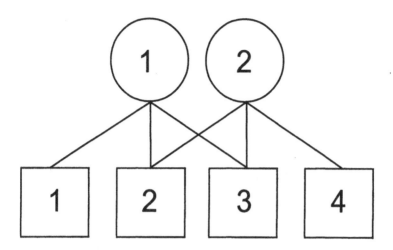

Figure 7.1 Efficient network

All buyers are marked with a box and are involved in some link formation. All sellers are marked with a circle and make specific investments. The industrial structure of Figure 7.1 is characterised by the fact that two buyers (precisely 2 and 3) establish two links, with the remaining buyers establishing only one link. The reason why two buyers may have an incentive in setting up more than one link (providing that link costs are sufficiently small) is that, in doing so, they maximise the probability of obtaining the input, provided their valuation is sufficiently high. Since two buyers are already linked with all sellers, buyers 1 and 4 have no incentive to establish additional links (the gain in probability of obtaining the input would not be sufficient to cover the additional link cost). Both sellers have an incentive to invest, since, according to the competitive rule, they are guaranteed to sell their input with a positive return. In other words, the industrial structure of Figure 7.1 represents equilibrium of the underlying network game.

This equilibrium is also Pareto efficient. Efficiency here is measured by the ability to maximise industry's expected profits. In the context of our simple example, an industrial structure with four buyers and two sellers is efficient if it is able to allocate the inputs to the two buyers with the highest valuations, independently of how these valuations are distributed. If, for example, buyers 1 and 2 hold the highest valuations, by the competitive rule, buyer 1 will win seller 1's auction, while buyer 2 will win seller 2's auction; if, buyers 1 and 3 hold the highest valuations, by the competitive rule, buyer 1 will win seller 1's auction, while buyer 3 will win seller 2's auction (and so on). In consequence, Figure 7.1 identifies *an equilibrium network which is also efficient.*

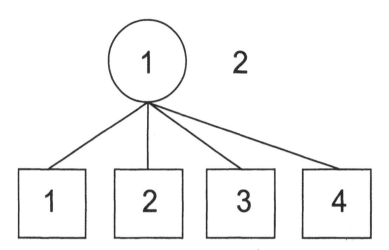

Figure 7.2 Non efficient equilibrium

Things change dramatically when we look at the network of Figure 7.2 which also demonstrates equilibrium within the network game. Seller 2 has not made specific investments, so no buyer has an incentive to establish a link. By the same token, seller 2 is not linked with any buyer and has no incentive to make specific investments. Competition will be harsher in seller 1's auction compared with the situation described in Figure 7.1. This is because all four buyers are bidding for a single specialised good. This, of course, will raise seller 1's profits at the expense of the winning buyer, but will lower industry's aggregate profits. In consequence, the equilibrium network of Figure 7.2 *is not efficient*, since only one specialised input is produced.

5. Evolution and Innovation: A Dynamic Approach

We are now in a position to introduce our evolutionary dynamics. At each point in time, every buyer and seller is assumed to receive a new opportunity with the same independent probability $p \in (0,1)$. If a new opportunity does not occur, a player will simply adopt the same strategy as in the previous period. Otherwise, they will switch strategy to the current best-reply, given the strategy profile selected by the rest of the population in the previous period.[12] We disturb these learning dynamics by allowing for some small probability that players 'mutate'. Such a mutation admits several possible interpretations. One natural possibility is simply to conceive the phenomenon of mutation as embodying players' experimentation. But, alternatively, it could also be taken to reflect the possibility that players make

---

[12] In presence of multiple best-replies, I shall assume that each strategy which may be selected has some (fixed) positive probability.

mistakes, or even view mutation as formalising some extent of population renewal (i.e. a process by which some of the incumbent players are randomly replaced by fresh and uninformed newcomers).

Whatever its particular motivation, the mutation adopted here is as follows. In every period, and once the learning stage is over (i.e. after all agents have completed any possible revision according to the best-reply dynamics), every player is subject to some independent probability $\varepsilon > 0$ of mutation. If this event indeed happens, the player in question is assumed to replace her ``interim'' strategy choice resulting from the learning stage by some other pure strategy. Once this mutation stage has been completed, play occurs in the time period, and players then obtain their corresponding payoffs.

It can be shown that the perturbed process can be modelled as a Markov chain on the same state space as for the original (unperturbed) process. Furthermore, for any $\varepsilon > 0$, this perturbed Markov chain is *ergodic*, that is, converges to a unique distribution independent of initial conditions. This unique invariant distribution, which we call μ_ε, summarises the long-run behaviour of the process, independently of initial conditions, as a function of the noise parameter ε.

Naturally, we want to conceive the magnitude of the noise (i.e. the probability ε), as quite small. Or, to be more precise, we are interested in studying the long-run behaviour of the process when $\varepsilon \downarrow 0$. Formally, such a long-run state of affairs is captured by the *limit invariant distribution*

$$\mu^* - \lim_{\varepsilon \to 0} \mu_\varepsilon$$

The above limit can be shown to be well defined. The states in the support of the induced limit distribution μ^* are called the *stochastically stable sets*. They are to be conceived as the only states which are visited a significant fraction of time in the long run when $\varepsilon \downarrow 0$. They represent, therefore, the 'selection' induced by the evolutionary learning process when an arbitrarily small amount of noise removes any long-run dependence of initial conditions.

We are now in the position to state the main result of the paper.

Theorem 1: *For any pair of link formation and investment costs for which there exists an efficient equilibrium network, this corresponds to an asymptotically stable set of the perturbed dynamics.*

Proof. See Cottica and Ponti (2002), Theorem 1.

We leave aside the technical details of the proof, providing instead an application for the simple two buyer-four seller example of section 4. First, notice that no state can be stochastically stable if it is merely transient for the unperturbed dynamics. In other words, only equilibria can support the limit invariant distribution indicated above. Moreover, since equilibrium conditions for buyers are aligned with economic welfare under networks, vertical integration and not investing, the best-reply dynamics alone will ensure that, in any stochastically stable set, buyers will make the efficient choice between vertical integration, networks, and not investing.[13] In consequence, to prove the theorem, it is sufficient to show that, in all stochastically stable sets, sellers' behaviour is also efficient. Take, for example, the equilibrium network of Figure 7.2 and assume that seller 2, by mutation, changes strategy to investing. Buyers will then have an incentive to form a link with seller 2 (i.e. seller 2 will have no incentives to return to not investing) and the system will gradually move to the (efficient) equilibrium network of Figure 7.1.

6. Towards a Cognitive Theory of Innovative Networks

Network theory has recently developed into a promising tool for investigating innovative activities. Bipartite networks, stylised as they may seem against real-life business activity, do seem to capture an important feature of innovation in many industries since they tend to develop within the context of frequent buyer-supplier relationships between firms who invent and firms who use new technology and new products.

Kranton and Minehart's (1998) original contribution on the efficiency of network equilibria has been improved by the same authors in 2000 to take specific investment in R&D into consideration. In this paper, we have adjusted their model in the direction of realism by including bounded rationality considerations, such as trial-and-error behaviour, link formation and R&D investment. This also allows us to restore the desirable features of efficiency of network equilibria displayed by the simpler no-investment static model (1998), but not by the static model allowing for specific investments (2000).

The economic interpretation of this result is straightforward: agents engaged in innovative activities face, almost by definition, conditions of severe uncertainty. In order to cope with it, they adopt trial-and-error heuristics in all dimensions of the innovation process. One of the more relevant of these dimensions is, consistent with the cognitive approach, the choice and nurturing of one's business partners. The pattern of business relationships between technology suppliers and technology users is therefore subject to evolution. In other words, networks are not 'just there', they evolve. This implies that, in the long run, only the fittest (i.e. the most efficient) link patterns will survive. This efficiency result adds a new meaning to the statement that network links are intangible assets: an efficient structure evolved over time is indeed an intangible asset for the industry as a whole, just as are individual business links for individual firms. The combination of bipartite network games and evolutionary dynamics provides a simple, elegant tool for explaining both the development of networks and their durable success in innovation-dependent industries.

---

[13] See Kranton and Minehart (2000), proposition 5.

In the time-honoured tradition, we conclude by recommending further research. In this paper we have used a cognitive argument to justify the introduction of perturbed evolutionary dynamics into models of innovation in networks. The deviation from best-reply behaviour in a repeated games framework, in fact, translates into new links being created (and old ones being dismantled) in our network model. This in turn is consistent with the recommendation of cognitive economists to experiment with different business relationships when facing complex foresight conditions. Consistency does not imply subtlety however, and we do of course realise that simply assuming that agents will deviate from best-reply with probability ε does not do justice to the richness of the cognitive vision. Further inquiry into the matter is therefore advocated, especially as far as a more finely tuned modelling strategy is concerned.

References

Arrow, K. (1962), 'Economic Welfare and the Allocation of Resources for Invention', in *The Rate and Direction of Inventive Activity: Economic and Social Factors*, National Bureau of Economic Research, Princeton University Press.

Bagnasco, A. and Pini, R. (1981), 'Sviluppo economico e trasformazione socio-politica dei sistemi territoriali a economia diffusa', Quaderni Fondazione Feltrinelli, Milano.

Beath, J., Katsoulacos, Y. and Ulph, D. (1995), 'Game-Theoretic Approaches', in P. Stoneman (ed.), *Handbook of the Economics of Innovation and Technological Change*, Basil Blackwell, Oxford.

Becattini, G. (1989), 'Riflessioni sul distretto industriale marshalliano come concetto socio-economico', *Stato e Mercato*, 111-128.

Brusco, S. (1982), 'The Emilian Model: Productive Decentralisation and Social Integration', *Cambridge Journal of Economics*, 167-184.

Capecchi, V. (1992), 'L'industrializzazione a Bologna', *Storia illustrata di Bologna*, vol. VIII, Il Mulino, Bologna.

Carlton, D. (1978), 'Market Behaviour with Demand Uncertainty and Price Inflexibility', *American Economic Review*, 68, 571-87.

Coase, R.H. (1937), 'The nature of the firm', *Economica*, 4: 386-405.

Cottica, A. (1994), 'The Micro Economics of Environmental Innovation in the European Packaging Industry', Paper prepared for the Fifth Annual Conference of the European Association of Environmental and Resource Economists - Dublin, 22-24 June.

Cottica, A. and Ponti, G. (2002), 'The Evolutionary Stability of Vertical Networks', University of Ferrara, mimeo.

Giussani, B. (2001), *Roam - Making Sense of the Wireless Internet*, Random House, London.

Goyal, S. and Joshi, S. (1999), 'Networks of Collaboration in Oligopoly', mimeo, Erasmus University.

Jackson, M., and Wolinsky, A. (1996) 'A Strategic Model of Social and Economic Networks', *Journal of Economic Theory*, 71, 44-74.

Katsoulacos, Y. and Ulph, D. (2000), *The Economics of Research Joint Ventures*, mimeo, University College London.

Kranton, R. and Minehart, D. (1998), 'A Theory of Buyer-Seller Networks', *American Economic Review*, 1, 570-601.

Kranton, R. and Minehart, D. (2000), 'Networks versus Vertical Integration', *RAND Journal of Economics*, 1, 570-601.

Lane, D. and Maxfield, R. (1997), 'Foresight, Complexity, and Strategy', in Arthur Durlauf and David Lane (eds), *The Economy as an Evolving Complex System II*, Addison-Wesley.

Lazerson, M. (1993) 'Factory or Putting-Out? Knitting Networks in Modena,' in Grabher, G. (ed.), *The Embedded Firm: On the Socioeconomics of Industrial Networks*, New York, Routledge, 203-226.

Marshall, A. (1916), *Principles of Economics*, London, Macmillan.

Pavitt, K. (1984), *Technology, Management and Systems of Innovation*, Eldward Elgar, Cheltenham.

Piore, M.J. and Sabel, C.F. (1984), *The Second Industrial Divide*, Basic Books, New York.

Poni, C. (1990), 'Per la storia del distretto industriale serico di Bologna (secoli XVI-XIX)', *Quaderni storici*, n.1.

Poyagou-Theotoky, J.A. (ed.) (1997), *Competition, Co-operation, Research and Development: The Economics of Research Joint Ventures*, Macmillan Press Ltd, London.

Putnam, R.D. (1993), *Making Democracy Work*, Princeton University Press, Princeton.

Richardson, G.B. (1972), 'The Organisation of Industry', *Economic Journal*, 82, 883-96.

Russo, M. (1985), 'Technical Change and the Industrial District: The Role of Inter-Firm Relations in the Growth and Transformation of Ceramic Tile Production in Italy', *Research Policy*, 14, 118-42.

Russo, M. (2000), 'Complementary Innovations and Generative Relationships: An Ethnographic Study', *Economics of Innovation and New Technologies*, 14, 517-557.

Scott, A.J. (1999), 'The US Recorded Music Industry: On the Relations Between Organisation, Location and Creativity in the Cultural Economy', *Environment and Planning*, 31, 1965-84.

Uzzi, B. (1996), 'The Sources and Consequences of Embeddness for the Economic Performance of Organisations: The Network Effect', *American Sociological Review*, 11, 674-698.

Uzzi, B. (1997), 'Social Structure and Competition in Interfirm Networks: The Paradox of Embeddedness', *Administrative Science Quarterly*, 11, 49-64.

Winograd, T. and Flores, F. (1986), *Understanding Computers and Cognition*, Ablex Publishing, Norwood.

Chapter 8

Intangibles and Intellectual Capital: An Overview of the Reporting Issues and Some Measurement Models

Stefano Zambon[°]

It is now commonly accepted that we are in the midst of a phase of evolution in the major global economies which is characterised by new performance and value drivers that are mainly intangible in nature. Accordingly, the so called 'intangible' or 'knowledge economy' is the environment that companies and institutions have to learn to cope with. This new phase is having profound implications also for corporate accounting and reporting. It is well known that there is a wide gap between the accounting book value and the market value of many listed companies, especially if they operate in knowledge- and technology-intensive sectors. Some companies have recognised this new phase and started producing reports which are different from the traditional, financially-oriented ones. These reports may take different names (intellectual capital statement, report on intangibles, etc.), but they have a common goal of enriching the financial dimension in order to try to identify and track the new value drivers – mainly of an intangible nature – which could permit long-term, sustainable growth of the company. This diverse economic order poses challenges and offers innovative opportunities also to the audit profession and financial analysts. In particular, the so-called 'intellectual capital statement' poses a problem of verification of the data which is disclosed to institutional investors and the general public. The procedures for verification of this new information set are immature, and need to be standardised and agreed at an international level.

The aim of this chapter is to provide an overview of the complex issues and various approaches regarding the area of accounting for, and reporting of, intangibles. In particular, the analysis deals with the issues linked to the recognition, measure, and disclosure within and outside the traditional financial statements which are posed by the intangible economy to private organisations. The concept of intellectual capital will also be examined, as well as some of the innovative methods and forms of reporting which have been put forward to deal with such a problematic area.

[°] The assistance of Adele Del Bello (University of Ferrara) is gratefully acknowledged.

1. Traditional Accounting for Intangible Assets

Financial accounting and reporting practices have traditionally provided a basis for evaluating a company's business performance. Outside of the firm, financial reporting should provide information that is useful to present and potential investors and creditors in order to make rational investment and credit decisions. Within the firm, accounting information is essential for the purposes of efficient managerial decision making, as managers need timely and accurate information in order to carry out the budgeting process and implement effective control mechanisms. Consequently, any event that is likely to affect a firm's current financial position or its future performance should be reflected in its annual accounts. Unfortunately, conventional financial statements appear to be rapidly becoming less adequate for today's dynamic business environment.

Why are Traditional Financial Measures Becoming Less Relevant?

Conventional accounting, as well as national accounts systems used in all industrialised countries, were developed for manufacturing economies where most wealth was in the form of property, plant and equipment (Blair and Wallman, 2001). These systems were designed to provide accurate and reliable cost-based information about the value of assets used in production, and about the net value (adjusted for depreciation) of the output produced by these assets. However, in recent years, also cost-based accounting information has become increasingly less relevant. According to many commentators, principal factor behind this growing irrelevance of conventional financial statements has been the global transition towards a knowledge-driven economy, where investments in human resources, information technology, R&D and advertising have become essential in order to strengthen a firm's competitive position and ensure its future viability.

Intangible factors play a predominant role in the ability of companies to innovate and their subsequent competitiveness within a knowledge-based economy. Such assets enable knowledge-intensive economies to maintain their competitive position compared to resource- or labour-intensive economies. There is a growing awareness in OECD member countries that an increasing part of total investment in the business enterprise sector is directed towards intangible 'investment products' such as R&D, marketing, training, software. Nevertheless, OECD data on intangible investment is still relatively scarce (Vickery, 1999), as it is in the national statistics.

With the transition to a knowledge-based economy, the principal source of economic value and wealth is no longer the production of material (tangible) goods but the creation, exploitation and manipulation of intangible assets. In other words, economic growth is not as much influenced by investments in physical capital (i.e. land, machinery) as by knowledge, which is a critical determinant for the productive application and exploitation of physical capital. Consequently, companies depend also on their capacity of being able to measure, manage and develop their knowledge.

However, conventional accounting systems still largely concentrate on, and measure only, the value of financial and physical assets (plant, equipment, inventories, land and natural resources). There presently exists no adequate accounting techniques for determining and reporting the value of intangible assets such as the skills of workers, IP, business infrastructure, brand names, patents, databases and relationships with customers and suppliers (Lev, 1999).

On top of that, while intangibles are most often internally generated, conventional accounting is transaction-based (cf. double entry principle) and financially-oriented. Indeed, as has been pointed out, in a world of increasing technological change and shortened product life cycles and where 'knowledge work' and intangible assets are of profound importance, future financial performance is often better predicted by non-financial indicators than by financial indicators (Mavrinac and Siesfeld, 1998, pp.3-4).

Problems with Conventional Accounting for Intangible Assets: The Capitalisation Issue

Research has shown that traditional financial accounting performed reasonably well when a company's investment in intangibles was high and stable. However, traditional accounting does not perform so well when companies increase their investment in innovation, for example to open up a new market. It is hard for investors and accountants to value this additional investment, particularly because the future earnings it might generate are very uncertain (Leadbeater, 1999).

Nevertheless, the greatest challenge to conventional accounting is not just that of quantifying the level of investment in intangibles, but also that of accounting for the latter's rate of change (Gröjer and Johansson, 1999). Changes in investment in intangibles are difficult to track. Those investments can lead to a marked and unpredictable change in business performance. Traditional accounting measures have been undermined by this faster, less predictable rate of change because accountants find it increasingly difficult to match costs and investments in one period with earnings and revenues in another. This more rapid rate of change is in part due to deregulation and technological change which has exposed companies to new competition and opened up new markets. However, intangible investment – R&D to create new products for example – also plays a significant role in driving such a change.

Conventional accounting performs particularly poorly with internally generated intangibles such as R&D, brands and human capital, that are the very items considered the engines of modern economic growth. Accountants generally agree that in principle any internally generated intangibles should not be treated as an asset. On the other hand, according to Gröjer and Johansson (1999, p.42), if intangibles are separable from the operations of a business, and acquired at an arm's length transaction, they may be classed as an asset, and valued at market price (such as purchased licensing agreements or franchises). For example, for a long time generally accepted accounting principles have called for the immediate expensing of R&D costs. But, unlike rent and interest payments, intangibles investments may often produce rich future rewards. Expensing them now produces serious distortions in reported earnings and detracts from the relevance of financial reports. Studies have shown that investors implicitly recognize R&D expenditures as assets rather than expenses. For example, Lev and Sougiannis (1996) found that net annual R&D investment (i.e. R&D expenditure minus the amortisation of the R&D capital) is positively and significantly associated with stock prices, despite the fact that this amount is expensed in the income statement.

Nakamura (1999) explains how investment, profit and savings are understated in corporate and national accounts, particularly since the mid-1970s, because of the accounting treatment of intangible assets. Nakamura (1999) shows that if investment in R&D had been treated similarly to investment in tangible assets, profits (and hence retained earnings) would have been higher and reported business savings would have increased enough to raise US reported gross national savings during the 1990s from 15.9 per cent to 17.1 per cent of GDP. This percentage would be even higher if investment in R&D was extended to include investments in intangibles.

The immediate expensing of practically all intangible investments, while obviously inappropriate given the consistent evidence about the substantial future benefits associated with such investments, is often justified by the conservatism principle (Lev et al., 1999). Conservative accounting procedures, like the immediate write-off of intangibles – goes the argument – counter a company management's general inclination to paint a rosy picture of the firm's performance and potential (to beat analysts' forecasts of earnings, to enhance compensation, etc). A conservative treatment of intangibles, it is further argued, is appropriate given the generally high level of uncertainty associated with such investment.

However, others see immediate expensing as being both biased and inaccurate (Lev, 1999). For example, expensing is only conservative when outlays on intangible investments exceed their revenues – which usually occurs early in a company's life. Later on, as investment in intangibles subsides whilst revenues from intangibles increase, reported profitability is often overstated.

Frequently, even internally generated corporate data is insufficient to support appropriate analysis and evaluation of the firm's intangible investment activities. Thus, both internal and external performance evaluation and monitoring of investment in intangibles are hampered by the absence of adequate accounting information.

In sum, traditional accounting techniques do an unacceptable job when measuring the value of the principle activities of a knowledge-intensive business. According to conventional accounting practices, tangible acquisitions such as computers, land and equipment are treated as company assets. Investment in knowledge-building activities such as training and R&D are, however, still largely treated as costs. This occurs despite such activities being a primary source of organisational wealth in intangibles-based economy.

Consequences of Inadequate Accounting for Intangibles

Interest in accounting for intangibles is based on the assumption that the present non-accounting of intangibles is causing harmful effects. Supporters for the inclusion of human capital and structural capital into the balance sheet argue that such capitals may largely explain the gap between book value and market value, namely intellectual capital. Opponents argue that balance sheet is not designed to be speculative and that determining precise figures/numbers is highly subjective and difficult to measure. The main argument for accountability and accounting regulation is (capital) market failures, e.g. appropriate accounting regulation would reduce the amount of market failures (Gröjer and Johansson, 1999). If intangibles are not reflected in the balance sheet, and intangible investments are fully expensed as they are undertaken, both earnings and the book value of equity are argued to be understated by the conventional accounting model. This makes it practically impossible for investors and company managers to:

- assess the rate of return (productivity) of investment in intangibles, and changes over time in the efficiency of the firm's investment activity;
- evaluate shifts in the characteristics of intangible investments, such as from long-term research to short-term development, or from product development to 'process (cost reducing) R&D'; and
- determine the value of a firm's intangible capital, and the expected lives (benefit duration) of such assets (Blair and Wallman, 2001).

There is considerable evidence that this lack of information about asset and true sources of value in corporations is already an urgent problem for corporate investors and managers (Nakamura, 1999). However, because valuation and disclosure issues related to intangibles are complex and little understood, accounting standard-setters around the world encounter great difficulties in attempting to improve disclosures about intangible assets.

Traditional Accounting for Intangible Assets: Some Recent Developments

The increased importance of intellectual capital to business competitiveness has driven change in the accounting treatment of intangibles. So far there are two broad streams of development. One approach is to improve information about intangibles by making it easier to treat them as assets in financial statements, thereby increasing their visibility in financial accounting and reporting. The International Accounting Standards Committee (IASC) took a step in this direction with the 1998 approval of International Accounting Standard (IAS) 38, a standard on intangibles, including advertising, training, start-up and R&D activities (IASC, 1998). To be recognised as assets, intangibles are required to meet definitions spelled out in the standard, generate a flow of benefits that are likely to accrue to the company, and to be measured reliably.[1] Although this places businesses under the obligation of recognising intangible assets on the balance sheet, it does impose

---

[1] 'Intangible assets as non-monetary assets without physical substance that are held for use in the production or supply of goods or services, for rentals to others, or for administrative purposes: (a) that are identifiable; (b) that are controlled by an enterprise as a result of past events; and (c) from which future economic benefits are expected to flow to the enterprise.' (IASC, IAS 38, 1998).

certain strict conditions on the capitalisation of such assets in order to get greater certainty on their future realisability (IASC, 1998). This fact, to a certain extent, limits its applicability in measuring and valuing a number of intangible assets.

Another approach is to increase the availability of non-financial information about investment in and management of intangibles. This strategy is most evident in Europe, where some countries require companies to report certain information about human resources, for example, and where many companies have voluntarily disclosed non-financial information about everything from training efforts to customer networks and in-process R&D (e.g. Skandia, Ramboll and Ericsson). This second approach is promising, as it does not run afoul of objections by accountants and accounting standards. In contrast to reporting requirements linked to accounting standards, though, the disclosure of non-financial information about intangibles has been far less transparent (Wurzburg, 1999). There is little clarity concerning definitions, measurement and verifiability of information; the consistency over time and the comparability of information across companies is not ensured.

A Short Note on Company Goodwill: The US Developments

Goodwill is often described as the corporate reputation of the acquired party; it might also flagship value, customer relationships, and a range of equally difficult to describe, much less to quantify, business intangibles. Goodwill is often thought of as the value of the company's trade identity (Sullivan, 1998, p.287). An accountant would describe goodwill as the market price of the business as a whole less fair value of other assets acquired (International Federation of Accountants, 1998). An economist would define goodwill as the consequence of a firm's above-normal ability to generate future earnings, or as a set of assets controlled by an acquired company.

Historically, the accounting treatment of goodwill has served as a convenient category in which to allocate intellectual assets. However, goodwill is only valued when a business is sold (acquired) and is therefore not valued for firms that have not been acquired. This does not, of course, imply that such firms do not own any intellectual assets. From July 2001, the US Financial Accounting Standards Board (FASB) no longer allows the accounting consolidation method called 'pooling of interests' as this does not reflect the creation of goodwill on purchase/acquisition (SFAS 141). The FASB was concerned that pooling obscured the true cost of acquisitions. Companies will also have to break down goodwill into its component elements (i.e. intangibles), which will be no more amortised, but subject annually to an impairment test aimed to verify whether the value of these intangibles has decreased (SFAS 142).

Moreover, as aforementioned, conventional accounting only recognises intangibles on a company's balance sheet when that company is acquired by another company. In the accounts the line item 'goodwill' represents the difference between the revalued net assets of a company and what is actually paid. It represents value in the eye of the buyer – not in the company value. The buyer might perceive value in trademarks, brand names and other intangibles not recorded in the books of the company being taken over. Under conventional accounting practices, 'goodwill' is only assigned a value when a company is sold.

Some Further Issues Relating to Traditional Accounting for Intangibles

Some further conceptual challenges, which are posed by intangibles to the traditional accounting, and which are to a large extent derived by the previously illustrated points, can be summarised as follows:

- *Relevance vs. reliability*: the knowledge of the value of company intangibles is certainly relevant owing to the today's business conditions and environment. However, this value is generally less reliable, verifiable and stable than that of a tangible asset: therefore, to switch the pendulum towards relevance of data may produce problems with their reliability.
- *Recognition vs. disclosure*: should the intangibles be recognised as a value within the traditional financial statements, or simply be accounted for in the disclosure section of the annual report ('Management Discussion and Analysis')? In the former case, we clearly face a measurement issue, while in the latter case we lend towards a more qualitative recognition.
- *Internal vs. external reporting*: should the intangibles be reported upon only in the internal accounts and statements of a company (e.g. internal managerial reports) or also in the external, publicly-available reports?
- *Voluntary vs. mandatory*: should the production and diffusion of information relating to intangibles be left voluntary, or somehow be made mandatory through ad hoc regulations (e.g. Denmark regulation in 2001)?
- *Audit and litigation*: who can audit this new information on intangibles and how, and how can companies avoid litigation consequences potentially linked to this type of information?

Some Concluding Remarks

With the transition to a knowledge-based economy, the competitive position of a firm is being increasingly determined by its investment in intangible assets such as human resources, information technology, R&D and advertising. As such investments are largely not tangible, most expenditures on intangibles are not being recognised as investments in either companies' financial accounts or national income and product accounts.

Therefore, it would be highly desirable that companies can provide a reliable and accurate insight into their 'intangible strength' to both investors and managers. Unfortunately, conventional financial statements and internal management reports presently provide insufficient information on the factors that really contribute to a company's success (Lev, 1999). As a consequence, the conventional book value of a company is often far removed from its true value.

Accountants have long argued that there are sound reasons for not treating intangibles as assets on a company's balance sheet (Wurzburg, 1999). Problems of definition and measurement hamper the degree to which data on intangibles is robust and comparable. This complicates valuation on the basis of historic costs, and valuation on the basis of expected future economic benefits is not appropriate for the balance sheet, which is backward-looking. A similar phenomenon occurs when valuing intangibles such as customer or supplier networks, which are difficult to separate from other aspects of the business. Furthermore, human capital cannot be easily treated as a financial asset because – as mentioned above – companies do not own their employees. Finally, tax policies often encourage the immediate expensing of investment in intangibles as a way of reducing tax liability. There is also strong opposition, among accountants, to recognising internally generated intangible assets, particularly research and development costs. Many accountants believe that this would allow management the flexibility to capitalise virtually every expenditure as an asset in an attempt to increase book value and defer expenses. This means that companies will be able to manipulate earnings both in the short term by determining economic feasibility, and in the long term by the judicious use of amortisation and impairment tests.

However, in the knowledge-driven economy – where the key factors are complexity, intangibility and dynamics – managers clearly need new management tools and stakeholders need other measuring methods to form a clear view of a company's true economic potential. Such tools should provide transparency about the quality and value of a company's intangible assets and their potential value in the future. Unfortunately, there are also evident difficulties in quantifying immaterial attributes such as openness to change or even degrees of competence.

The above problems are nowadays widely recognised at international level, and an increasing number of countries, scholars and practitioners are working on developing a viable system of accounting for intangible assets (for more depth, see Zambon, 2003).

2. Intellectual Capital: Definition and Classification

Definitions of Intellectual Capital (IC)

Intellectual capital can be described simply as knowledge that can be converted into profits (Intellectual Capital Management – ICM – Gathering, 1999). There is, however, a multitude of other IC definitions and experts have yet to reach a consensus on a commonly accepted definition. Researchers and other large accounting/consulting firms have played an important role in the search for suitable classification of intangibles. Other definitions of intellectual capital/assets include:

> ... is intellectual material – knowledge, information, intellectual property, experience that can be put to use to create wealth. (Stewart, 1997)

> 'Knowledge that can be converted into value.' (Edvinsson and Sullivan, 1996)

'Intellectual material that has been formalised, captured and leveraged to produce a higher valued asset.' (Klein and Prusak, 1994)

Components of Intellectual Capital

In order to pursue the objective of valuing and measuring IC, it is necessary to understand the different components that make up intellectual capital. Intellectual capital encompasses inventions, ideas, general know-how, design approaches, computer programs, processes and publications. Distinguishing between the different components of IC will help to improve the understanding of what IC is, and will hopefully allow us to apply the concept at a strategic and operational level. Some components of intellectual capital are difficult to measure, and the costs and benefits are difficult to quantify.

Table 8.1 Classification of intellectual capital

Human Capital	Structural Capital	Relational Capital
• Knowledge, competence, skills and experiences of employees; • Training; • Networks.	• Organisational processes; • Databases; • Software; • Manuals; • Trademarks; • Laboratories and market intelligence; • Assembled workforce: relationship between business and employees; training, contracts; • Leadership; • Organisational capacity for saleable innovation; • Organisational learning capacity; • Leaseholds; • Franchises; • Licenses; • Patents; • Mineral rights.	• Customer relationship; • Customer loyalty and satisfaction; • Distribution relationships and agreements; • Relationships with other partners and other stakeholders.

Source: Adaptation from Bontis (1999).

For example, quantifying the value of customer relationships is highly subjective and determining a monetary measure would be very difficult.

One of the most popular models for classifying IC is the Hubert Saint-Onge model (1998), which is largely based on the Sveiby one (1988). The Saint-Onge model, developed in the early 1990s, classifies intellectual capital into 3 parts:

human capital; structural capital; and customer capital. A slight variant of this model, devised by Dr Nick Bontis, Director of the Institute for Intellectual Capital Research, restates customer capital as relational capital to include relationship with suppliers and other strategic partners and stakeholders. Adopting Bontis' classifications (1999), intellectual capital can be divided into the following three broad categories (see above Table 8.1).

Human capital is often recognised as one of the largest and most important intangible assets in an organisation. It is the capital which ultimately provides the goods or services which customers require or the answers to their problems. Human capital includes the collective knowledge, competency, experience, skills and talents of people within an organisation. It also includes the creativity and innovativeness of the organisation. Improving productivity through the provision of employee training is not a new phenomenon, but the financial commitment and scale at which companies are now investing in human capital is growing. The effects of human capital formation are hard to determine, even how difficult they are to measure. Apart from the measurement difficulties, many argue against the inclusion of human capital on the balance sheet because (1) human capital is not owned by the organisation: it is only for rent, and (2) for ethical reasons, placing a price on individuals runs the risk of making employees appear substitutable for other forms of capital. However, in spite of these shortcomings, considerations of human capital provide another approach on training and human resource management policies, ultimately improving the management of an organisation.

Structural capital is often referred to as 'what is left when the employees go home at night' and is considered the 'hard' assets of the firm. It consists of the supporting resources and infrastructure of a firm and includes all of the assets found in the financial statements of a firm, such as cash and equivalents, property, buildings, and equipment. It reflects the collective capabilities of the organisation that enable it to function to meet market requirements. Unlike human capital, structural capital is company property and can be traded, reproduced and shared within the firm.

Relational capital comprises not only customer relations but also the organisation's external relationships with its network of suppliers, as well as its network of strategic partners and stakeholders. The value of such assets is primarily influenced by the firm's reputation. In measuring relational capital, the challenge remains in quantifying the strength and loyalty of customer satisfaction, longevity, and price sensitivity.

3. Valuation of Intellectual Capital

Why Do Companies Want to Measure Intellectual Capital?

Before going into the issues surrounding the measurement and reporting of intellectual capital, we need to examine why firms should want to measure IC. There is a general consensus among managers, investors, financiers and accountants that intangibles are important factors in company performance.

Businesses are discovering that fostering growth in their intellectual capital can improve profits and are attempting to quantify this in their financial statements. Reporting such information has the potential to improve internal management and the efficiency of the allocation of resources by providing more explicit recognition of assets. Other benefits include increased transparency, better information for investors and lenders, and more effective and efficient allocation of investments in the capital market. Firms that are actively measuring and reporting IC obviously see value or benefits in such activities, otherwise they would choose not to engage in such activities. Companies starting to measure their intangible assets cite several reasons for doing so. Reasons for reporting on intellectual capital can be broadly classified into internal and external reasons.

Reasons for IC Internal Reporting

- To align IC resources to strategic vision. To support the implementation of a specific strategy via a general upgrading of the work with the company's human resources (support and maintain a strategy concerning the composition of staff as regards seniority, professional qualifications and age. Through the description of the staff profile, measuring, discussion and adjustment become possible).
- To support or maintain various parties' awareness of the company. In particular, to make the company appear to the employees as a name providing an identity for them.
- To help bridge the present and the past (it stimulates the decentralised development of the need for constant development and attention towards change).
- To assess the effectiveness of a firm's IC utilisation.
- To allocate resources between various business units.
- To extract full value from acquisitions and joint ventures.
- To determine the most effective management incentive structures and, more in general, to relate employees' contribution to IC to profits.
- To reply to the growing demand for effective governance of intangibles, of which social and environmental reporting are already evident.
- To focus on protecting and growing those assets that reflect value ('What gets measured, gets managed').
- To report on current and future income from IC.

Reasons for IC External Reporting

- To reflect the actual worth of the company by giving more useful information to current and potential investors.
- To improve the accurateness of stock prices through providing a more comprehensive picture of a firm's assets. In this sense, external reporting supports a corporate goal of enhancing shareholder value.
- To reduce the uncertainty about a company's growth potential and, this way,

to have a positive effect on the cost of capital.

- To stimulate the pursuing of a set of policies – by means of the knowledge embodied in the employees – aimed at increasing customer satisfaction and loyalty.

- To help young and knowledge-intensive organisations, which generally encounter great difficulty in attracting external financiers, to develop a reliable and accepted way to quantify their intellectual capital to investors and financiers.

The attempt to measure IC has largely been driven by companies that rely heavily on knowledge as a key input to production. Companies that are creating measurement and reporting requirements are choosing to engage in benchmarking activities because they believe that such activities create value for them. To gauge the relative profitability of such investments, firms should be able to measure their IC Firms which develop a deep understanding of the role of knowledge in their business and treat it as an asset, cultivate and exploit it, are gaining significant business benefits as a result.[2]

---

[2] The following examples are companies that have benefited from the reporting of their intellectual capital. A wide variety of different IC measurement tools has been used by such companies:

- PLS Consult, a Danish consulting firm has worked with intellectual capital issues since the early 1980s. PLS Consult credits their considerable growth (in particular, the systematic and future-oriented management of this growth) experienced in the past five years to their use of their IC accounts. At PLS Consult, the IC accounts focus on objective statistical information about the education, age and experience of their human resources (The Danish Trade and Industry Development Council, 1999, p.32).

- Skandia, the first company to release an intellectual capital supplement to its annual financial report, found that its stock price rose by approximately 40%. Leif Edvinsson, its former vice president for intellectual capital, reports that Skandia considers 25 of those percentage points to be a direct response to the IC supplement (Sullivan, 1998, p.301). In addition, Skandia, through the reuse of knowledge and transfer of experiences, have been able to reduce the time involved with the administration aspects of acquisitions by 60-70%.

- ABB Sverige is Sweden's largest industrial company and has an internal and external IC management system. Since introducing the system, ABB has become more productive with an increase in turnover per employee from approximately SEK 65,000 to approx. SEK 150,000. In addition, there has been important lead time reduction. ABB have been using human resource accounting (for external purposes) and their EVITA system (for internal purposes such as developing corporate strategies) to bring the upgrading of employee qualification and responsibilities into focus and improve the co-operation with suppliers and customers.

- At WM Data, Sweden's fastest growing IT company, intellectual capital accounts have been used to identify problems with the composition of the company's staff, such as age structure, seniority, and educational background. Staff turnover ratio is used to assess whether knowledge crucial to the company can be maintained.

The Valuation of Intellectual Capital: Holistic and Analytical Models

The measurement models of intellectual capital can be divided into two large categories. Some models provide a global valuation of it, without identifying its individual components: these models can be labelled as *holistic*. A second type of models provides a visualisation/valuation of each of the elements constituting the IC: these are known as *analytical* models. An examination of the main models amenable to those two macro-categories follows.

Some Holistic Models

This section examines the four major models used to value intellectual capital as a whole (*holistic methods*). The growing interest in benchmarking intellectual capital stock between firms has led to the development of four broad indicators: market-to-book ratios, Tobin's Q, Calculated Intangible Value (CIV), and the Economic Value Added (EVA). It is worth pointing out that these measures of intellectual capital should be interpreted as stock valuations, not flows. Further, this section considers also the use of real options methodology as a way of valuing the anticipated/expected benefits from investments in intellectual capital. This model attempts to utilise the workings of the market to determine a price and value of assets that are expected to yield future economic benefits. Unlike the previously mentioned static models, real options provide a forward looking approach to the valuation of IC.

Market-to-Book Ratios

The value of intellectual capital is frequently – and roughly – expressed as the difference between the market value of the company and its book (equity) value.[3] This divergence is a signal that there is something not accounted for on the balance sheet.[4] Acquisitions show that the price paid for an acquired company is almost invariably higher than its book value, and this difference has been incorporated under conventional accounting practices as goodwill. In today's increasingly fast-paced business environment, where mergers and acquisitions are occurring more frequently, what has increasingly changed is the size of the value of goodwill that has been paid.

The today's common disparity between market value (MV) and book value (BV) is largely based on the intangibles of the business providing the foundation for future growth. The largest disparity occurs in high-tech and knowledge-intensive industries, where investment is heavily weighted in intangible assets such as R&D and brands. Foe example, in June 1997 the market-to-book value for all Dow Jones Industrial companies was 5.3, while for many knowledge-intensive

---

[3] The book value is also known as net asset value.

[4] There are many other explanations for the gap between market value and book value. One claims that it is due to knowledge (e.g. Buckman Laboratories), while another attributes it to the brand (e.g. Coca-Cola) or the ownership of a standard (e.g. Microsoft).

companies (e.g. Microsoft, pharmaceutical companies) the ratio was more than 10. Moreover, it has been pointed out by many commentators that between 1973 and 1993, the median ratio of MV to BV of American public companies doubled; the difference has grown with the boom in high-tech shares and the differences being the biggest for firms that have most rapidly boosted spending on R&D.[5]

It is important to point out that, despite the explosion of the financial bubble in the years around 2000, the market-to-book ratios remained on average constantly above 1-1.5 for the vast majority of companies listed on the most advanced markets.

From an internal perspective, differences between MV and BV are due primarily to assets that are not currently included in the conventional balance sheet total, such as knowledge, relationships, and image. From an external perspective the gap between MV and BV is due primarily to the company's future opportunities and these are currently not valued in the conventional balance sheet. These results suggest that there are important hidden values in such companies, which are not visible in traditional accounting. Yet increasingly larger investments are being made in precisely these hidden assets. Such investments concern customer relations, information technology, networks and competence.

Market-to-book ratios as measure of intangibles raise both theoretical and practical problems. First, the stock market is volatile and responds, often strongly, to factors entirely outside the control of management. Stock market price data are a highly volatile series, which can often be dominated by irregular, seasonal and cyclical factors. Furthermore, market-to-book values ignore exogenous factors that can influence MV, such as deregulation, supply conditions, general market nervousness, as well as the various other types of information that determine investors' perceptions of the income-generating potential of the firm, such as industrial policies in foreign markets, media and political influences. Companies with large intangible values tend to have share prices that fluctuate more than other companies. In a publicly traded company, the greater the ratio of intangible to book value, the more uncertain the investment,[6] as witnessed by recent falls in

---

[5] Research undertaken by Margaret Blair (2000), a Brookings Institute economist, has demonstrated that the value of hard assets represented 62 per cent of the companies market value in 1982. In 1992, this figure had dropped to 38 per cent. In 1995, health care and personal care companies had the highest market-to-book value in the world with almost 75 per cent of MV attributable to intangible assets. Recent estimates suggest that 50-90 per cent of the value created by a firm comes not from management of traditional physical assets, but from the management of IC (International Federation of Accountants, 1998, p.4). In May 1997, for example, the market-to-book ratio for General Motors was 1.6 compared with 13.4 for Microsoft. Moreover, at the time, only about 7 per cent of Microsoft's stock market value was accounted for by traditional tangible assets (land, buildings, machinery and equipment) recorded on it's balance sheet. Intangible assets (e.g. brands, R&D and people) were seen as constituting the remaining 93 per cent of the company's assets.

[6] In addition, organisations that are not traded in public markets do not have a market value that is easily determined. Presumably, this organisations still have IC which has value to the organisation.

technology stocks.

Second, there is evidence that both MV and BV are usually understated. To encourage companies to invest in new equipment, US Internal Revenue Services rules deliberately permit companies to depreciate assets faster than the rate at which they actually wear out. Calculations of IC that use the difference between market and book values can also suffer from inaccuracy because book values can be impacted if firms choose, or are required, to adopt tax depreciation rates for accounting purposes (International Federation of Accountants, 1998, p.17). Other changes to US accounting standards also impact on the book value of the companies of that country, such as the FASB Standard no. 115 (1993) which affects reported book value. Under Standard 115, returns on equity for a given company will fluctuate inversely with the book value and will be unusually high when the book value is depressed because of high interest rates.

Third, adopting the market-to-book approach for valuing intangibles suffers from timing inconsistencies because market value is determined and revised constantly whereas book value is only updated periodically.

The reliability and usefulness of the difference between MV and BV can be enhanced by looking at the ratio between the two, rather than at the raw number. One can then compare a company with similar competitors – or benchmarked against the industry average – and also make year-to-year comparisons of the ratios. While the market-to-book method of valuing IC is subject to several problems, it has served to draw attention to the undeniable existence of IC, and for that reason alone has been a constructive innovation.

Tobin's Q

Traditionally, Tobin's Q (1969) was used as a method for predicting investment behaviour.[7] Tobin's Q compares the market value of a company with the replacement cost of its assets. It uses the ratio (the 'Q') to predict the investment decisions of the firm, independent from macro-economic conditions such as interest rates. The replacement cost of fixed assets can be calculated as the reported value of a company's fixed assets plus the accumulated depreciation and adjusted for inflation.

As with market-to-book ratios, Tobin's Q is most revealing when similar companies are compared over a period of several years (Stewart, 1997, p.226). Both Tobin's Q and the market-to-book ratio are best suited to making comparisons of the value of intangible assets of firms within the same industry, serving the same markets, that have similar types of hard assets. These ratios are useful for comparing the changes in the value of IC over a number of years. When both the Q and the market-to-book ratio of a company are falling over time, it is a good indicator that the intangible assets of the firm are depreciating. This may provide a signal to investors that a particular company is not managing its intangible assets effectively and may cause them to adjust their investment portfolios towards companies with climbing, or stable Q's. An advantage of

---

[7] The Nobel laureate James Tobin proposed the idea of 'Q' in 1969.

Tobin's Q over the market-to-book ratios, is that the Tobin's Q approach neutralises the effects of different depreciation policies.

Technology and human capital assets are typically associated with high 'Q' values (International Federation of Accountants, 1998, p.18). An Australian study by the Department of Industry Science and Resources, using Tobin's Q as an indicator of company valuation, found that the market does value more highly those firms which invest in R&D and patents. Indeed, there is a relationship at work between these intangible assets, such that R&D is valued more highly if it is effective in leading to patent applications.[8]

Tobin's Q can be a useful measure of intellectual capital because it can reflect the value markets place on assets which are not typically reported in conventional balance sheets. By making intra-industry comparisons between a firm's primary competitors, these indicators can act as performance benchmarks that can be used to improve the internal management or corporate strategy of the firm (International Federation of Accountants, 1998). The information provided by these ratios facilitates internal benchmarking, enabling the organisation to track its progress in the area that it has defined as being integral to its success.

Calculated Intangible Value (CIV)

Developed by NCI Research in the late 1990s, Calculated Intangible Value should allow us to place a monetary value on intangible assets. This method permits to calculate the fair value of an intangible asset. CIV computes the value of intangible assets by comparing the firm's performance with an average competitor that has similar tangible assets. An advantage of the CIV approach is that it allows firm-to-firm comparisons using audited financial data and, as such, CIV can be used as a useful tool for benchmarking.

Determining the CIV:

1. Calculate average pre-tax earnings.
2. Calculate average year-end tangible assets (from balance sheet).
3. Return on assets (ROA) = Average pre-tax earnings / Average year-end tangible assets.
4. Benchmark/compare the ROA against the industry's average ROA. If a company's ROA> Industry ROA proceed to step 5.
5. Excess return = Pre-tax earnings - [industry - average ROA * company's average tangible assets].
6. (1-t) * excess return = premium attributable to IA (where t = average income tax rate and IA= intangible assets).
7. $NPV_{premium}$ = premium / company's cost of capital = CIV.
    Where NPV stands for Net Present Value.

---

[8] Markets value investment in these intangible assets five times greater than investment in physical assets. This is consistent with US studies, which find that R&D spending is capitalised into a firm's market value at a rate between 2.5 and 8 (with most estimates centred between 5 and 6).

However, CIV also has several limitations. First, the CIV uses average industry ROA as a basis for determining excess returns. By nature, average values suffer from outlier problems and could result in excessively high or low ROA. Secondly, the NPV of intangible assets will depend on the company's cost of capital. However, for comparability within and between industries, the industry average cost of capital should be used as a proxy for the discount rate in the NPV calculation. Again the problem of averages emerges and one must be careful in calculating an average that has been adjusted for outliers (International Federation of Accountants, 1998, p.19).

Economic Value Added (EVA^{TM})

EVA^{TM} is a measure developed in the 1980s by New York consultancy firm Stern Stewart & Co as an indicator of returns to shareholders.[9] EVA is common in many large US companies, including AT&T and Coca-Cola, though less used elsewhere. EVA strips out many of the anomalies of the accounting system, and represents the difference between profit and the cost of capital. It provides a measure directly linked to return on capital employed. In simple terms:

EVA = net operating profit after taxes – (capital x the cost of capital)

Put most simply, EVA is the net operating profit minus an appropriate charge for the opportunity cost of all capital invested in an enterprise. As such, EVA is an estimate of the amount by which earnings exceed or fall short of the required minimum rate of return that shareholders and lenders could get by investing in other securities of comparable risk. By taking all capital costs into account, including the cost of equity, EVA shows the monetary amount of wealth a business has created or destroyed in each reporting period. The related measure MVA (Market Value Added) compares total market value (less debts) with the money invested in the firm, represented by share issues, borrowings and retained earnings.

According to Stern Stewart, when used as a management tool, EVA shifts managers' focus to balance sheet rather than on income statement:

> By assessing a charge for using capital, EVA makes managers care about managing assets as well as incomes, and for properly assessing the trade-offs between them. All key management decisions and actions are thus tied to just one measure, EVA.[10]

According to Stern Stewart, conventional financial balance sheets often need restating to give an accurate picture of the capital employed in the business, and frequently this involves adding in intangibles. They have identified over 160 possible balance sheet adjustments, of which an obvious one is to write back

---

[9] See http://www.sternstewart.com.
[10] *Ibid.*

goodwill that has been written off. Other adjustments may include adding back R&D costs, and appropriate parts of marketing expenditure as well. If this was not done the EVA would show a short-term reduction even though the investment may ultimately increase the MVA.

Despite its popularity, measures like EVA have numerous critics. First, among analysts there is a feeling that EVA relies too much on accounting profits and adjustments, whereas cash flows might be a more reliable indicator. Analysts are beginning to recognise that EVA should be complemented with measures that create stronger linkages between long-range plans, financial and stock price goals. Critics also argue that EVA is still a too historic measure and does not provide any sense of the linkages between a company's investments in intangibles and its financial performance (Leadbeater, 1999). Furthermore, EVA has also been criticised for its inability to explain why firms can be successful one year and a complete failure the next.

> EVA and the like is all well and good, but there is absolutely no evidence whatsoever that it is a guide to whether companies can sustain good performance. What we are looking for are the measures which really create shareholder value over the long term (Phillips, 1997).

Real Options-Based Approach

Another market approach to the valuation of intangibles is now gaining currency. Over the past twenty years, there has been a growing body of academic research that has taken the theory and methodology of financial options and applied it to the valuation of intangible assets. This is known as 'real option theory', an extension of 'financial option theory'.[11] An option is the right, but not the obligation to buy (or sell) an underlying asset at some fixed price for a predetermined period of time. A real option is an option that is based on non-financial assets. It applies the same techniques and variables as the well-known Black and Scholes (1972) model on which financial options are based, but uses non-financial inputs. Real options can be applied by using non-numeric strategy options to determine the value to proceed, defer, expand or abandon investment. By drawing on financial markets' techniques, benchmarks, and information, businesses can discipline their investment decisions and align them with the investment decisions of the market. They can potentially close the gap between strategy and shareholder value (Amram and Kulatilaka, 1999, p.96).

Reporting intellectual capital is often criticised by accounting professionals for the high uncertainty associated with the returns on intangible assets. Intellectual capital by its very nature derives its value from the opportunities it creates. Unlike the previous measures of IC – market-to-book value, Tobin's Q, CIV, and EVA – real options (option pricing models) provides an approach which values the

---

[11] The item 'real option' was coined in 1977 by Stewart C. Myers of Massachusetts Institute of Technology. Its earliest applications were in oil, gas, copper, and gold, and companies in such commodity businesses remain some of the biggest users.

opportunities arising from IC.[12] Deciding how much to spend on R&D, or the kind of R&D in which to invest, translates to the valuation of opportunities. Companies with new technologies, product, development ideas, defensible positions in fast-growing markets, or access to potential new markets own valuable opportunities. For some companies, opportunities are the most valuable things they own (Luehrman, 1997) and the question is how do we map the opportunity to reality (Partanen, 1998, p.50). The analysis of real options is more than simply a valuation tool. It is also a formal strategic tool, offering a proactive rather than just reactive flexibility.[13]

However, it is fair to say that the real options approach is in its infancy. There are real limits to how far it can go. Historically, R&D and other forms of knowledge capital are difficult to value because knowledge is not actively traded. According to an OECD study by Charles Leadbeater (1999), a market for knowledge capital is developing at least in the United States.[14] The emergence of markets where R&D and other intangibles are traded should be closely watched since prices established as reliable in these markets could provide guidelines for changes in accounting procedures. Natural resources companies have been the early keen experimenters in the use of real options, largely as a result of their ability to link the future value of their assets to traded commodities, for which

---

[12] Rapid change has also exposed the weaknesses of these less flexible valuation tools.

[13] A project's full value is the value of all the options it creates, not just the value when it is successful. Spending money to exploit business opportunities is analogous to exercising an option on, for example, a share of stock. The amount of money expended corresponds to the option's exercise price. The length of time the company can defer the investment decision without losing the opportunity corresponds to the option's time to expiration (Luehrman, 1998, p.52). The possibility of deferral gives rise to two additional sources of value. First, *ceteris paribus* we would always prefer to pay later than sooner, because we can earn the time value of money on the deferred expenditure. Second, while we are waiting, the world can change. The more uncertain and volatile the pay-offs from the project, the more it makes sense for a company to hold an option. Hypothetical examples of the most common types of real options: timing options; growth options; staging options; exit options; flexibility options; operating options; learning options.
Traditional net present value (NPV) analysis misses the extra value associated with deferral, because it assumes the decision cannot be delayed. In contrast, option pricing presumes the ability to defer and provides a way to quantify the value of deferring. However, we must note that value may be lost as well as gained by deferring, and the proper decision depends on which effect dominates. Any time there are predictable costs to deferring, the option to defer an investment is less valuable, and we would be foolish to ignore those costs (Luehrman, 1998, p.53).
Option valuation tools and models are constantly being improved, and additional types of risk are constantly being securitised. Many risks that once had to be considered private risks have turned into market-priced risks. For example, the establishment of a trading market for sulphur dioxide emissions has enabled manufacture and energy companies to think systematically about the most economic way to reduce pollution (Amram and Kulatilaka, 1999, p.104).

[14] Internet growth has produced new online marketplaces which bring together potential buyers and sellers of patents, licences and intellectual property on a global scale.

market information is readily available. It is now gaining appeal to a wider corporate audience.

Advocates of the real options approach believe that it provides greater substance to management intuition. Real options analysis is a big step beyond static valuation measures such as price-earnings and market-to-book-ratios. Because the options approach handles simple contingencies better than standard Discounted-Cash-Flow (DCF) models, option-pricing theory has been regarded as a promising approach to valuing business opportunities since the mid-1970s. However, a combination of factors – large, active competitors, uncertainties that do not fit neat probability distributions, and the sheer number of relevant variables – makes it impractical to analyse real options formally. As a result, option pricing has not yet been widely used as a tool for valuing opportunities (Luehrman, 1997). According to McKinsey, option pricing has not been much used in the evaluation of corporate investments for three reasons: the idea is relatively new, the mathematics are complex, making the results hard to grasp intuitively, and the original techniques required the source of uncertainty to be a traded world commodity such as oil, natural gas, or gold (Copeland and Keenan, 1998, pp.38-39).

Although this new measure may also seem attractive for valuing intangibles and intellectual capital, there are significant drawbacks. Determining the value of real options remains an inexact science. Substantial difficulties remain in valuing non-financial assets accurately at a firm level. Unfortunately, most business opportunities are unique, so the likelihood of finding a similar option is low. The only reliable way to find a similar option is to construct one. Furthermore, real options is often too complex to be worthwhile for minor decisions. The use of real options presents two other fundamental problems: first, quantifying real option value; and, second, persuading an organisation to change the way they traditionally think about valuation and investment. There are a number of other limitations such as model risk, imperfect proxies, lack of observable prices, lack of liquidity and private risk.

Some Concluding Remarks About Holistic Methods

Intellectual capital measurement can be approached from several viewpoints: internal versus external; qualitative versus quantitative; and monetary-based versus non-monetary-based. The valuation techniques discussed in this section are aggregate measures that attempt to assign a value to a firm's stock of intellectual capital. These economic valuations measure the extent to which intangible assets comprise a firm's total value. For purposes of comparability between firms, the models outlined in this section would be more useful.

In the following section, the intellectual capital models considered have more of an internal-analytical measurement focus – such as budgeting, patent counts and staff turnover/levels – than those discussed in this section. Such micro-level measures of IC are largely designed to support management's decision making process and for reporting purposes. Given the difficulties associated with determining precise values for IC, most of the metrics considered in this section do not attempt to put a monetary figure on the value of intangibles, but instead measure processes or results that are dependent on it. Focusing on such aspects of IC, much of the metrics considered are of a non-financial nature.

Some Analytical Measures and Models for Representing IC

A growing number of analytical measurement systems are appearing, and one of the challenges for their users is to determine their relative merits, scope and suitability. In this section four popular analytical approaches to intellectual capital measurement will be briefly discussed. These four models are presented below.

Human Resource Accounting

Human Resource Accounting (HRA) is a set of accounting methods that seek to settle and describe the management of a company's staff. It focuses on the employees' education, competence and remuneration. HRA promotes the description of investments in staff, thus enabling the design of human resource management systems to follow and evaluate the consequences of various HR management principles (The Danish Trade and Industry Development Council, 1999). There are four basic human resource accounting models (The Danish Trade and Industry Development Council, 1999).

- *The anticipated financial value of the individual to the company.* This value is dependent on two factors: the person's productivity, and his/her satisfaction with being in the company.
- *The financial value of groups,* describing the connection between motivation and organisation on one hand, and financial results on the other. This model does not measure value, but concepts such as motivation and welfare. Under this model, measurements of employee satisfaction are represented with great importance.
- *Staff replacement costs,* describing the financial situation in connection with recruitment, re-education and redeployment of employees. This model focuses on replacement costs related to the expenses connected with staff acquisition, training and separation. The acquisition covers expenses for recruitment, advertising etc. Training covers education, on-the-job training, etc. Separation covers lost production, etc., when a person leaves a job. This model can be used to describe the development of costs in connection with replacements. In many firms, such replacement costs are included in accounts as an expression of staff value to the company.
- *Human resource accounting (HRA)* as complete accounts for the human resource area. This model concentrates on cost control, capitalisation and depreciation of the historic expenses for human resources. One effect of such a system is the visualisation of the impacts of human resource management, through revealing the consequences of inexpedient human resource management routines.

The basic aims of HRA are several. First, it improves the management of human resources from an organisational perspective, through increasing the transparency of human resource costs, investments and outcomes in traditional financial statements. Second, HRA attempts to improve the bases for investors' company-valuation. Unfortunately, for several reasons, the accuracy of HRA is often called into suspicion (Ernst & Young Centre for Business Innovation, 1997). This doubt stems from difficulties with several major human resource evaluation methods:

- *Input measurement.* Inputs (such as training) are not necessarily effective, so cost is not always a good proxy measure of output value. Trained personnel may also move to another employer through higher labour mobility, thus inhibiting the returns from corporate training investment.
- *Output measurement.* Virtually no firm actively measures the output benefits from training.
- *Replacement values.* Such values are rare, usually calculated to help product sales or the sale of the company, and are often highly debatable.

Intangible Asset Monitor

The Intangible Assets Monitor (IAM) was developed by Karl-Erik Sveiby[15] as a management tool for organisations that wish to track and value their intangible assets. Sveiby was one of the first to develop a method for measuring intangible assets in the late 1980s, in an attempt to demonstrate how the intangible assets account for the difference between a company's market value and book value. The 'Konrad Group', to which Sveiby belonged, introduced the 'family of three' concept of intellectual capital, that is the division of IC into external structures, or customer capital, internal structures, or organisational capital, and individual competence, or human capital.[16] This concept has become the basis for many IC measurement systems, including Sveiby's Intangible Asset Monitor.

The IAM is based on the fundamental premise of people being an organisation's only profit generators. According to Sveiby, people are the only true agents in business; all assets and structures, whether tangible physical products or intangible relations, are the result of human action and depend ultimately on people for their continued existence.[17] Therefore, according to the IAM, human actions are converted into both tangible and intangible knowledge 'structures'. Such structures are either directed outwards (external structures) or inwards (internal structures). These structures are assets, because they affect the organisation's revenue streams. According to the IAM, the profits generated from people's actions are signs of that success, but not the originators of it.

---

[15] See Karl-Erik Sveiby (www.sveiby.com.au).
[16] The Konrad Group ('Konradgruppen') consisted of members from several Swedish knowledge companies. See Sveiby *et al.*, 1989.
[17] See http://203.147.220.66/InvisibleBalance.html.

Table 8.2 Celemi intangible asset and monitor

Intangible Assets					
Our Customers (External Growth/ Renewal)	199	**Our Organization (Internal Growth/ Renewal)**	199	**Our People (Competence) Growth/Renewal**	199
Revenue growth	22%	Organization-enhancing customers	49%	Average professional competence	8
Image-enhancing customers	70%	Revenues from new products	71%	Competence-enhancing customers	65%
		Intangible investments % value added	27%	Growth in professional competence	47%
				Experts with post-secondary degree	68%
Efficiency		**Efficiency**		**Efficiency**	
Revenues per customer	269	Proportion of administrative staff	21%	Value added per expert	753
		Revenues per administrative staff	8,5	Value added per employee	620
Stability		**Stability**		**Stability**	
Repeat orders	54%	Administrative staff turnover	0%	Expert turnover	6%
Five largest customers	40%	Administrative staff seniority	2	Expert seniority	3
		Rookie ratio	55%	Median age all employees	35

Source: Celemi Annual Report, 1997.

The IAM is a stock/flow theory. It assumes that some of the organisation's assets are intangible assets and the purpose of the IAM is to guide managers in how they utilise the intangible assets, identify the flows that are increasing and renewing them and guard against the risk of losing them.[18] According to the IAM the intangible part of a company's balance sheet can be said to consist of three parts: individual competence, internal structure and external structure.

---

[18] *Ibid.*

- *Individual competence*. This is one's ability to act in various situations. It includes skills (including social skills), education, experience, and values. According to Sveiby, a key determinant of an organisation's success is the competence of its staff. This competence is directed in two ways, externally and internally.
- *Internal structure*. These assets are organisational in nature, in fact they include patents, processes, systems, concepts, and computer and administrative systems. Such structures are generally created by the employees and are thus generally 'owned' by the organisation, and adhered to. A key feature of such structures, is that they largely remain intact even if people leave the organisation.
- *External structure*. This consists of relationships with customers and suppliers, brand names, trademarks and organisational reputation or 'image'.

For a concrete application of the IAM to a Swedish consultancy company called Celemi see the above Table 8.2.

The Skandia Navigator

The world's first annual intellectual capital report was prepared by the Swedish financial services firm, Skandia. Skandia's 1994 IC report, *Visualising Intellectual Capital*, represented a coherent first attempt to report the value of intellectual capital in an organisation. The Skandia 'Navigator' is perhaps the best known business model developed to identify the intangible assets that are key to company performance. A feature of the Skandia Navigator is its definition of the intellectual capital as not just the skills and expertise of its workforce, but also the systems and processes that it has put in place to capture and exploit all the knowledge it can. The Navigator is based upon the same broad conceptual framework as the IAM (see Figure 8.1).

The Navigator is designed to provide a balanced picture of the financial and intellectual capital. Consequently, it incorporates measures in categories similar to those of the balanced scorecard (cf. next section). The focus on financial results, capital and monetary flows is complemented by a description of intellectual capital and its development. The Navigator framework, as expected, has at its top end a series of measures relating to the *financial focus*. But it also has 'below the line' measures of intellectual capital. These involve four areas and two dimensions. The four areas are:

- *customer focus*, which quantifies how the organisation is to look to its customer;

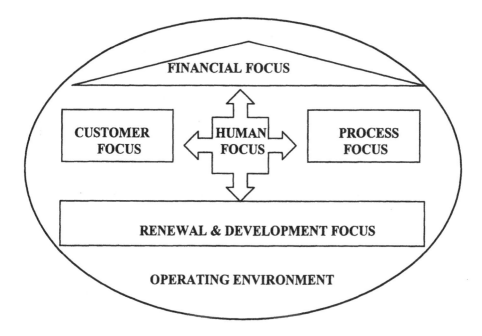

Figure 8.1 – *Skandia Business Navigator*[19]

- *process focus*, which quantifies key aspects of the organisation's process performance;
- *renewal and development focus*, which quantifies what is being done to renewal and develop the intellectual asset base; and
- *human focus*, the 'virtual' binding force of customer, process, renewal and development and finance.

The Navigator incorporates a total of about 30 key indicators in the various areas, which are monitored internally on a yearly basis.[20] Almost more importantly, the Navigator includes two dimensions. The measures in each focus are specified in terms of today's performance and tomorrow's performance; this is a clear view of articulating 'targets' for the Navigator.

---

[19] Source: Intellectual Capital Report, Skandia 1998.

[20] The key indicators for customer focus include the number of accounts, the number of brokers and the number of lost customers. The key indicators for process focus include the number of accounts per employee and administrative costs per employee. The key indicators for human focus include the personnel turnover, the proportion of managers, the proportion of female managers and the training and/or education costs per employee. The key indicators for development/renewal focus include the satisfied employee index, the marketing expense/customer and the share of training hours.

The Skandia Navigator is used to identify the important areas of know-how in the organisation which need to be developed and shared. Each of Skandia's strategic business units have used the Navigator framework to develop their own specific measures of intellectual capital. By identifying important assets like its customer and innovation capital more systematically, Skandia says the Navigator has improved its management of these assets, benefited overall performance and increased its share value.[21] Skandia says that its ability to identify and draw upon the relevant know-how easily has enabled it to set up foreign offices much more quickly than in the past. The Skandia Navigator model has been applied by the Swedish Government and also developed by other companies.

The Skandia Navigator and Intangible Assets Monitor are two popular methods for calculating and visualising the value of the intangible capital. Despite this widespread popularity, both approaches are not without their critics. Both approaches share the presupposition that IC represents the difference between market and book value of a company. Some authors, however, have expressed concerns that two other important aspects of evaluation and value creation remain unresolved by the Navigator and IAM (Pulic, 2000).

1. Market-based IC value cannot be calculated for companies which are not listed on the stock market, so that these companies need an alternative way to determine their market based IC value.
2. There is no adequate system monitoring the efficiency of current business activities performed by the employees, indicating whether their potential is directed towards value creation or value destruction.

Another criticism of these two models revolves around how they define intellectual capital. Both models define IC as being divided into essentially three parts: human, customer and structural capital. The problem arising from this approach, critics argue, is how to measure IC performance defined as such. For the analysis of human, customer and structural capital many indicators have been developed, but most of them are subjective. Many critics argue that one common objective indicator is needed, so as to facilitate comparisons between companies (Pulic, 1998).

The Balanced Scorecard

The Balanced Scorecard (BSC) is an organisational framework for implementing and managing a strategy at all levels of an enterprise by linking objectives, initiatives and measures to an organisation's vision and strategy (Kaplan and Norton, 1992). The BSC translates a business's vision and strategy into objectives and measures across four balanced perspectives: financial performance, customers, internal business processes, and organisational growth, learning and innovation. Put simply, a BSC is a structured way of communicating measurements and targets, and is becoming a widespread way of managing, measuring and

---

[21] See http://www.skandia-afs.com/purpose/intellectual/pdf/intell/intell1.pdf.

communicating the financial, non-financial and intangible assets of a company. The BSC allows an organisation to monitor both its current performance (financial, customer satisfaction and business process) and its efforts to improve processes, motivate and educate employees and enhance its ability to learn and improve. The BSC is closely related to the concept of intellectual capital and comprises not only tools for the measurement of intangible resources but also a vision of continuous learning and change as to create value for the future (Johansson *et al.*, 1999). Since being introduced in 1992, the balanced scorecard concept has been implemented at the corporate, strategic business unit and even individual level in hundreds of public and private sector organisations worldwide.[22]

Despite its widespread use, the balanced scorecard concept does suffer from several shortcomings (Leadbeater, 1999).[23] First, the creation of a BSC can involve a considerable amount of time on the part of everyone whose performance is to be measured. The selection of appropriate measures for the four perspectives can be especially time consuming. This is due to that fact that in any company there is a large number of potential goals and targets, and even more ways to measure them. People are likely to disagree about which objectives should be measured and how to measure those objectives, and it will take time until consensus is achieved. Second, a well-designed scoreboard will be useless without the participation and commitment of staff in implementing and using it. Third, companies using BSC often come up with too many measures. For example, a division of one company came up with 500 important measures for its scorecard on the first pass. This is a problem because it is very difficult to accurately track a large number of measures. Fourth, the BSC does not have an explicit focus on intellectual capital – unlike some later IC measurement models. Finally, the fact that a BSC gathers all key indicators of business performance (and their linkages) into one management tool may deprive a company's executives of the various information flows required to remain competitive in today's challenging business environment.

4. Conclusions

The issues linked to the intangibles and their role vis-à-vis accounting, audit and financial analysis are complex and very broad. Much of the extant literature has focused on these issues, so that one could say that this is at the same time one of the largest but also one of the most investigated fields in the new intangibles literature.

There are several substantial difficulties associated with the valuation of intangibles; in fact, values are subject to frequent changes and many intangible assets are produced internally, rather than acquired in an arm's length transaction. In addition, the value of an intangible asset often depends on the value of other related intangible and/or tangible assets. According to Mavrinac and Siesfeld (1998), empirical results collected using revealed preference analysis suggest that

---

[22] See: www.abctech.com.

[23] See: www.isds.bus.lsu.edu.

non-financial measures of quality and strategic achievement have a profound effect on investment and valuation.

One particular problem is represented by the economic issue of how to price intangible assets in the absence of proper functioning markets. From an economic standpoint, the challenge is to create an internal market for IC, where buyers and sellers can exchange intangible assets at fair market prices (Klein, 1998, p.6).[24] In practice, however, markets for knowledge and information depend critically on reputation, on repeated interactions and on trust. Through the internet, a variety of companies such as 'yet2.com', 'pl-x.com', 'Patentauction.com, and 'Inventions for Sale' have been providing a forum/marketplace for the trading of technology, patents, licences, and intellectual property.

More strictly on the reporting aspects, despite a rapid and spreading success – at least in some countries – of the above described new forms of company statements and valuations (both at the internal and external level), it is also clear that there are some issues and problems which are linked with those forms. These issues and problems can be summarised as follows:

- *attribution of a value in absence of a market price*: this can be seen as the re-emergence of the old problem of value in use vs. value in exchange, bringing about problems of credibility and meaningfulness vis-à-vis these new reports;
- *interpretability of these reports*: it is not clear how the new metrics should be interpreted in the light of the many qualitative variables used;
- *specificity vs. generalisability*: very often these new forms of reporting are based on indicators, parameters, and measures that are specific to the reporting organisation. This of course causes problems of consistency, comprehensiveness, and comparability of data (at least between companies);
- *regulation vs. voluntary compliance*: shall the new forms of reporting be left only to a voluntary decision of the company management, or should some forms of (soft) regulatory framework be imposed on companies in this subject area?
- *atomistic vs. holistic measurement approach*: when comparing the methods proposed in section 3 and the EVA and the remaining ones presented in section 4, it is easy to detect that there are two rather different approaches to the measurement and representation of intellectual capital: one is more holistic and it looks at the comprehensive value of this capital, while the other is far more analytical leading to an 'atomistic' representation/quantification of the various components of the intellectual capital;
- *common measurement unit vs. different measurement unit*: in the new forms of reporting there seems to be a lack of a common measurement unit (like it is money in the traditional financial statements), and this reinforces the above mentioned interpretability problem due to the lack of a synthesis;

---

[24] It has been estimated that the non-commercialised technology lying dormant in US companies is worth more than $179 billion (Walker, 1999).

- *relevance vs. reliability*: this aspect has also been mentioned before with regard to the traditional accounting and its problems vis-à-vis intangibles. Also with the 'new accounting' the relevahce of the data can be in conflict with their reliability, in that the intangibles phenomena represented by this data are difficult to measure with a sound degree of reliability;
- *intended users*: who are the intended users of these new reports: e.g. management, shareholders or stakeholders, or a combination of these categories?

The current lack of visibility of investments in intellectual capital have several consequences. If IC or human capital is not regularly accounted for, the result risks generating an under-investment in the companies. If we can develop a better way to account for such investments, we will achieve a more efficient allocation of resources and benefits will accrue to the economy. The measurement and accounting systems we use today actually depress intangible investments. In other words, the poorer the information that investors have about the companies they invest in, the greater the information asymmetry, the less efficiently the capital markets can allocate capital and the higher the cost of capital. As a result of the complexity and involvement of many fields of study/research in the valuation of intangibles and intellectual capital, a multi-disciplinary and multi-institutional approach which engages economists, accountants, regulators, investors and intellectual property specialists needs to be undertaken.

References

Amram, M. and Kulatilaka, N. (1999), *Real Options: Managing Strategic Investment in an Uncertain World*, Harvard Business School Press.

Black, F. and Scholes, M. (1972), 'The Valuation of Option Contracts and a Test of Market Efficiency', *Journal of Finance*, Vol. 27, No. 2, pp.399-417.

Blair, M. (2000), 'New Ways Needed to Assess New Economy', 13 November, *Economic Studies*, The Brookings Institution, Washington D.C.

Blair, M. and Wallman, S. (2001), *Unseen Wealth*, The Brookings Institute, Washington D.C. (www.brookings.edu).

Bontis, N. (1999), 'Managing Organizational Knowledge by Diagnosing Intellectual Capital: Framing and Advancing the State of the Field', *International Journal of Technology Management*, Vol. 18, Nos. 5/6/7/8, pp.433-462.

Copeland, T.E. and Keenan, P.T. (1998), 'How much is flexibility worth?', *McKinsey Quarterly*, No. 2, pp.38-49.

Danish Trade and Industry Development Council (1999), *Intellectual Capital Accounts: Reporting and Managing Intellectual Capital*, available at www.oecd.org/dataoecd/16/50/1948022.pdf

Edvinsson, L. and Sullivan, P. (1996), 'Developing a Model for Managing Intellectual Capital', *European Management Journal*, Vol. 14, No. 4, pp.356-364.

Ernst & Young Centre for Business Innovation (1997), *Measures that Matter*, available at www.businessinnovation.ey.com.

Financial Accounting Standards Board (FASB) (1993), *Accounting for Certain Investments in Debt and Equity Securities*, SFAS no. 115, May.

Financial Accounting Standards Board (FASB) (2001), *Business Combinations*, SFAS no. 141, June.

Financial Accounting Standards Board (FASB) (2001), *Goodwill and Other Intangible Assets*, SFAS no. 142, June.

Gröjer, J.-E. and Johansson, U. (1999), Voluntary guidelines on the disclosure of intangibles: A bridge over troubled water?, working paper presented at the Workshop 'Manage and Account for Intangibles', 15-16 February, 1999, Brussels.

Intellectual Capital Management Gathering (1999), *Introduction to Intellectual Capital*, available at http://www.icmginc.com/gp.asp?pId=4.

International Accounting Standards Committee (IASC) (1998), *IAS 38 – Intangible Assets*, London, IASC (available at http://www.iasc.org.uk/frame/cen2_138.htm)

International Federation of Accountants (IFAC) (1998), *The Measurement and Management of Intellectual Capital: An Introduction*, International Management Accounting Study No. 7, October, IFAC, New York.

Johansson, U., Eklöv, G., Holmgren, M. and Mårtensson, M. (1999), *Human Resource Costing and Accounting Versus the Balanced Scorecard. A Literature Survey of Experience with the Concepts*, OECD Report, Paris.

Kaplan, R.S. and Norton, D.P. (1992), 'The balanced scorecard - Measures that drive performance', *Harvard Business Review*, January-February, pp.71-79.

Klein and Prusak (1994), *Characterizing Intellectual Capital*, Ernst & Young Center for Business Innovation.

Klein, D.A. (1998), *The Strategic Management of IC*, Boston, Butterworth-Heinemann.

Leadbeater, C. (1999), *Living on Thin Air*, Viking: Penguin Books, London.

Lev, B. (1999), 'R&D and Capital Markets', *Journal of Applied Corporate Finance*, Vol. 11, No. 4, Winter, pp.21-35.

Lev, B., Sarath, B. and Sougiannis, T. (1999), 'Reporting Biases Caused by R&D Expensing and Their Consequences', unpublished paper, New York University.

Lev, B. and Sougiannis, T. (1996), 'The Capitalization, Amortization and Value-Relevance of R&D', *Journal of Accounting and Economics*, February, pp.107-138.

Luehrman, T.A. (1997), 'What's It Worth?: A General Manager's Guide to Valuation', *Harvard Business Review*, May-June, pp.132-142.

Mavrinac, S. and Siesfeld, T. (1998), *Measures that Matter: An Exploratory Investigation of Investor' Information Needs and Value Priorities*, Ernst & Young Center for Business Innovation, OECD.

Myers, S.C. (1977), 'Determinants of Corporate Borrowing', *Journal of Financial Economics*, Vol. 5, No. 2, pp.147-176.

Nakamura, L. (1999), 'Intangibles: what put the new in the new economy?', *Federal Reserve Bank of Philadelphia Business Review*, July-August, pp.3-16.

Partanen, T. (1998), *Intellectual Capital Accounting*, Master Thesis, Helsinki School of Economics and Business Administration, Spring.

Phillips, R. (1997), *Innovation and Firm Performance in Australian Manufacturing*, Industry Commission Staff Research Paper, AGPS, Canberra (September).

Pulic, A. (1998), Measuring the performance of intellectual potential in knowledge economy, available at www.measuring-ip.at/Opapers/Pulic/Vaictxt.vaictxt.html

Pulic, A. (2000), 'VAIC^{TM}. An Accounting Tool for IC Management', University of Graz, available at www.measuring-ip.at/Papers/ham99txt.htm

Roos, J., Roos, G., Dragonetti, N. and Edvinsson, L. (1997), *Intellectual Capital: Navigating in the New Business Landscape*, New York, New York University Press.

Saint-Onge, H. (1996), *Measuring and managing intellectual capital: A comprehensive guide*, unpublished paper.

Stewart, Th. (1997), *Intellectual Capital: The New Wealth of Organisations*, Doubleday.

Sullivan, P. (1998), *Profiting From Intellectual Capital. Extracting Value From Innovation*, Wiley.

Sveiby, K.E. (ed.) (1988), *Den osynliga balansräkningen (The invisible balance sheet)*, Affärsvärlden/Ledarskap, Stockholm.

Tobin, J. (1969), 'A General Equilibrium Approach to Monetary Theory', *Journal of Money, Credit and Banking*, No. 1, pp.15-29.

Vickery, G. (1999), *Intangibles and Competitiveness: An Empirical Approach*, Edward Elgar Publishing, Cheltenham.

Walker, D.M. (1999), *IT: Taking the intangibles off the shelf*, available at www.it.fairfax.com.au/industry.

Wurzburg, G. (1999), *Promoting Disclosure*, available at www.ey.com.

Zambon, S. (ed.) (2003), *Study on the Measurement of Intangible Assets and Associated Reporting Practices*, European Commission, DG Enterprise, Brussels.

Chapter 9

Towards a More Effective Investment Analysis of Intangibles Sensitive Companies

Mike Hall and Richard Youngman

In a knowledge-based economy, where business models and organisational forms are in transition, providers of capital need access to new types and forms of information. Knowledge has become central to the production of value in a world in which access to resources ('assets') is more important than ownership. Value creation is increasingly less dependent on tangible assets and largely takes place beyond the legal boundaries of the firm. Since traditional accounting principles mainly accommodate only tangible assets, there is often a great material difference between book value and market value.

Investment analysis dependent on historic data often results in major challenges for companies trying to raise finance. If current practice does not adapt, this lack of understanding about intangibles represents a potential block on growth opportunities for European businesses.

Although we need to understand and measure intangibles and knowledge beyond the intuitive approaches prevalent today, there is widespread ignorance and much institutional resistance to change the current methods of corporate reporting and analysis. Intangible assets are difficult to identify and measure and as such their processes and causal links are complex and poorly understood. The current system of financial reporting and investment analysis risks polarising between standardised, XBRL[1]-assisted financial accounts and sector indicators; and more idiosyncratic and holistic measures of a company's value creation processes not captured by traditional financial and non-financial indicators.

Bankers, for example, work in risk aware cultures. They often assume that historical financial performance provides a more objective view than qualitative measures, which, when used, consist of simple checklists instead of a true examination of cause and effect. It is often assumed that banks are not concerned with measuring and evaluating intangibles beyond goodwill, brands, and patents, etc. which currently feature in established accounting standards. Intangible and

---

[1] eXtensible Business Reporting Language (industry standard XML for tagging standard sets of data reportable en masse and viewable in customised format) - http://www.xbrl.org.

latent competencies such as competitiveness or quality of management have in fact been incorporated in credit risk analysis for some time, albeit intuitively and subjectively and with neither a common language nor explicit measurement. Traditional key performance indicators (KPIs) are in fact only the visible effects of interdependent intangibles working beneath the surface of the value creation process.

Since banks do not thoroughly analyse intangibles, the majority of the borrowing universe of innovative SMEs is largely avoided by the biggest banks. Although this leads to customer drift from large banks to small banks, some borrowers become just too big for the small banks to cope with. Do they get the same value for money or attention from the bigger banks? Treacy and Carey (1998) recognised these problems, noting that SMEs usually have limited access to external finance and often have few or no assets that can be sold in an emergency without disrupting operations. Larger firms have more ready access to alternative financing, more saleable assets, and a more firmly established market presence. For these reasons, many banks require that small borrowers be assigned relatively risky grades even if their financials might suggest a more favourable rating. Uncertainty due to a lack of sufficient forward-looking data augments perceived risk and often results in decisions not to lend.

We need to challenge our assumptions about intangibles. PRISM's conceptual framework for intangibles (shown in the diagram) goes beyond the typical capital markets' focus on a snapshot view of asset values and indicators of cash flow. By highlighting how banks incorporate intangibles within credit assessment, this paper will suggest how companies whose core value drivers and assets are mainly intangible can portray themselves more positively, and enhance their interaction with their providers of debt finance. We shall also propose how the various stakeholders can work together towards a common language for intangibles, and conclude with some recommendations for further work and co-operation in this important field.

The findings here are based upon recent empirical research undertaken by the multi-disciplinary research group PRISM, with the help of international commercial lending banks and credit analysis companies, into how providers of finance incorporate intangibles into their lending decisions (Hall, 2003).

1. Intangibles and Credit Risk Analysis

Hall surprisingly uncovered no dedicated credit risk models or processes that solely incorporated measures for intangibles. There was little evidence moreover of the systematic inclusion of intangibles in *any* models. When considering qualitative factors, analysts rely on their intuition and experience as well as some limited guidance offered by their employers. Culture plays a major role. The dominant mindset of many credit analysis teams is to avoid risk and to over-depend on historical financial performance which is widely considered to provide the most objective view of quality of management and other intangibles. As far as ratings agencies are concerned, even though they develop commercial products to meet the business needs of the investment community, there is surprisingly little evidence of any explicit consideration of intangibles in their corporate ratings products.

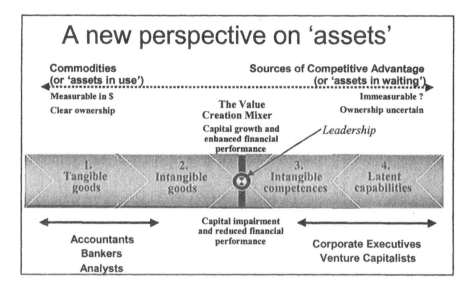

Figure 9.1 A new perspective on assets

Quality of management and competitive positioning are the two most heavily emphasised qualitative factors taken into account by credit analysts. Measures of operating performance are designed from a defensive viewpoint at the expense of their usefulness as forward looking indicators. Too much focus is given to 'surface' performance factors instead of systematic measures of the true intangibles that drive value creation. These surface factors are in reality the effects of underlying intangibles. Differences in currently-measured KPIs between companies are therefore accounted for by intangibles. Credit analysis can be a very people-intensive business in which culture, context, and individual and collective knowledge all play an important role. Process and efficiency cannot replace unwritten know-how. The intuition of the credit analyst is only reliable however after many years of individual and collective experience and knowledge-sharing within the bank.

There is much diversity in banks' internal credit rating systems, which lie on a continuum between the statistical modelling of historic quantitative data, and judgemental models relying on subjective opinions about borrowers' qualitative characteristics. Banks rely on models mainly to allocate internal ratings which reflect the probability of default on a loan (PD) and the loss given default (LGD). PD and LGD represent the two main credit risk metrics that determine the regulatory capital that banks must set aside against losses in their lending businesses. Factors that determine a company's PD consequently range between historical financial data and immeasurable factors such as the quality of its top management team. The main drivers of LGD are the characteristics of collateral assigned to mitigate eventual losses. To illustrate intangibles within this context, here is an adjusted version of the PRISM framework which conceptualises a firm's key value drivers in four asset groups (see diagram).

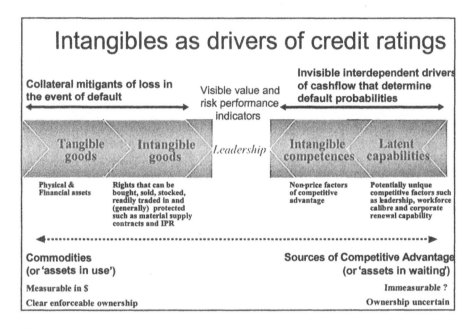

Figure 9.2 Intangibles as drivers of credit ratings

Debt financiers require unambiguous company reporting and the understanding of how a company's value creation processes drive cash-flow, collateral value and subsequently determine PD and LGD. But this is hindered by data limitation, which is compounded when we attempt to explicitly introduce intangibles into risk models (BCBS 2000). In fact, the *Financial Times* reported that one Basle II impact study revealed that large international banks are unable to allocate a credit rating to 62 per cent of their corporate loans due to lack of information (FT, 2003).[2]

If the value 'in-use' of an intangible asset is zero in the event of company failure, it cannot really be considered as collateral. Asset-based lenders need to identify, disentangle and measure collateral for usage as security. The need for institutional and legal frameworks to adopt intangible goods as potential collateral is a process which has required first movers such as David Bowie (music back catalogue) to undertake such activities. Regulatory definitions of collateral,

---

[2] Basle II aims to create more efficient and safer banking by allowing banks to align more closely the capital they are required to hold against the risks they undertake.

however, exclude most if not all intangibles from eligibility as security against vanilla lending. It is therefore necessary for traditional lenders to focus on intangibles as drivers of cash-flow and PD, and less on their impact on collateral value and LGD.

In the context of Basle II, it is increasingly important for banks to have a better handle on borrowers' credit risk since they can gain both top and bottom line benefits through reduced credit losses *and* lower capital allocation. Tests show that large EU banks adopting the advanced approach would require six per cent less capital than today (BCBS 2003). Although it does not accommodate the explicit inclusion of intangible competencies and latent capabilities, understanding and incorporating intangibles is implicitly compatible with certain Basle II approaches. But although much effort is being put into understanding and implementing Basle II, banks' focus is overwhelmingly on controlling the cost and bureaucratic effort of this seemingly very complicated task. It is sufficient, if they so choose, to include goodwill, copyright and other such intangible goods as inputs into their credit models, but not much more beyond what is already reported on the balance sheets of their borrowers.

The greatest challenge ahead will be to better establish cause and effect linkages between intangibles and cash-flow. Common definitions for classes of intangibles and an understanding of their interdependencies will be a starting point. There is a danger however that checklists are used as a substitute for a true examination of causation at the expense of the establishment of appropriate measurement mechanisms. Banks need to reduce where possible their over-reliance on backward looking financial data and need to ask what are the real costs of their lack of understanding of the value creation processes of the majority of their borrowers. This uncertainty augments perceived risk and results in higher PDs, lower credit ratings, the need to allocate more capital to the loan, and decisions not to lend since models say it would be better to lend elsewhere, where data is more 'available'.

If the scale of lending and/or margin merits the cost to further understand the borrowers' business models, then banks will invest to make better decisions. The inclusion of intangibles will however need to be incremental rather than revolutionary, principally due to legacy IT systems and the need to abstract context and knowledge within broader credit metrics. The key question therefore seems to revolve around how banks can deliver credit services at the most cost-effective price. The majority of lending decisions are taken (or soon will be) with the minimum of human intervention and the vast majority of banking relationships are now low cost and low touch. Reconciling the powerful and conflicting forces surrounding intangibles and credit analysis represents a potential nirvana for both providers and lenders of debt capital. The answer may lie in focussing on key sectors within a portfolio of customer relationships and recognising that seeking a solution with more widespread appeal is likely to miss the target.

Some of the responsibility lies with companies, who must work better to understand more deeply their value creation processes, and subsequently communicate more effectively to their providers of capital. After all, since the indicators of intangibles are idiosyncratic to each company, they are best understood and measured from within.

2. How Companies can Differentiate their Disclosure to Debt Financiers

Although few would argue that intangibles increasingly drive value creation within the modern enterprise, the need to understand, identify, measure and communicate information about intangibles is constrained by their inherent invisibility and ambiguity and consequent potential for misinterpretation. This greatly impacts disclosure.

The growing role of intangibles has caused a blurring of sector boundaries and significant information asymmetries between insider managers and close investors on the one hand, and the rest of the investing universe on the other. Holland (2001) shows that management's communication of their understanding of value creation increasingly takes place through private disclosure with select equity fund managers and analysts These insiders then piece together and interpret the various elements through the mosaic of information disclosed by a company and with the contextual support of management's 'strategic story'.

Holland defends private disclosure as the main stage for a discussion of intangibles, assigning it to managerial preferences, problems of definition and measurement, and the lack of external disclosure standards and guidance on intangibles. He states that iterative learning by management through dynamic, private interchanges of information is itself an important influence on corporate disclosure behaviour and a key means to overcoming the new information asymmetries arising from the growth of intangibles. Non-disclosure or secrecy decisions are much influenced by the characteristics of intangibles, their potential or actual role in creating value, and their imitability. Despite the efforts of various accounting standards to remove opportunities for the manipulation of financial statements, these efforts have actually reduced corporate flexibility for the disclosure of goodwill and internally generated brand values, and have reduced the scope for companies to voluntarily release information on intangibles, especially if measurement of asset values is involved.

Does private disclosure harm other providers of finance, such as commercial banks, whose current business models do not permit the same depth of analysis and contact as that of venture capital and equity investors? Is it really necessary for companies to differentiate their disclosure to lenders when the latters' priority over assets in default already acts in compensation for their less clear picture? Some banks are confident that they obtain an equal if not better perspective on their borrowers than fund managers.

> If our relationship managers are doing their job properly, our decisions are better informed than those of fund managers. The relationship manager will go truly inside the company, often meeting operations' management and will receive monthly management accounts in many cases. This is in contrast to private, but still controlled, meetings between fund managers and senior management. The information asymmetry

assumption that banks do not get the right information is incorrect, particularly vis-à-vis SMEs. Especially due to the lack of secondary markets for many loans, we have no choice but to stay very close to our borrowers and nurse them back to health which necessitates knowing 'warts and all' what's going on (Hall, 2003).

Notwithstanding the above quote, which was from an LBO specialist, company leaders should encourage close(r) relationships with key debt providers to develop common language and communication structures for intangibles alongside their current disclosure practices. They should internally promote a wider appreciation of intangibles and set in place measures to identify and communicate to financiers the intangibles that drive their most important value creation processes. This is even more necessary for companies given the absence of systematic measures within banks to identify the real driving forces behind generalities such as 'quality of management'. Such general indicators in fact comprise of components which are driven by, or leverage off, underlying invisible intangibles. They are the matching 'effects' to the underlying intangibles 'causes'. KPIs or value drivers might come close to being such components but are often limited to being common industry measures and not representative of the idiosyncrasies of the company.

Banks increasingly use KPIs to measure and monitor borrower risk more closely than metrics such as interest coverage, which is linked more directly to debt covenants. Although this represents progress, there is still a long way to go for intangibles. The challenge is compounded by the interdependencies that exist between different intangibles and between intangible and tangible assets. One could compare this search for component metrics to indicators of the existence of sub-atomic particles used in the absence of a means to identify and measure the particles directly. We might not need to spend the time and money to identify and measure intangibles if we can establish more credible linkages between company-idiosyncratic indicators of the intangibles and how these drive cash-flow and collateral value. To support this we turn to Heisenberg:

> Heisenberg's Uncertainty Principle basically says that there is no way to precisely measure most essential properties of sub-atomic behaviour. Or rather, the more precisely you measure one property – say, the momentum of an electron – the less precisely you can know another – in this case, its position. The more certain the one, the more uncertain the other..... The essential aspects of a particle (position, velocity, momentum and energy) can never be precisely observed at once – the act of observation itself inevitably and irretrievably distorts at least one of those qualities. The best we can hope for is to take measurements and make predictions that are *probable* or statistical (Macrone, 1999).

Banks therefore need to more effectively capture data to underpin judgements made on the basis of statistical probabilities. Whatever the measures used and however subjective the analysts' judgements, we can assume that metrics for 'intangibles' identified and scored so far are the surface factors masking a whole raft of intangibles underneath. Differences in KPIs between two companies from the same sector could in reality be accounted for by relative differences in their intangibles. Creating company-specific measures for these differences could be a starting point on the path to better identifying and measuring intangibles and, since there is a chance that XBRL might soon automate the reporting of KPIs, this could free up time for considering and communicating the true drivers of cash-flow.

If metrics can be established to measure intangibles and their effect on cash-flow, a further challenge is to avoid the claims made of CSR and Corporate Governance initiatives that they are ignored by management who just take the minimum surface actions. There is a real danger that checklists are used as a substitute for a true examination of cause and effect and the establishment of appropriate measurement mechanisms for intangibles. We are of the opinion nevertheless that checklists can be useful indicators of differentiation where external validation is available, in national or Europe-wide certifications of product quality for example.

We suggest that companies learn from these insights from banks to instil a deeper understanding and capability to communicate about intangibles and how they drive value creation. Lessons towards this objective will undoubtedly come from the UK Kingsmill report into how companies can present information on human capital in their annual reports. The ongoing UK Department of Trade and Industry working group towards a statutory operating and financial review (MD&A in US parlance) will also help.[3] There is no 'one best way' however. As such we do not suggest a list of possible metrics for intangibles. A realistic minimum 'easy win' is to motivate finance and investor relations professionals to think in other directions than the traditional ways. A longer term approach will require the joint efforts of not just providers and demanders of finance but also intermediaries such as auditors which already have in place the channels for the capture and communication of information on intangibles. These parties together with other stakeholders in the business reporting and investment analysis world should work together to establish some form of common language for intangibles.

3. Towards a Common Language and Understanding for Intangibles

Our investigations into commercial bank lending and intangibles considered whether providers and recipients of capital have, or even understand, the required data to incorporate intangibles into their investment analysis. Where specialist teams exist, it is not clear that they conduct any specific analyses beyond knowing better the assumed key success factors in their respective industries. Many banks use external sources to assist in arriving at their internal ratings. These include systems such as Credit Monitor from Moody's/KMV: 'very useful'; ratings agencies grades: 'sometimes reactive'; and equity analysis: 'has a somewhat different focus and sometimes independence can be questioned'. Since these tools rely heavily on historic company and market data, they suffer from the same weakness as existing bank credit models when it comes to intangibles.

---

[3] See respectively http://www.accountingforpeople.gov.uk/ and
http://www.dti.gov.uk/cld/financialreview.htm.

If we assume that data insufficiency and the lack of a common language for intangibles are hurdles to more accurate credit risk appraisal, what might be the required knowledge, and which knowledge and information flows can make it easier, to identify and capture the requisite data and system inputs? Work by the accountants Price Waterhouse Coopers and Cap Gemini Ernst & Young's former Centre for Business Innovation, for example, has gone a long way to establishing lists of possible metrics for intangibles and intellectual capital, and have conceptualised hierarchies of information such as 'financial reporting to company specific measures'.[4]

Banks will not invest however to create idiosyncratic measures for each and every borrower, not just for cost reasons but due to the levels of abstraction that their credit risk models require to produce comparable ratings. Whilst this does not mean that *no* banks will develop their own metrics for intangibles, it does imply that a common language for intangibles across the banking sector (and perhaps the investing universe) might be difficult to achieve. This is due to the differing individual contexts and operating environments of the universe of borrowers and to the diversity of banks' legacy credit risk analysis systems.

In the near future at least, banks will rely as before on audited financial accounts, sector specific metrics and KPIs, and on a certain number of softer factors such as quality of management where some understanding of the borrower, or at least a detached judgement of the analysts, is required.

Communication needs to evolve between providers and demanders of capital in order for increased consistency and reliability of analysis. Although this clearly requires more transparency and disclosure, the inherent tensions and uncertainties regarding corporate disclosure are a potential blocking factor. The investment to achieve this transparency and understanding must be shared. Since banks will not invest to create their own metrics, this begs the question of which players in the business reporting value chain are best equipped to act as catalysts for/suppliers of the correct information to help banks better assess intangibles. An initial answer is that companies such as auditors and ratings agencies, which have existing infrastructures for determining and delivering sets of data and information in standardised formats, can definitely act as catalysts for the automation via XBRL of much of the supply of sector specific metrics once they are agreed. This might free up the time of bank credit analysts to more closely consider the idiosyncrasies of their borrowers.

Taking this further, one might imagine some form of 'assurance standard' for intangibles similar to emerging standards such as AA1000 in CSR.[5] A challenge would be to develop a truly practical and useful discovery and communications tool and to avoid just another checklist. This would involve the company or a third-party producing metrics and narratives which would demonstrate the achievement of certain standards set by the assurance framework covering the full range of possible intangibles. Similar to AA1000, the process would, inter alia, focus on the materiality of these intangibles to investment analysis and returns; examine the

---

4 http://www.valuereporting.com/pwcvr/index.jsp ; http://www.cbi.cgev.com.
5 http://www.accountability.org.

completeness of the borrower's own understanding of its value creation processes and the role played by intangibles therein; and provide forward-looking indicators of an organisation's ability to carry out stated policies and goals, as well as to meet future standards and expectations.

Two elements in the process towards a higher institutional appreciation of intangibles have been recorded by Mouritsen (2002). One is the process of disentanglement, where 'new' intellectual assets are identified and recognised as separable assets. The other is the process of entanglement, whereby investment companies help develop the conditions under which their financial capital will assist the company, thus making clearer how intangibles and intellectual resources work in practice. The first process towards increased disentanglement goes via accounting rules and standards. The second process via increased entanglement goes through an appreciation of the production function/ business model of knowledge.

The challenge for lenders will be first of all to decide whether or not they need a closer understanding of the intangible drivers of value creation. Then they should examine the cost versus the benefit, not just of arriving at such an understanding, but of incorporating measures for intangibles into their existing processes. Banks may in fact wish to adopt follower strategies. Other investors with high risk thresholds might well be better placed to act as first movers in this space.

If lenders are to pursue a common language for intangibles, the individual and collective understanding and knowledge of the bankers themselves is where we should focus. Simplistically put, there is no point investing in data and systems if the softer aspects are not considered. Analysts' knowledge and the ability to share it are the key success factors for incorporating intangibles in credit risk processes. This is implicitly supported by the Danish IC Guidelines[6] for company managers and by Holland's work concerning private disclosure between fund managers and companies (Holland, 2002).

There is a need for specialist and generalist knowledge and the appropriate mindset to be able to spot the emerging patterns in the mosaic of information disclosed by a company. Somehow we have to create a means to better and more quickly understand what is needed to be known; to better communicate this knowledge such that others can understand the context and reason behind a credit decision; and to enable this knowledge to be distributed throughout the bank and, where possible, entered into information systems and credit risk models. Providers of finance need to examine their own intangibles in order to better understand those of their customers.

4. Conclusion

We have highlighted the challenges faced by companies and their financiers to understand, measure, communicate and analyse the intangibles that drive value creation. A lack of understanding leads to lack of funding and company failure,

---

[6] http://www.vtu.dk/jaccounts.

especially of SMEs, which although perhaps not a serious pandemic today, can only deteriorate with the increasing intensity of intangibles within companies in the knowledge economy.

Much of the current work on intangibles demonstrates a need for new measurement tools for the knowledge-based economy and rejects a good deal of the rhetoric of the industrialist society. Our work will be successful if we open the minds of the decision making champions within demanders and providers of finance. We must convince them of the need to better include intangibles in their performance measurement and investment decisions

Further investigation into intangibles and investment analysis should aim to develop scaleable methods to more effectively provide innovation capital to European SMEs, achievable through a more widespread understanding of intangibles. This work should encourage the various players to develop their own intangible and latent capabilities as a means to better understanding, communicating and leveraging for their advantage the real underlying drivers of (corporate) value creation. We encourage companies and capital market participants to take their own actions and to lobby their industry bodies and national and supranational policy makers for encouragement and support. We suggest as a starting point four interdependent initiatives to develop intangible investment techniques:

1. Develop a core investment analysis and management 'approach' for intangibles intensive organisations which can be overlaid to bank credit portfolios, equity and bond fund management, etc.
2. Develop training courses in new skills and competencies to understand and analyse intangibles for (i) the new 'approach' and (ii) how to make it scaleable.
3. Communicate the 'approach' to demanders (and other providers) of finance as an incentive for them to better understand, communicate and analyse intangibles.
4. Develop new forms of disclosure mechanisms for intangibles to be used by demanders of finance.

There is currently much duplication of effort in investment analysis, especially within universal providers of finance. This repetition will be reduced by developments such as XBRL, and continuous auditing, one of whose main applications will be to increase the visibility of corporate malfeasance.[7] Such initiatives for smarter, more effective analysis will leave more time to develop and express judgements about intangibles and company-specific measures.

In corporate lending for example there could be scope for a greater segmentation of credit risk and capital market activity as took place when IT tools were applied in the credit card and mortgage markets and which might not be limited to collateralised intangible goods. Discontinuities affecting legacy industries that require investment in IPR could become the lending domain of specialists. Traditionally minded analysts could still fulfil vital roles distilling

---

[7] http://www.continuousauditing.org.

financial information and industry specific measures. One could for example imagine a separate set of analysts specialising in intangibles and responsible for an 'X factor' of value and risk, not taken into account by traditional metrics. This complementary analysis would account for the positive or negative differences between raw and final investment grades and offer contextual explanations to enable others to understand and monitor any consequent investments.

A central issue for investment analysis is that intangibles' disclosure will require more bespoke and detailed analysis, something that will make the provision of research yet more expensive. One could imagine the new 'approach' being used at the entry level into investment portfolios and perhaps implemented as a bottom up screening/analysis by separate/specialist people from traditional analysts.

Since measures for intangibles are often borrower specific, they have to be tacitly understood both at the initial lending decision as well as during the lifetime of the loan. Such knowledge management and cultural challenges require new skills and competencies acquired via techniques borrowed from complex adaptive systems theory which challenge the orthodoxy of scientific management and mainstream consultancy, and which require an understanding and clear separation of context, narrative and content management (Snowden, 2002). Tools and techniques for accelerated learning, experience capture and knowledge sharing, instilled via training courses, can help analysts more quickly and more effectively map cash-flow drivers beyond the checklists and measures of effect (rather than cause) widespread today. This will require an understanding of the generic and specific cultural challenges for intangibles and might consider how to create 'enabling cultures' to encourage the requisite behaviour appropriate for different financing arenas.

Such training courses can help investors become more attuned to intangibles and the need to more proactively embrace them in their financing decisions, particularly as they pertain to SMEs. This could also explore capital supply issues such as how to improve investment performance among intangibles-rich firms and how to shift the boundary between tacit and codified information in the interests of improved capital allocation.

We need to encourage co-operation between the demanders and providers of capital and their information infomediaries through, for example, feasibility studies into new forms of 'assurance standards' or 'kite marks'. Attaining such standards would reduce the level of uncertainty and ambiguity in a business reporting of its value creation processes (and how intangibles drive them). A challenge however would be to avoid producing 'just another checklist' of factors for a company to produce and to instead develop a practical and useful discovery and communications tool. This could incorporate learning from the various sustainability and CSR efforts and perhaps even offer them new insights via a better mapping of underlying intangibles to non-financial risk drivers.

Common to all financiers is an appetite to make better informed investment decisions and in doing so to satisfy the requirements of a wider population of businesses. In many if not most businesses however, the ambiguities and disclosure issues surrounding intangibles makes directors and owners uncomfortable. Although little evidence in the banking world can be uncovered of conscious and systematic efforts to incorporate intangibles into credit risk systems, our conclusion is that even though banks are not reinventing the wheel, they are nevertheless asking themselves serious questions about how to better understand value creation processes and drivers of cash-flow. It is now up to borrowers to help their banks to better put the pieces of the jigsaw together.

References

Basle Committee on Banking Supervision (BCBS) (2000), 'Range of Practice in Banks' Internal Ratings Systems', Discussion Paper, Jan 2000:
http://www.bis.org/publ/bcbs66.htm.

BCBS (2003), 'Quantitative Impact Study 3. Overview of Global Results', May 5, p.3:
http://www.bis.org/bcbs/qis/qis3.htm.

Financial Times (2003), 'Banks' loan data are inadequate, warn regulators', 6 May, p.17.

Hall, M. (2003), 'Measures to Increase the Effectiveness of Credit Risk Analysis in Corporate Lending Through a Better Understanding of the Role of Intangibles', PRISM Group, April: http://www.euintangibles.et/library/.

Holland, J. (2001), 'Corporate Value Creation, Intangibles and Disclosure', Working Paper 2001/3, Dept. of Accounting & Finance, University of Glasgow:
http://www.law.gla.ac.uk/dbase/Accfin/Department/Library/Wp2001-3.pdf.

Holland, J. (2002), 'Fund Management, Intellectual Capital, Intangibles and Private Disclosure', Working Paper 2002/4:
http://www.law.gla.ac.uk/dbase/Accfin/Department/Library/Wp2002/jbh2002.pdf.

Macrone, M. (1999), *Eureka! 81 Key Ideas Explained*, Barnes & Noble Books, London.

Mouritsen, J. (2002), 'Intellectual Capital and the Capital Market: The Circulability of Intellectual Capital', PRISM Group:
http://www.euintangibles.net/research_results/ic_in_capitalmarkets.pdf.

Snowden, D. (2002), 'Complex Acts of Knowing – Paradox and Descriptive Self-awareness.' Special Issue of the Journal of Knowledge Management, 6(2):
http://www.1.ibm.com/services/files/Complexactsoftknowing_1.pdf.

Treacy, W. and Carey. M. (1998), 'Credit Risk Rating at Large US Banks,' Federal Reserve Bulletin, November, 897-921:
http://www.federalreserve.gov/pubs/bulletin/1998/1198leadw.pdf.

Index

For Product Safety Concerns and Information please contact our EU
representative GPSR@taylorandfrancis.com Taylor & Francis Verlag GmbH,
Kaufingerstraße 24, 80331 München, Germany

Printed and bound by CPI Group (UK) Ltd, Croydon, CR0 4YY
01/05/2025
01858407-0001